W9-BBK-473

PERGAMON INTERNATIONAL LIBRARY
of Science, Technology, Engineering and Social Studies

The 1000-volume original paperback library in aid of education,
industrial training and the enjoyment of leisure

Publisher: Robert Maxwell, M.C.

PSYCHOLOGICAL CONSULTATION IN THE COURTROOM

THE PERGAMON TEXTBOOK
INSPECTION COPY SERVICE

An inspection copy of any book published in the Pergamon International Library
will gladly be sent to academic staff without obligation for their consideration for
course adoption or recommendation. Copies may be retained for a period of 60 days
from receipt and returned if not suitable. When a particular title is adopted or
recommended for adoption for class use and the recommendation results in a sale
of 12 or more copies the inspection copy may be retained with our compliments.
The Publishers will be pleased to receive suggestions for revised editions and new
titles to be published in this important international Library.

Pergamon Titles of Related Interest

Apter/Goldstein YOUTH VIOLENCE: Programs and Prospects
Brassard/Germain/Hart PSYCHOLOGICAL MALTREATMENT OF
CHILDREN AND YOUTH
Calhoun/Atkeson TREATMENT OF VICTIMS OF
SEXUAL ASSAULT
Weisstub LAW AND MENTAL HEALTH: International Perspectives,
Volume 1
Weisstub LAW AND MENTAL HEALTH: International Perspectives,
Volume 2

Related Journals *

CLINICAL PSYCHOLOGY REVIEW
INTERNATIONAL JOURNAL OF LAW AND PSYCHIATRY
JOURNAL OF CRIMINAL JUSTICE

*Free sample copies available upon request

PSYCHOLOGY PRACTITIONER GUIDEBOOKS

EDITORS

Arnold P. Goldstein, Syracuse University
Leonard Krasner, SUNY at Stony Brook
Sol L. Garfield, Washington University

PSYCHOLOGICAL CONSULTATION IN THE COURTROOM

MICHAEL T. NIETZEL
RONALD C. DILLEHAY
University of Kentucky

PERGAMON PRESS
New York   Oxford   Toronto   Sydney   Frankfurt

Pergamon Press Offices:

U.S.A.	Pergamon Press Inc., Maxwell House, Fairview Park, Elmsford, New York 10523, U.S.A.
U.K.	Pergamon Press Ltd., Headington Hill Hall, Oxford OX3 0BW, England
CANADA	Pergamon Press Canada Ltd., Suite 104, 150 Consumers Road, Willowdale, Ontario M2J 1P9, Canada
AUSTRALIA	Pergamon Press (Aust.) Pty. Ltd., P.O. Box 544, Potts Point, NSW 2011, Australia
FEDERAL REPUBLIC OF GERMANY	Pergamon Press GmbH, Hammerweg 6, D-6242 Kronberg-Taunus, Federal Republic of Germany
BRAZIL	Pergamon Editora Ltda., Rua Eça de Queiros, 346, CEP 04011, São Paulo, Brazil
JAPAN	Pergamon Press Ltd., 8th Floor, Matsuoka Central Building, 1-7-1 Nishishinjuku, Shinjuku, Tokyo 160, Japan
PEOPLE'S REPUBLIC OF CHINA	Pergamon Press, Qianmen Hotel, Beijing, People's Republic of China

347.7366
N55p
141723
apr.1987

First printing 1986

Library of Congress Cataloging in Publication Data

Nietzel, Michael T.
    Psychological consultation in the courtroom.

    (Psychology practitioner guidebooks)
    Includes index.
    1. Psychology, Forensic. 2. Evidence, Expert--
United States. I. Dillehay, Ronald C. II. Title.
III. Series.
KF8922.N54   1986   347.73'66   85-28361
ISBN 0-08-030956-9   347.30766
ISBN 0-08-030955-0 (pbk.)

Printed in the United States of America

To Geri and Val

Contents

Preface   ix

Chapter

1. INTRODUCTION: THE PSYCHOLOGY-LAW
   INTERACTION   1
   Trial Procedures   4
   Scope of Consultation   12
   Overview of the Book   14

2. VOIR DIRE: STRUCTURE AND METHODS   17
   Purposes of Voir Dire   17
   Voir Dire Consultation   20
   How the Consultant Should Be Identified   59
   Evaluation   60

3. PUBLIC OPINION SURVEYS AND CHANGE OF VENUE   62
   Three Uses of Public Opinion Surveys   62
   Legal Status of Change of Venue and Other Remedies
   for Pretrial Publicity   65
   How to Conduct a Venue Survey   70
   Results of the Surveys   79
   Methodological and Interpretive Issues   90

4. PSYCHOLOGISTS AS EXPERT WITNESSES   97
   Topics for Expert Psychological Testimony   99
   Coping on the Witness Stand   109

5. WITNESS PREPARATION IN CIVIL CASES   116
   Who Is Being Prepared for Trial?   117
   Is There a Literature on Witness Preparation?   118
   The Consultant's Own Preparation on Facts of Case   118

Introducing the Consultant to the Witness   120
Major Areas of Witness Preparation   120
Appearance   127
Threats to Credibility   128
The Assessment-Intervention-Evaluation Sequence   130
The Escalation of Preparation   132
Do Witnesses Change?   133

6. CONVINCING THE JURY: EVIDENCE AND
   OTHER INFLUENCES   134
   The Communication Paradigm: Applicable but Limited   135
   Trial Segments and Juror Influence   137

7. EVALUATION AND PROFESSIONAL ISSUES   156
   Epistemology and the Behavioral Consultant   156
   Assessing the Effects of Consultation   159
   Ethical Issues   166

Appendix A: Special Juror Questionnaire   173

References   175

Author and Case Index   187

Subject Index   193

About the Authors   197

Psychology Practitioner Guidebooks List   198

Preface

The impetus for writing this book was our 10 years of experience in consulting with trial attorneys about jury selection, courtroom dynamics, and trial strategy. On the basis of this experience, we gradually developed a model of consultation, a set of interventions, and a program of research that addressed many of the practical and intellectual demands that face the courtroom consultant. Our ideas about juries and the courtroom come from many sources—attorney lore and logic, our own "clinical" intuitions, prior and ongoing empirical research, interviews with jurors, advice from other consultants, and analyses driven by psychological theory.

In writing this book, we aimed to (a) describe how we implement our model of consultation in criminal and civil litigation and (b) summarize the empirical, theoretical, and experiential bases for this work. Our intended audience includes professional psychologists and advanced graduate students who would like to expand their consulting activities to include the courtroom and who need a systematic but efficient guide on how to begin.

This book represents the contributions of many students, lawyers, judges, and colleagues, and we want to acknowledge the assistance and education they have given us over the several years of work described here. First, we wish to thank the attorneys who shared with us the challenges and problems of their litigation and who gave us the chance to participate in some exceedingly complex trials. Our special gratitude in this regard goes to Bob Reeves and other attorneys in the firm of Stites and Harbison (Lexington, KY); Pete Partee, the Public Defender for Greenville, South Carolina; the attorneys with the Kentucky Office of Public Advocacy, especially Vince Aprile, Bill Radigan, Ernie Lewis, Gail Robinson, Ed Monahan, and Kevin McNally; and Larry Roberts, former Fayette County Commonwealth's Attorney. Professors William Fortune and Robert Lawson of the University of Kentucky College of Law were helpful to us in many ways and were always willing to give us the benefit of their legal expertise on trial practice. Members of the National Jury Project, especially

Beth Bonora, Emily DeFalla, and Elissa Krauss, have provided both ideas and encouragement for consultation.

A number of graduate students assisted us on the research projects described throughout the book. We would like to recognize the practical and intellectual contributions of Ron Davis, Melissa Himelein, Greg Morrow, Mike Neises, and Glen Rogers, all from the University of Kentucky Department of Psychology and Mike Davidson from the UK College of Law. Our research also depended on the cooperation of many trial judges who gave us access to their courtrooms; special appreciation is expressed to James Park, Jr., Armand Angelucci, L. T. Grant, M. Mitchell Meade and their fellow judges from the Fayette County Circuit Court. Court administrator Donnie Taylor never failed to answer whatever requests we had for him during the several trials for which we impaneled an "alternative jury" (see chapter 3).

Portions of the research described in the book were supported by Grant #SES-8209479 from the National Science Foundation, by a James McKeen Cattell Fellowship (R.C.D.), and sabbatical leaves from the University of Kentucky. We thank these institutions for their support of our work.

Last, we want to thank two people who worked far beyond the call of duty in bringing the manuscript to final form: Kelly Hemmings who spent countless hours reading the manuscript, trudging to the library, and coordinating the bibliography, and Shirley Jacobs who does all jobs that need to be done and does them better than anyone has a right to expect.

Michael T. Nietzel
Ronald C. Dillehay
July, 1985
Lexington, Kentucky

Chapter 1
Introduction: The Psychology-Law Interaction

Psychologists were already consulting on courtroom phenomena at the turn of the twentieth century. William Stern reported that he began to study the correctness of recollection in 1901 by presenting pictures to students for 45-second study, and then asking them to report on the content of the pictures they could remember at various intervals (Stern, 1939). These *aussage* (testimony) experiments were the antecedents of today's research on the reliability of eyewitness testimony and led Stern to conclude that "perfectly correct remembrance is not the rule but the exception" and that "leading questions are capable of exercising a well-nigh fatal power" (Stern, 1939).

Stern (1939) acknowledged that his *aussage* experiments were "determined by theoretical interests in the realm of memory rather than by practical considerations," but that he soon realized the importance of the results for evaluating trustworthiness of testimony at trial. As we intend to show in this book, the value of sound psychological theory as a basis for courtroom consultation remains as essential today as it was in Stern's time.

Although Hugo Munsterberg, the controversial Harvard psychologist, is often credited as the first forensic psychologist, his book, *On the Witness Stand*, was not published until 1908, several years after publication of Stern's work, and also after the discussion by Alfred Binet of the potential forensic utility of word association research (Whipple, 1909). In addition, as early as 1906, Freud proposed the use of reaction-time experiments and word association tests in determining the guilt or innocence of defendants (Rothgeb, 1973).

Munsterberg was the first psychologist to insist that psychological methods surpassed existing legal tools in their ability to assess memory, uncover deception, evaluate confessions, and even to prevent crime. In contrast to teachers, physicians, artists, businessmen, ministers, soldiers, and politicians, attorneys, Munsterberg complained, were the most "obdurate" in accepting psychology as a help to them:

1

The lawyer and the judge and the juryman are sure that they do not need
the experimental psychologist. . . . They go on thinking that their legal in-
stinct and their common sense supplies them with all that is needed. . . .
(Munsterberg, 1908, pp. 10–11)

Munsterberg's bombast did not sit well with attorneys. In the best-
known reply, Professor John Wigmore (1909), that era's leading expert
on legal evidence, brought a mocking libel suit against Munsterberg for
overselling the usefulness of psychology, for ignoring the difference between
laboratory findings and legal requirements and realities, and for glossing
over many disagreements among psychologists themselves. Wigmore en-
tered his suit in the mythical Wundt County. Plantiffs were licensed
attorneys represented by Mr. Simplicissimus Tyro. Munsterberg's counsel
were "the celebrated Mr. R. E. Search, assisted by Mr. Si Kist and Mr.
X. Perry Ment." The case was heard by one Judge Wiseman. Plaintiffs
sought damages for injury to their good names in the sum of one dollar.
After listening to lengthy crossexamination of Munsterberg by Mr. Tyro,
"The jurors, after a few moments' whispering, announced that they did
not need to retire, being already agreed on a verdict . . . for the plaintiffs
with damages of one dollar."

The antagonisms contained in the Munsterberg–Wigmore exchange
typified the psychology–law interaction through the 1920s and squelched
any chance of a rapprochement. In his book, *Social Research in the Judicial
Process*, Wallace Loh (1984) called this period the "Yellow Psychology"
phase in which psychologists were ready to market their product but in
which attorneys were not buying what the psychologists were selling.

Loh (1984) described the 1930s as the "Psychologism in the Law" stage
in which psychology was applied to the practice of law and was used to
critique legal doctrines and decisions. This period corresponded to the
"legal realism" movement, which argued that the law was influenced by
social, economic, personal, and psychological influences in addition to
formalistic factors such as precedent, logic, deduction, and legal analysis.

During this period, Dwight McCarty's book, *Psychology for the Lawyer*
(1929), presented "the new psychology," a science that "explain(s) the
very thing with which the legal practitioner is dealing day by day." Harold
Burtt's (1931) book, *Legal Psychology*, was organized into three sections:
the psychology of testimony, the psychology of the criminal, and the
psychology of crime prevention. Burtt, one of Munsterberg's students,
attempted to present various psychology-in-law topics to "both the student with somewhat of a psychological background and the lawyer who
has perhaps no formal psychological training but who may be a pretty
good psychologist withal."

A major section of M. Ralph Brown's (1926) book, *Legal Psychology*, ad-
vised attorneys on "trial psychology" including such topics as examin-

ing witnesses, selecting juries, and presenting arguments. Brown believed that:

Psychology can make justice more certain. If all lawyers were required to study the principles of psychology, and to learn the applications thereof so that both sides of every case were presented in the best psychological as well as best legal manner, the personal element would tend to become equal or eliminated. Greater justice would result. . . .

Edward Robinson's (1935) book, *Law and the Lawyers*, was important because it sought to apply the methods of naturalistic science to the law, decried by Robinson as an "unscientific science." Robinson was especially enthusiastic about the utility of behaviorism and believed that psychological "facts" had to be substituted for legal concepts.

Loh (1984) credits Robinson's book with introducing the idea that legal psychology should not attempt to apply existing psychological theories and knowledge to legal problems as, for example, Munsterberg had done, but that it should first conduct a psychological analysis of the legal problem concerned and then perform new empirical research on that problem. (Loh cites the research of Hutchins & Slesinger, 1929, on the psychology of evidence as an example of this perspective.) Of course, these two approaches to a psychology of the courtroom are compatible; they constitute two of the foundations for the consultation we describe in the remainder of this book.

The courtroom consultant can derive his or her recommendations from any one of three knowledge sources (Dillehay & Nietzel, 1980a). First, the consultant can draw on generic psychological theory and research. After evaluating the theory's potential for extrapolation to practical settings and judging the research on its methodological merits, the consultant can decide whether the theory and/or the research has something valid to say about the question at hand. This method was practiced by Munsterberg, except that he failed to restrain his tendency toward wholesale transportation of concepts beyond their justified range of applicability.

A second source of knowledge is derived from a careful diagnosis of the psychological issues at play in the courtroom followed by empirical examinations of those phenomena. This is the approach advocated by Robinson, and it is well represented by Thibaut and Walker's (1975) experimental analysis of adversary versus inquisitorial systems of dispute resolution.

The third research strategy is to study, as directly as possible, courtroom phenomena as they naturally occur. Jury interviews, courtroom observation, and use of archival data are the means to this end. Some of the best known examples of this approach are represented by the research known as the Chicago Jury Project (e.g., Broeder, 1965).

The 1950s commenced what Loh (1984) termed "The Forensic Stage" where psychologists were predominantly occupied in offering expert testimony to juries and appelate courts on various subjects. The two areas receiving the most attention were expert opinions on the relationship between mental disorders and responsibility for criminal conduct and testimony about the psychological effects of school segregation. Both topics sparked debate about the proper role of social scientists in adjudication, a conflict that continues today (Haney, 1980; Morse, 1978; Robinson, 1980). Chapter 4 presents the practical issues facing the psychologist who testifies as an expert in the courtroom and surveys several topics for such testimony.

Loh's (1984) fourth stage of psychology–law interaction was "New Research on Procedural Justice," a product of the political activism of the 1960s, which in the 1970s and 1980s concentrated on procedural issues in the trial process, particularly criminal trials. James Marshall's *Law and Psychology in Conflict* (1966) announced this research agenda, one that has been pursued in the last two decades—empirical evaluations of legal procedures and assumptions. Loh divided research in this stage into four categories that concentrated on jury functioning: pretrial influences on the jury, selection of the jury, presentations of testimony and law to the jury, and decision-making by the jury. We examine each of these topics in the remaining chapters because they provide much of the data with which the effective consultant should be acquainted.

This fourth era saw the emergence of specialists in psycholegal research, the beginning of interdisciplinary training programs for psychologist-lawyers, and the initiation of several publication outlets for psycholegal studies (e.g., *Law and Human Behavior, Criminal Justice Journal, Law and Psychology Review*, and *Criminal Justice and Behavior*). Finally, a large number of books analyzing psychological research on courtroom phenomena have been written in the past few years. Most of this scholarship attempts to integrate the psychological literature with the legal procedures one finds in daily courtroom use. In the best of these volumes, the psychologist is educated about the realities of the legal system, whereas the attorney is appraised of the potential application of social science methods to adjudication (Bartol, 1983; Ellison & Buckhout, 1981; Greenberg & Ruback, 1982; Hastie, Penrod, & Pennington, 1983; Horowitz & Willging, 1984; Kaplan, 1986; Kassin & Wrightsman, 1985; Kerr & Bray, 1982; Lippsitt & Sales, 1980; Monahan & Walker, 1985; Saks & Hastie, 1978; Sales, 1981).

TRIAL PROCEDURES

The right to a jury trial in a criminal matter is guaranteed by the Sixth Amendment to the U.S. Constitution. In civil disputes, the right to a jury trial is provided by the Seventh Amendment. Psychologists who consult in the courtroom must know the basic sequence of events in criminal and civil litigation and must be knowledgeable about the differences between the two types of trials. Many of the questions that attorneys pose to consultants deal with variations in trial procedures that attorneys will try to turn to their advantage.

Adversary Model

Criminal and civil trials are conducted according to an *adversary model* of litigation. In an adversary system, the opposing attorneys contend against each other for a result favorable to themselves. The judge functions as an independent arbiter of the proceedings but has no responsibility for investigating or preparing the case as would a judge under the *inquisitorial system* that is practiced in many European countries. Presumably, this role frees the judge to be an impartial referee of the contest being waged by the contending advocates. The advocates are responsible for representing their clients as zealously as the law allows and are expected to use whatever tactics the rules allow in gaining a victory.

The adversary system has been likened to trial by battle, a "dramatic duelling of opposing counsel" (Wigmore, 1909), in which the less skillful advocate loses, an altogether acceptable outcome according to laissez-faire policy. There are some special obligations imposed on both counsel in a criminal trial. The prosecutor is responsible for seeing that justice is done, not for obtaining convictions at any cost. In the words of one court decision, "While [the prosecutor] may strike hard blows, he is not at liberty to strike foul ones" (*Berger v. United States*).[1] On the other hand, the ethics of defense attorneys require them to defend the interests of their clients and to promote any permissible construction of the law that is favorable to their clients.

The adversary conduct of trials is often cited as one of the major philosophical differences that separates lawyers and psychologists in their respective approaches to "truth." As a scientist, the psychologist's search for truth is a public, objective, impersonal inquiry conducted according to methods that can be repeated by others, one that yields results that are interpreted by predetermined standards. "Truth" is reached only probabilistically; hypotheses and theories are always subject to the revisions required by the results of the next experiment. Trial advocates, on the other hand, require dichotomous answers (e.g., guilty vs. not guilty) and seek them through the use of artful persuasion, rational argument, emotional appeal, *ad hominem* attacks, and well-practiced theatrics.

The socialization processes, the preferred style of communication, the educational experiences, and the rules of decorum are quite different for lawyers than for psychologists. The adversary system magnifies these discrepancies. However, we believe that many of the so-called fundamental differences between the two disciplines are not as divisive as is believed. We question first whether psychologists are unfamiliar with adversary approaches to decision-making or, second, whether they oppose an ethical position that emphasizes loyalty to one's client.

Bartol (1983) claims:

> The adversary model presents problems for empirical psychology, since it not only concentrates on one particular case at that particular point in time, but also encourages lawyers to dabble in and out of the data pool and pick and choose that segment of psychological information they wish to present in support of their position.

This is an accurate depiction of what lawyers do, but why it should be problematical to psychologists is less clear. Much psychological literature is rife with selective citation of studies, biased interpretation of data, and differential standards for methodology. Any psychologist familiar with the published controversies over the efficacy of psychotherapy or whether a psychologist should testify about the limited accuracy of eyewitness identification can attest to the presence of passion, subjectivity, and partiality in those scholarly debates. These characteristics will surprise few current philosophers of science (Feyerabend, 1970; Kuhn, 1962) who argue that science progresses through a clash of paradigms, not through the slow increments of empiricism; progress is guided by personal, political, and social factors as much as by the brute facts of careful empiricism. Psychology should not replace experimental methods with adversary ones, despite the arguments of some commentators (e.g., Levine, 1974). However, those who are most alarmed that psychologists "dirty their hands" in the courtroom may have an overly sanitized notion of what psychologists do outside it.

Consulting in the Adversary System

Psychologists may nonetheless still feel uneasy about the ethics of consulting in our adversary system of justice. They are reluctant to believe that the "fairest" outcome is achieved by having two opposing forces enter into combat against each other to achieve a result favorable to themselves. This reluctance often progresses to outright aversion when the psychologist is asked to enlist on one of the sides and act in a partisan fashion. Some experiments on bargaining show that the best joint outcome results from efforts by the negotiators to maximize their individual profits rather than to attempt to cooperate in pursuit of a mutual goal (Kelley & Schenitzki, 1972). Extensive experimental research conducted by Thibaut, Walker and their colleagues (Thibaut & Walker, 1975) on procedural variables in dispute resolution indicated that, as compared with "inquisitorial" systems in which disinterested third parties determine the facts, the adversary system is favored for its fairness, satisfactory performance, and other features. Our training and many of our professional values, however, seem to contradict the expectations and the ethics of an adversary process. Yet our involvement as trial consultants forces us to evaluate whether we can function in the partisan fashion required by such work.

We do not believe there is a complete answer to many of the ethical dilemmas that will be faced by the trial consultant, as we discuss more fully in chapter 8. Colleagues whom we respect often resolve a problem such as defending a client they believe to be guilty differently than we do. We believe the principles of the adversary system are ethically defensible and, in many instances, are not far removed from the psychologists' ethical standards of respecting the integrity and protecting the welfare of the person or group with whom they work. However, we need not work for every client, nor need we work with every attorney. We believe our work as trial consultants must be viewed in the context of the adversary system, which *requires* that attorneys represent their clients zealously within the bounds of the law and professional regulations. Increasingly, this zealousness results in requests for consultation on the psychological dimensions of jury selection and case presentation. Although psychologists should not accept the ethics of attorneys as their own, trial consultants must reach some decision about whether the value the adversary system places on partisan functioning is sufficient justification for their own partisanship. Without some resolution of this question, consultants' days in court are likely to be numbered and unpleasant.[2]

Criminal Trials

Criminal trials are concerned with violations of the criminal law as set forward in federal, state, and local statutes that proscribe certain conduct and set penalties for those persons convicted of a transgression. Criminal law applies to violations against the state or public order; therefore, a criminal case is brought to trial by a representative of the federal, state, or local government (the *prosecutor*) who accuses the *defendant* of a violation of a specific law.

This process begins when a crime is reported and an alleged offender is arrested. The police collect evidence, and the suspect is either charged with an offense or released if there is insufficient incriminating evidence. Within days, a *preliminary hearing* may be held, in which the prosecutor must show *probable cause* that the accused is responsible for the crime charged. This hearing allows the accused and the defending attorney to hear some of the evidence the prosecutor has gathered to prove guilt, a process known as *pretrial discovery*.

For serious crimes, the prosecutor next presents evidence to a *grand jury*, which meets in secret to evaluate whether there is sufficient evidence to indict the defendant formally for a crime. (Not all jurisdictions use a grand jury; those that do not require the prosecutor to go before a judge and present the charge in an *information*.) The grand jury indicts the accused when it returns a *true bill*; if it returns a *no bill*, the case is usually dropped unless new evidence can be discovered by the prosecution. Following return of a true bill, defendant is *arraigned*, at which time the defendant, through defense counsel, enters either a plea of guilty, or not guilty, or no contest to the formal criminal charges.

Between the time of the preliminary hearing and the trial, most defendants (up to 90% in some jurisdictions) *plea bargain*; in this process defense counsel and prosecutor negotiate an arrangement by which the defendant will plead guilty to lesser charges if the more serious charges are dropped; thus, the severity of sentence faced by the defendant is reduced. Judges are not obligated to accept these bargains, although they usually do. Plea bargaining is a much-criticized procedure, but it is grudgingly accepted as a necessity without which the court system would be smothered by the backlog of cases waiting to go to trial.

After arraignment, defense counsel will engage in *motion practice* in an attempt to improve the defendant's chances for acquittal at trial. Motions may be made to suppress evidence, limit publicity, change the venue of the trial, dismiss some or all of the charges, limit the prosecutor's ability to call certain witnesses, evaluate defendant's competence, or to seek a *continuance* of the trial. Prosecutors respond to these motions and may file some of their own. As illustrated in chapters 2 and 3, psychologists are often asked to write affidavits in support of some of these motions.

The criminal trial begins with jury selection or *voir dire*. A panel of prospective jurors or *venirepersons* are called to the courtroom by the court and are questioned about their ability to judge the case impartially. After a jury is selected (see chapter 2 for a thorough presentation of the mechanics and objectives of jury selection), the prosecution makes its *opening statement* to the jury, stating what it believes the evidence will prove in the trial. The defense may then make its opening statement, or may reserve its statement until just before presenting its evidence; defense may also waive the statement. Opening statements offer a preview of the evidence; they should not be argumentative or evaluative about the credibility of the evidence.

The order in which evidence is presented is determined by the fact that the prosecution has the *burden of proof* in criminal trials. Therefore, the prosecution is usually first to make an opening statement, first to present evidence and, usually, first to make closing arguments. Evidence is presented through witnesses who testify under *direct examination* by the prosecution. The defense may confront each of the witnesses through *cross-examination*, a type of inquiry that permits leading; controlling questions not allowed in direct examination. A round of *re-direct* and *re-cross* is permitted, but the scope of the questioning is limited to the content brought out in the immediately preceding inquiry.

After the prosecution finishes, the defense will often ask for a *directed verdict* from the judge. This request seeks a ruling that the prosecution has failed to present enough evidence to justify sending the case to the jury. If the judge does not direct a verdict, the defense then has the opportunity to present evidence. The defense has no burden to present any evidence. The defendant cannot be compelled to testify, and the jury is ordered not to draw any conclusions about the defendant's guilt if the defendant elects to remain silent. Any witnesses testifying on behalf of the defendant are subject to cross-examination by the prosecutor.

After the defense presents its case, the prosecutor and the defense are allowed the chance to present *rebuttal evidence* to the jury. Rebuttal is limited to evidence that attempts to counter some part of the other side's evidence.

After both sides have finished presenting their evidence, they present *closing arguments* aimed at persuading the jury to evaluate the evidence in a manner favorable to one or the other advocate's side. The form and content of closing arguments are less abridged than are those of opening statements. They are presented with partiality and a concentrated effort to sway the jury's commitment to one side. The closing arguments are the last opportunities for the attorneys to influence the jury directly; during these arguments, attorneys dominate center stage. In federal courts and in many state courts, the prosecution makes the first closing argument; the defense follows. The prosecution then has a final chance to rebut the defense's closing argument. However, this sequence does not occur in all states. In some jurisdictions, the defense makes the first closing argument, and the prosecution follows; the defense is not allowed a rebuttal argument.

Although the jury decides the facts of a case, the judge determines the law that applies to these facts. The judge conveys the meaning of the law in *instructions to the jury* given immediately after closing arguments. These instructions discuss legal principles such as burden of proof and proof beyond a reasonable doubt. They identify the elements of the crime in question that must be proved by the prosecution to obtain a conviction; they also instruct the jury on the meaning of defenses such as insanity and self-defense that may be raised by the defendant. These instructions also inform the jury about the possible verdicts it can reach. In jurisdictions in which the jury sentences defendants, information about sentence options will be given.

Jury instructions are prepared by the judge in a conference with the opposing attorneys. Each side drafts a version of the instructions it prefers,
and the judge then writes a final set of instructions that, in the judge's
opinion, best fits the case. The judge reads the instructions to the jury in
open court (an activity sometimes called *charging the jury*), and the jury
is usually given a copy to use during its deliberations. In some states, the
instructing of the jury may precede the attorneys' closing arguments.

After receiving its charge, the jury retires to a special room to deliberate
and to reach its verdict. These deliberations are private and should be conducted in an atmosphere free of any "outside" contamination. The decision rule for reaching a verdict varies. Most states still require a unanimous
verdict for either conviction or acquittal of serious crimes; some jurisdictions allow majority verdicts. A jury that is not able to reach a verdict
because it has deadlocked short of the decision rule is called a *hung jury*.
A judge may urge a deadlocked jury to continue its deliberations, point-
ing out that they are the people best prepared to render a fair decision
in the matter. This intervention is known as an *Allen charge* after the case
of *Allen v. United States*.[3]

The jury returns to the courtroom to announce its verdict. An acquittal
frees the defendant from jeopardy. A conviction may be appealed by the
defendant on the grounds that the judge committed *reversible error* in conducting the trial. Appellate courts review the written record of the trial,
study the written briefs and listen to the oral arguments made by both
sides and reach one of three decisions. If the reviewing court finds no
serious error, it will *affirm* the trial court's outcome. If it determines that
a serious error was committed, it will *reverse* the lower court's decision.
If serious error is found, the appellate court can also *remand* the case to
the lower court for a new trial.

The criminal trial can be viewed as a process that extends different advantages and disadvantages to the competing parties. The prosecution has
greater resources for investigating the evidence, the trial participants, and
even the potential jurors. Because it represents the public, the prosecution usually has pretrial community sentiment on its side except in the
rare instance of unpopular prosecution. Balanced against these advantages
of the prosecution is a set of procedural safeguards and legal principles
that help the defendant. The burden of proof is placed on the prosecution and the standard for proof is a stringent one—*beyond a reasonable doubt*.
Something less than complete certitude, reasonable doubt cannot be quan-
tified; in fact, it is painfully difficult to define, although it has been suggested that reasonable doubt is doubt for which one has a good reason.
Whatever its definition, the reasonable doubt standard reflects the legal
system's preference for mistaken acquittals rather than mistaken convictions.

In addition to this stringent standard of proof, the defendant is protected by an elaborate set of rules of evidence that limits the information the jury is allowed to consider in reaching a verdict. During a trial, many steps are also taken to insulate the jury from any outside, extralegal influences that might shape its verdict.

Civil Trials

Civil law regulates disputes between private citizens and businesses who seek to protect their rights by bringing a lawsuit against the party alleged to have violated their rights. In civil trials, the party bringing the suit is the *plaintiff*, who occupies a position similar to that of the prosecution in a criminal case. The party against whom the suit is filed is the defendant. Civil suits may involve allegations of malpractice against a physician, disputes over who was at fault in an auto accident, or charges that a company produced a defective product that caused injury to the plaintiff.

The order of procedure in civil trials is similar to that of criminal trials. The plaintiff has the burden of proof and therefore is first to make an opening statement, to present evidence, and to offer a closing argument. (In states in which criminal defendants make the first closing argument, civil defendants usually follow the same order.) In a civil case, the standard for plaintiff's burden of proof is a *preponderance of the evidence*, a threshold that implies that one side has prevailed in its presentation of evidence by a probability of more than .50. Preponderance of the evidence may be interpreted to mean "more likely than not likely," although Loh (1984) reviewed research which suggested that jurors and judges set a higher requirement than this interpretation implies. However the level is interpreted, it is clear that the law intends the plaintiff's burden of persuasion to be less demanding than that of the prosecutor because the consequences of a loss in a civil trial are thought to be less than those in a criminal trial, *considering all criminal and civil trials that will take place*.

A second difference between criminal and civil trials is that the civil defendant can be forced to testify by opposing counsel but the criminal defendant cannot. Plaintiff may call the defendant as an *adverse witness* and require that defendant answer questions posed by plaintiff's counsel.

There are numerous differences in the pretrial proceedings in civil and criminal investigation. There is no grand jury in civil proceedings. The use of *depositions* (sworn testimony made previous to trial) and *interrogatories* (written responses to questions from the other side) are frequent discovery tools in civil cases but are less common in criminal cases. In civil proceedings, the counterpart to the plea bargaining that occurs in criminal proceedings is known as *negotiating a settlement*; this mechanism resolves most civil suits before they reach the trial stage.

SCOPE OF CONSULTATION

We received our first request to serve as trial consultants in 1975 from a young public defender who was trying his first case. The defendant was a young black man accused of robbing and murdering an elderly white man who owned a small liquor store in Paris, Kentucky. The attorney asked us to help him select the jury, and using a selection model we now recognize as woefully simplistic, we did. The result was a jury that hung 11–1 in the direction of conviction, admittedly the most slender of threads from which to spin a theory of consultation. However, the notorious ability of the legal profession to define nondefeats as victories caused the hung jury outcome to be counted in the "win" column. Demand for our services increased; we had to develop our model of consultation.

We have now consulted in over 50 trials; in most, defendants were involved in criminal cases with capital charges. Most of our consultation in civil litigation has been with attorneys defending medical malpractice cases, although we have also worked with plaintiffs in personal injury and discrimination cases. The consultation model we describe here evolved from our work in these cases and reflects a blend of psychological theory, empirical data, clinical intuitions, and many insights from the attorneys with whom we work.

Requisite Knowledge for Consultants

The most valuable commodity that can be offered by the consultant to the attorney is the ability to think as a well-trained psychologist. Often it is difficult to maintain this psychological perspective. When you are consulting in the legal system, everyone else will be applying legal concepts to the phenomena of interest. At the beginning of a consulting relationship, communication is hindered, as though two different languages were being spoken. A "translator" will not be available, however. It is the consultant's task to decipher lawyers' language and to translate the jargon of psychology into everyday language. In addition, the excitement, drama, and real-world consequences of trials are captivating qualities that tend to seduce the consultant into identifying with attorneys and, at times, into an attempt to think of trial phenomena as a lawyer might. This outcome is not particularly desirable; and in its extreme form, the psychologist may decide to become a lawyer.

We do not discourage multidisciplinary training, nor do we oppose the increasingly popular law and psychology degree programs. However, good courtroom consultation does not require extensive legal training; if legal training either inhibits or replaces the psychological perspectives that should be provided by consultants, it can limit their contributions. One or more classes in criminal procedure, civil procedure, or torts are helpful but not essential preparation for effective consulting. Attendance at a number of criminal and civil trials and observation of the trials as they unfold is good preparation for consultants. Whatever form the preparation takes, the consultant must become thoroughly familiar not only with trial procedure, but also with the ways in which attorneys think about litigation and with the social–psychological factors at work in courtrooms. It may be beneficial for a consultant to discuss what is seen in the courtroom with an attorney in order to clarify any confusion about trial procedures and the permissible variations in them. In chapter 3, we describe the "method of alternative juries," a more elaborate method for studying trials.

If attorneys needed only another legal opinion they could more easily obtain it from their law partners. However, lawyers already spend too much time talking only with other lawyers, and that is why they are often willing to pay for another perspective.

The consultant must obtain adequate information about the case at hand and instruct attorneys in the ways in which the consultant can aid the litigation team. It is imperative that a consultant know the basic facts in the case, the theory of the case the attorney will attempt to develop, and the local rules for voir dire and jury selection. The consultant should have as much information as possible about the litigating parties, the major witnesses, the opposing counsel, and the presiding judge. The consultant need not know as much about the case as the attorney, but can serve best with thorough knowledge.

There are several ways to acquire this knowledge. The following sources provide good information: (a) copies of any media coverage, especially in cases in which one of the consultant's major tasks will be to nullify the adverse effects of pretrial publicity; (b) copies of depositions from the main witnesses in civil cases; (c) a personal interview in which the client discusses the events that the trial will cover and learns in turn about the proposed involvement of the consultant; (d) in instances of long-distance consulting when it is difficult to meet the client before the trial begins, a tape-recorded interview between the attorney and client that the consultant can hear before the trial; (e) a copy of the statutes and local rules covering voir dire if the consultant is not already familiar with how it will be conducted; and (f) a report from the attorney containing a summary of the major issues to be developed at trial, a clear statement of the theory of the case, and a preliminary indication of what contributions the attorney expects from the consultant.

The attorney's report is essential because it begins to focus the mind of the consultant on the unifying, inevitable, and ultimate question for every trial: "What is it that we want the jury to understand and to believe?" Most attorneys will already have written some type of trial outline that will serve this purpose well. If such an overview has not been prepared, the consultant's first important contribution to the litigation team will be a request for one.

Attorneys will usually recruit a psychological consultant for a specific activity. For example, a consultant may be asked to help select the jury or to conduct a public opinion survey. In most instances, this initial request will expand into other activities as the consultant and the attorney discuss the case. The directions this expansion will take are determined by the special needs of a given case, the consultant's own particular expertise, and the opportunities that are stimulated as the consultant and the attorney become acquainted and develop ideas that will improve and support the theory of the case.

With very few exceptions, we have found that trial attorneys, even those who are most experienced, are responsive to our psychological speculations and advice. During initial contacts attorneys are naturally somewhat skeptical of consultants' input. However, while working with the same attorney on several trials, an amicable professional relationship will probably develop, in which the attorney will defer to the consultant's opinion on the psychological aspects of the courtroom. As Saks and Hastie (1978, p. 100) have observed, "trial lawyers are, to a remarkable degree, professional applied social psychologists." This may explain why they are so willing to listen to and learn from what the consultant has to say.

All of the previous advice can be formed into the first principle of psychological consultation, a principle that should never be broken: *The consultant should learn as much about the case as early as possible through direct communication with the attorney and the client.* The range of consulting activities we describe in this book have resulted in large part from what we have learned through our strict adherence to this one rule.

OVERVIEW OF THE BOOK

The content of chapters 2 through 6 is devoted to a thorough description of a model of jury selection and courtroom consultation for psychologists who are interested in developing these skills as part of their professional work. We know that many of our colleagues have been asked by attorneys for assistance in jury selection and trial preparation but that they often decline the offer because they lack experience in this area and have no convenient guidebook to serve as a working tool. This book is aimed at those deficiencies.

We include material that psychologists need in order to begin jury and trial consultation. Although the book has a practical emphasis, we also try to establish the theoretical and empirical bases that psychologists will require for their interventions.

In chapter 2, we discuss the objectives and methods of jury selection and describe a research-based role for psychologists directed at securing the best conditions for selecting jurors. We present a 4-factor model of jury selection and the techniques used in assessing potential jurors.

Chapter 3 outlines the step-by-step procedures used in public opinion surveys, a very valuable tool for the jury/trial consultant. We pay special attention to the results and implications of change-of-venue surveys and discuss the utility of survey results for drawing juror profiles, developing the theory of one's case, and pretesting trial strategy and tactics. An alternative technique for evaluating pretrial hypotheses, known as the trial simulation, is also described in this chapter.

Chapter 4 deals with issues pertaining to psychologists who testify as expert witnesses in the courtroom. This function is different from any of the other activities addressed in the book. As a consultant, the psychologist is a behind-the-scenes advisor whose influence on the course and outcome of the trial is an indirect one; as a witness, however, the psychologist is one of the trial's central participants, one who presents direct evidence relevant to the trial's outcome. We will discuss expert testimony because it is the activity that brings most psychologists to the courtroom and because our observations of psychologists as expert witnesses suggest that they are uncomfortable and uncertain in that role, often doing a poor job of communicating their opinions effectively in the courtroom. We concentrate not on the substantive issues of expert testimony (e.g., questions as to whether the insanity defense should be abolished or as to what constitute the criteria for legal competence or criminal responsibility), but on matters relevant to expert witness behavior in general (i.e., the most appropriate attitudes and roles for the psychologist to assume when testifying as an expert). We recommend specific ''coping strategies'' for expert witnesses with a particular emphasis on planning the testimony and ''on-the-stand'' performance.

Chapter 5 describes the preparation of witnesses in civil and criminal trials. Methods of rehearsal, feedback, and influence are illustrated; we show how these training components can be combined to assist attorneys and their witnesses in enhancing credibility and the impact of courtroom testimony.

Chapter 6 deals with the presentation of evidence at trial. We discuss the structuring and presentation of opening statements; attorneys' styles and behavior in the courtroom; strategies and decisions during the trial; juror attitude formation and change; and closing arguments.

Chapter 7 examines the multiple sources of verification that can and should be used by consultants in evaluating their impact. Observation, evaluation research, archival investigations, juror interviews, and experimental methods can be integrated as a science of jury behavior and courtroom phenomena that guide our interventions and understanding of what occurs during a trial. We also cover various issues pertaining to the professional and ethical implications of courtroom consultation. Reactions to courtroom consultants by the public, attorneys, judges, and other psychologists are examined, and reasons for resentment of this type of consultation are discussed.

NOTES

[1]295 U.S. 78, 88 (1935).

[2]It is important to distinguish the role of expert witness who testifies about substantive matters before a jury from the role of consultant who assists attorneys in the development of their trial advocacy. Although most of this book concentrates on the consultation role, Chapter 4 discusses expert testimony. The ethical dilemmas facing the expert witness and the trial consultant are often different and may require different resolutions (see chapter 7).

[3]164 U.S. 492 (1896).

Chapter 2
Voir Dire: Structure and Methods

During the part of a trial known as voir dire, defined by *Black's Law Dictionary* (5th ed., 1979) as "to speak the truth," venirepersons (potential jurors) are questioned under oath[1] about their ability to sit as impartial evaluators of the issues at trial. This stage of the trial is often called *jury selection* because its product is the impaneling of a jury to decide the case. The term jury selection inaccurately connotes the idea that attorneys are allowed to recruit the jurors they favor from a large group of eligible candidates. In fact, a jury is composed of those venirepersons who are not removed by the judge or the attorneys for various reasons (see below). It is a group of survivors, not recruits, and the process is one of deselection, not selection, as is often implied by critics of social science consultation in voir dire (Etzioni, 1974).

PURPOSES OF VOIR DIRE

Voir dire has five purposes, three of which are sanctioned by the courts and two of which are not officially recognized and vary considerably in the degree to which judges will tolerate them.

Assessment of Statutory Requirements

The first recognized function of voir dire is to determine whether jurors meet statutory requirements for serving on a jury. In Kentucky, for example, a juror is disqualified from jury service if he or she:

1. Is not a citizen of the United States; or
2. Is not a resident of the county; or
3. Is unable to speak and understand the English language; or
4. Is incapable, by reason of physical or mental disability, or rendering effective jury service; or
5. Has been previously convicted of a felony and has not been pardoned

by the governor or other authorized person of the jurisdiction in which the juror was convicted; or

6. Is presently under indictment; or
7. Has served on a jury within the past twelve (12) months. (KRS 29A.080, 1977).

Juror qualifications are often assessed with a juror form that not only asks for information regarding these requirements but for further biographical information. Later in this chapter, we will further discuss juror questionnaires as a consultation tool. Use of these forms lessens the time spent in voir dire questioning jurors on their qualifications. It is rare for a juror to be disqualified on statutory grounds.

Discovery of Bias

The second recognized purpose of voir dire is to discover bias in a juror that would render that juror partial and therefore subject to a *challenge for cause*. A challenge for cause is raised when a juror indicates either actual or implied bias against one of the parties at trial. If the judge finds actual or implied bias, the juror is removed by the judge. *Actual bias* is revealed by a juror's own statements that (s)he holds a bias that would be verdict relevant (e.g., that the juror has formed a firm opinion that the accused is guilty). *Implied bias* arises when the juror does not admit to bias but the circumstances suggest that bias is probable (e.g., the juror is the sheriff's brother and the sheriff will be the prosecutor's main witness; despite the juror's assurances of impartiality, bias is implied). There are an unlimited number of challenges for cause in any trial, although judges tend to be conservative in granting them.

Obtaining Information for Peremptory Challenges

A set number of *peremptory challenges* is granted to each side in a trial for the purpose of letting that side remove jurors it believes to be unsympathetic to it. Peremptory challenges can be exercised for any reason, and are not subject to judicial interference except in very unusual circumstances. In criminal trials, the defense will have either the same number or a greater number of peremptories than the prosecution, depending on the jurisdiction. In civil litigation, defendant and plaintiff are granted the same number of peremptories; this number is usually less than that granted in criminal trials in the same jurisdiction.

Most of the questions posed by attorneys in the voir dire are aimed at uncovering information on which the attorneys can base the intelligent

exercise of their peremptory challenges. Courts usually recognize this justification for questions but may require attorneys to show how a given
question is relevant to the case at trial. Questions are likely to be permitted
if they include inquiries into education, occupation, family residence, past
jury experience, experiences as a victim of crime, attitudes about punishment, exposure to pretrial publicity, and other sources of influence outside the courtroom.

Judges are allowed great discretion in conducting voir dire and in the
questions they permit jurors to be asked. Unless it can be shown that a
party has been prevented from obtaining an impartial jury, a judge's limits
on voir dire will be upheld even to the extent that attorneys may be pre-
cluded from learning jurors' names or asking about their ethnic backgrounds (*United States v. Barnes*).[2] In studying the material that follows,
the consultant must remember that judges may properly refuse to allow
jurors to be questioned on topics regarded by the consultant as the pivotal
ones for exercising peremptory strikes.

Ingratiation

Most attorneys will attempt to use the voir dire as a means to persuade
jurors to like them or to identify more strongly with them. Suggs and Sales
(1981) distinguish this "unofficial" objective from the development of "effective rapport" necessary for productive questioning and include as examples of ingratiation the following tactics: (a) making a show of not asking venirepersons any questions after saying to them that "I'm confident
that you will all be fair jurors and I'm not going to waste any more of your
time with a lot of questions," (b) displaying great solicitousness toward
potential jurors, (c) commenting on similarity of background with certain
jurors ("Mr. Penn, the fact that we're both Quakers won't bias your opinion at all, will it?"), and (d) trying to be humorous with jurors. Attempts
at ingratiation can be risky and often backfire. Jurors may believe that the
attorney is too casual about the case or too obvious in attempts to manip-
ulate their feelings. Attorneys will often ask consultants to help them influence the jury more satisfactorily during voir dire. Usually, the consultant should advise attorneys to eliminate the more theatrical attempts at
ingratiation from their repertoire.

Indoctrination

The second unofficial function of voir dire is indoctrination, whereby attorneys attempt to prepare potential jurors to be receptive to their theory
of the case. "Priming the pump" and "gaining a toehold" describe the
indoctrination techniques practiced by attorneys in voir dire when the

judge permits it. The most common forms of indoctrination and ones which consultants are often asked to embellish are (a) desensitizing the jury to the negative aspects of one's case (e.g., "The evidence will show that my client, Rick Jones, is a drug user; will that fact alone make any of you so prejudiced against Rick that you won't be able to give him a fair trial?"); (b) acquainting jurors with the essential features of one's case (e.g., "You agree, don't you, that almost any product if used carelessly or improperly can be dangerous?"); (c) introducing key evidence for jurors to anticipate (e.g., "We will be presenting some pictures of Mr. Reeve's injuries. Do any of you feel that you won't be able to look at these pictures because you would become unduly upset?"); and (d) obtaining commitments from jurors to behave in certain ways (e.g., "You won't make up your mind, will you, on what sentence to give the defendant, if you find him guilty, until you've heard all the evidence from both sides?").

In voir dire, all attorneys seek to impanel the jury that will be most favorable for their clients. In fact, this is the goal required by our adversary system, which presumes that energetic pursuit of this objective in opposite directions by two competent advocates will culminate in a jury composed either of members whose prejudices and preferences cancel one another's or of members whose views cluster around a midpoint of a favorable-unfavorable dimension.

Attorneys will attempt to reach this goal by using the three judicially sanctioned functions of voir dire to prune the panel of the potential jurors they find most unfavorable while using the two unofficial strategies of voir dire to cultivate favorable tendencies in the remaining jurors. Attorneys involve jury consultants in the process to secure the maximum benefits from voir dire. Although consultants may modify the adversarial uses of voir dire by attorneys (i.e., challenges for cause, peremptory challenges, detailed questioning or investigation of jurors, and manipulation of jurors), attorneys will use the techniques whether or not jury consultants are used.

VOIR DIRE CONSULTATION

Evaluations of Consultation Techniques

The use of social scientists to deselect jurors began in the famous political trials of the late 1960s and early 1970s and was thoroughly described in several case histories published thereafter. The professional literature summarizes the "scientific jury selection" methods used in the trials of Joan Little (McConahay, Mullin, & Frederick, 1977); the "Harrisburg 7," (Schulman, Shaver, Colman, Emrich, & Christie, 1973); the "Gainesville 8" (Christie, 1976); Black Panther members Fred Hampton (Berk,

1976), and Huey Newton (Blauner, 1972); the "Attica brothers" (Levine & Schweber-Koren, 1976); Angela Davis (Sage, 1973); the Wounded Knee defendants (Christie, 1976); Pat Swinton (Buckhout, 1978); and John Mitchell and Maurice Stans (Zeisel & Diamond, 1976). Jury consultation is no longer confined to national showcase trials. Jury consultants are now frequently involved in death penalty trials, civil litigation, and the "typical criminal cases" (Bennett, 1977). Here, we focus our attention on criminal trials, because most jury research has been conducted on criminal cases, and because we believe the jury variance to be influenced is greater in criminal than in civil trials.

Initial reactions to jury consultation, whether unbridled enthusiasm or unrealistic fear, have been tempered somewhat by reviews that argue that there is no scientifically acceptable evidence to prove that scientific jury selection is anything more than marginally effective in influencing the outcome of a trial. The sophistication of these reviews range from naive attacks on rigging juries (Etzioni, 1974) and the patently false claim that "no defendant who has used scientific jury selection has ever been convicted, except on the most trivial charges . . . " (Silver, 1978), to thorough, provocative critiques of the methodology, conceptualization, and operation of jury selection techniques (Berk, 1976; Berk, Hennessy, & Swan, 1977; Berman & Sales, 1977; Saks, 1976a, 1976b; Saks & Hastie, 1978, pp. 61–71; Suggs & Sales, 1978). Skepticism about scientific jury selection occurs for at least four reasons; these reasons must be considered before we describe our approach to jury consultation and the evidence in support of its use.

1. Most often cited in support of the effectiveness of jury consultation is the evidence that most defendants who have used it have been acquitted or convicted only on minor charges. However, this high "batting average" may be because of several variables in these trials that are confounded by use of jury consultants. Most of the early trials involved political activists charged with conspiracy, an extremely difficult charge to prove and one that provokes large attitudinal differences among the public. Defense lawyers in these cases were zealous advocates whose spirited representation of their clients may have persuaded juries of almost any composition that the government had not proven its case. Finally, all aspects of the defense, not just the jury selection, were vigorously practiced in these trials, making it difficult to attribute the verdict to a favorable jury as opposed to unusually credible defense witnesses or successfully impeached government witnesses.

2. Jury selection critics object to the lack of research designs adequate to test claims of effectiveness and point out that comparisons of scientific jury selection versus selection by a good (or even bad) attorney are either not available or are not convincing (see the attempts at simulated comparisons by Penrod, Rosenblum, Stefek, & Hastie, 1979, and by Horowitz,

1980). For example, Saks & Hastie (1978, p. 62) argue that evidence for the superiority of scientific jury selection requires that the verdicts of scientifically selected juries be compared with those of traditionally selected juries hearing the same cases. Such studies have not been conducted, nor is it probable that they will be, given the requirements of trial procedure in our country. Although we agree that consultants are obligated to evaluate their work empirically, we question an insistence on a method that would, in all likelihood, be legally prohibited. Randomized experiments for evaluating a number of important procedures with personal significance (surgery vs. no surgery) or national implications (speed limits of 55 vs. 75 mph) are not possible; yet persuasive data from quasi-experimental designs can inform the use of such procedures (Cook & Campbell, 1979). Quasi-experimental data can serve the same purpose in the area of jury consultation.

3. The specific techniques that constitute the consultant's armamentarium have been criticized on standard psychometric grounds, with the more general observation that social scientists do poorly on most prediction tasks, of which predicting jurors' behavior is among the most difficult.

Berk (1976) has noted that juror surveys suffer from sampling problems, uncertain temporal reliability, and numerous criteria problems, and that they yield data that are probabilistic but that must be converted into binary, yes–no decisions. However, surveys permit gathering of information that attorneys cannot obtain in voir dire, and they are usually supported by other data from the voir dire that facilitate the necessary yes–no decision. Saks (1976a) has argued that, analogous to jury selection, clinical predictions by psychologists have been proved inferior to actuarial prediction. However, jury consultants often rely primarily on actuarial strategies, so this criticism may apply only to certain consultation methods. We agree that the reliability and validity of graphoanalysis, horoscopes, and body language are doubtful, but they are peripheral to the work of most jury consultants.

4. The most important objection to scientific jury selection is that jury characteristics account for much smaller amounts of verdict variance in comparison to the strength of the evidence (see Hepburn, 1980; Penrod, 1980). There is consensus on this point among opponents and proponents of jury consultation. Richard Christie (1976), a senior figure among jury consultants, acknowledges that there are cases in which "the evidence is so clearcut that no method of jury selection could outweigh [it]."

Research indicates that correlations between demographic variables and verdict-relevant attitudes seldom exceed .30. At the same time, results of mock jury studies (a literature we believe has limited relevance to jury consultation; see Dillehay & Nietzel, 1980a, 1980b) are not consistent on this point. We interpret the variance-accounted-for evidence to mean that there are some trials in which legal evidence will overwhelm other influences. In such cases, jury consultation may be a waste of time. However, in other cases in which the evidence is more ambiguous and in which there is sufficient heterogeneity among potential jurors, scientific jury selection may yield benefits. In addition, in some cases, control of 10% of the variance (a correlation of .30) is not trivial effect size. As Rosenthal (1983) said, "neither experienced behavioral researchers nor experienced statisticians (have) a good intuitive feel for the practical meaning of such common effect size estimations. . . . " An effect size accounting for 10% of the variance in a dichotomous outcome (guilty vs. not guilty) produces a 30% change in the "success rate" attributable to an intervention (Rosenthal, 1983), an outcome that is not trivial to trial participants.

On the basis of our research and experiences, we believe jury consultation has three beneficial effects in criminal trials.

First, deselection of the most unfavorable venirepersons from panels results in juries that have an increased tendency to evaluate ambiguous evidence more favorably and an increased tendency to return less severe penalties against convicted defendants than they would have had if consultation had not been used.

Second, conditions of the voir dire can be improved; thus, attorneys are better able to detect biased jurors and to exercise peremptory challenges intelligently.

Third, attorneys' confidence and positive expectancies about the "extra edge" they have received from jury consultants are increased. In addition to the morale boost that attorneys receive from using a technique they believe to be very powerful (similar to the expectancy effects associated with psychotherapy), use of jury consultants permits attorneys more free time to attend to pretrial preparation and matters of evidence, an outcome that even skeptics should appreciate.

Stages of Jury Consultation

Critics of jury consultation usually focus their criticisms on the deselection of jurors, that is, the ways in which consultants advise attorneys on exercise of their peremptory challenges. However, juror deselection is only one of three important activities in which consultants are involved in voir dire. We describe next the techniques of consultation in each of these stages together with the research that evaluates their effectiveness. Table 2.1 summarizes the goals and techniques of the three stages of jury consultation.

Table 2.1. Goals and Techniques of Jury Consultation

Stage of Consultation	Goals	Techniques
Stage I: Voir dire preparation	Learn about the case	Hold planning sessions with attorneys
	Educate attorneys about contributions that consultants can make	Review media, interview client, observe courtroom procedures
	Develop instruments	If necessary develop: juror questionnaires, survey questionnaires, trial simulations, and interviews with key informants
	Formulate initial theory of jury selection	Analyze data from above and propose theory of jury selection that is integrated with attorneys' theory of case
Stage II: Improving voir dire conditions	Structure voir dire in a manner that improves chances to uncover juror bias and to identify juror prejudice	Affidavits, expert testimony on: change of venue; individual, sequestered, attorney-conducted voir dire; struck versus "as you go" system; and composition challenge
	Improve voir dire skills of attorneys	Preparation of voir dire topics and training of attorneys in interviewing techniques
Stage III: Juror deselection	Develop final theory of jury selection	Coordinate pretrial data with in-court observation of venirepersons
	Impanel a jury as favorably disposed toward client and theory of case as possible.	Develop rating system to identify jurors for peremptory challenge by: juror experience, intelligence, sentiment, and social influence

Voir Dire Preparation

In preparation for voir dire, the consultant should: (a) learn as much as possible about the case; (b) instruct the attorneys as to what they may expect from the consultant in voir dire; (c) develop the instruments (surveys, juror questionnaires, simulations) that will be used for the consultation; and (d) formulate a theory of jury selection that is unique to the needs of the case at hand.

Planning Meeting. As explained in chapter 1, effective courtroom consultation requires that consultants and attorneys know each other's expectations and capacities. The consultant must be thoroughly knowledgeable about the case because its nature will determine to a great extent the consultation decisions. An essential rule of jury consultation is that no two trials are identical; therefore, decisions about jury characteristics must be tailored to the demands of each trial. There is no such thing as an "across-the-board" ideal defense juror or plaintiff juror; consultants who presume that will simply be substituting their stereotypes for those of lawyers.

We request a meeting with defense attorneys as far in advance of the trial as possible. At this meeting, we seek a description of the charges, the state's evidence, the theory of the defense, local rules for voir dire, and any special procedures of the particular court. We obtain a psychological portrait of all the important figures in the trial: defense counsel, prosecutor, judge, and all witnesses. After this meeting, we hold a personal interview with the client so that the client may understand our role in the case and so that we in turn may observe the impressions the client makes on other people. If a personal interview is impossible, we ask for a tape-recorded interview between the attorney and client that we can listen to prior to the trial. After meeting with the client and the attorneys, we usually visit the trial courtroom to observe the physical setting as well as the style and demeanor of the prosecutor and presiding judge.

Juror Questionnaires. In most jurisdictions, the venire from which the jury will be selected is asked to complete a questionnaire that assesses qualifications for jury duty and other facts such as education, current employment, and number and ages of children. Members of the panel either bring this form to court on their first day of service or return it by mail. Usually, it is then given to both the defense and prosecuting attorneys.

The consultant may draw up an expanded questionnaire that asks information about the juror's employment history; education and occupation of spouses and children; previous experiences as a litigant or crime victim; membership in religious, civic, and social organizations; reading habits; hobbies; etc. Pretrial survey findings can be linked to answers to these questions, thereby aiding in peremptory striking of the least desirable jurors. Such juror questionnaires offer attorneys and consultants early data about potential jurors and permit an initial classification of their desirability as prospective jurors. Judges are most responsive to motions for use of a special questionnaire if they can be convinced that it will save time in the voir dire proper. Appendix A is a special juror questionnaire that we have used.

Opinion Surveys. In cases that receive excessive publicity or that inflame community passions, it may be necessary to seek a change of venue. If so, the consultant will need extra time to conduct a competent survey of public opinion. For that reason, decisions about the venue must be made at the outset. Attorneys underestimate the time required to conduct a survey; therefore, the consultant must take the initiative in securing sufficient time. Venue surveying is described thoroughly in chapter 3.

The community survey is a key element in some applications of systematic case preparation and jury selection (see Bonora & Krauss, 1984). When time and resources permit, this technique can provide important and useful information about the attitudes of potential jurors on both general and specific aspects of the case, including the parties involved in the litigation. The venue survey (discussed in chapter 3) can be used for this purpose if considerable additional information on respondents' views and attitudes is obtained and additional social and demographic information on the respondents is gathered. In the venue survey, one determines the prevalence of belief and related beliefs concerning the guilt of defendants. The survey conducted for purposes of voir dire must be designed to permit an extensive analysis of the relationships among variables so that those persons who favor or disfavor one's side of the case can be identified. Based on the relationships discovered in the analyses between social and demographic variables on the one hand, and case-relevant attitudes, motives, and values on the other, profiles of desirable and undesirable jurors are developed in terms of variables ascertainable on the jury panel. These descriptors serve as the link for inferences about likely dispositions of members of the jury panel. Although the survey thus applied can be instructive, we seldom use it, both because of the time and expense involved and because the magnitude of relationships among the variables involved —although significant—are usually small. If time, money, and expertise are available, however, the community survey that focuses on relationships among relevant variables can inform case preparation and jury selection.

Trial Simulations. Chapter 3 also describes trial simulations, a time-consuming but very effective technique for developing the theory of the case and evaluating the impact of supportive and adverse evidence and various trial tactics. During the first stage of voir dire preparation, a major function of the consultant is to acquaint the attorneys with the availability of procedures such as simulations or "trial by surveys" (see chapter 3) that assist in case preparation. These methods are not necessary for every case and are not substitutes for the careful case analysis that should be practiced by attorneys. However, they yield some empirical data regarding the response of laypersons to the presentations of attorneys and permit precourse corrections of misdirected tactics. Attorneys often lose sight of the jury as the target in pretrial preparation; much of their time is spent debating with and attempting to influence other attorneys. The trial simulation or the trial by survey serves as a tether connecting attorneys to the reactions of the ultimate jury.

If time and money are limited, the consultant may find it necessary to play the role of the simulated jury in an attempt to imagine the range of

reaction one might receive from a group of people. Although this procedure is not ideal, primarily because it eliminates the opportunity for consensual feedback, it allows many of the insights on case analysis and initial jury profiling that are usually contributed by simulations.

Key Informants. Key informants living in the local community who are
asked about their knowledge of jurors as it pertains to verdict-relevant issues are the last source of pretrial information. We have not made extensive use of key informants for two reasons. First, jurors may discover that
other people are being questioned about them and resent the invasion of
privacy, disliking those who engage in what most people consider objectionable behavior. Second, the reliability and validity of informant data
are problematic. The data are collected second- or third-hand, are subject
to distortions along the lines of transmission, and often indicate not that
a person will make a "good juror" but that the person is honest, trustworthy, or a potentially desirable friend. When we have made use of key
informants, they have often been attorneys not connected with the case;
the validity and reliability problems were not eliminated.

Tentative Jury Profile. By the end of the preparation stage, the consultant
should be able to formulate an initial theory of jury selection, one that is
integrated with the theory of the case and that has been guided by results
of armchair reflection, juror questionnaires, surveys, key informant interviews, and trial simulations. Because use of peremptory and cause challenges guarantees only that unfavorable jurors can be removed, the consultant should concentrate on developing the profile of the unfavorable
juror and, with the help of the juror questionnaires, on identifying people on the venire who fit a negative profile. Profiling favorable jurors provides attorneys with a psychological benefit, reassuring them their case
can have a receptive audience; however, the mechanics of voir dire will
serve not to draft the best jurors, but to remove the worst.

Improving Voir Dire Conditions

Having drawn up the assessment instruments and having constructed a
tentative jury profile, the consultant next must help attorneys structure
the conditions of voir dire to maximize its chances of identifying biased
jurors and to permit the best use of peremptory challenges. In this pretrial stage, consultants also aid attorneys in improving their voir dire skills.

In most jurisdictions, judges have wide discretion as to who will conduct the voir dire; the length of time of the voir dire; the type of questions to be asked and their phrasing; whether the questions are to be
posed to individual jurors or to the panel as a group; and whether jurors

are to be present to hear the answers of other jurors. In federal courts and in many state jurisdictions, judges restrict voir dire by interrogating the jurors themselves and by directing their questions to jurors en masse rather than to individual jurors. Attorneys may submit questions they wish to ask jurors to the judge, but the judge is free to refuse or modify these questions. Judges prefer to conduct the voir dire themselves of the entire jury panel in the courtroom, because they believe this method is more efficient and less subject to adversarial excesses (Fortune, 1980–1981).

Limited voir dire proves an unpleasant reality for many attorneys, who often find themselves trying to predict jurors' behavior with no more than the scanty and possibly unreliable data rendered by traditional voir dire. The research skills of the consultant then become important. The consultant can provide effective identification of variations of voir dire that may influence its various outcomes and can then conduct evaluative research on such variations. Results of this research can be presented through affidavits and expert testimony in support of motions seeking to improve the conditions of voir dire. Although the research we later describe compares the effects of sequestered voir dire of individual jurors with open court voir dire of the panel en masse, other variations may be of more importance in different jurisdictions. Selecting the most important dimensions for investigation is a diagnostic task, one that is best performed by the consultant after learning from attorneys which voir dire conditions are the most constraining. In some courts, it may be best to evaluate the effects of voir dire conducted by the attorney as opposed to voir dire conducted by a judge. In others, it may be best to document the consequences of arbitrary time limits on voir dire.

Whatever the questions, we believe that the most convincing data are obtained by observational or archival studies of voir dire (Dillehay & Nietzel, 1980a, 1980b), although we acknowledge the value of theory-guided laboratory research (Saks & Hastie, 1978) and, under certain circumstances, juror analogue investigations (Haney, 1984a). An example of research on voir dire procedures is presented below.

Structuring Voir Dire. Several aspects of psychological research suggest that venirepersons are less likely to be completely candid and informative about their attitudes and beliefs concerning a specific case when voir dire is conducted by the judge in open court with all jurors present than when it is conducted by attorney and judge who question individual venirepersons separated from one another (see Suggs & Sales, 1981 and Bush, 1976 for reviews of this literature).

Although jury consultants (Ginger, 1977; Bonora & Krauss, 1984; Suggs & Sales, 1981) and attorneys (Clarke, 1980) agree on the desirability of attorney-conducted voir dire of individual jurors sequestered from one another, the data in support of this preference are scarce, consisting of Christie's (cited in Ginger, 1977, p. 323) analysis of different types of voir dire used in seven well-publicized political trials; Broeder's (1965) reports that in private post-trial interviews jurors give answers that are discrepant (and presumably more candid) than those that they give in voir dire; and Padawer-Singer, Singer, and Singer's (1974) mock jury study of attorney-conducted voir dire in comparison to absence of voir dire.

Our first study of this issue (Nietzel & Dillehay, 1982) examined whether individual questioning by judge and counsel of sequestered venirepersons produced more successful strikes for cause than did other forms of voir dire. A dismissal by the judge for cause favored by one side is a distinct advantage for that side, allowing that side to preserve a peremptory challenge that can be used on another unwanted potential juror. A dismissal for cause also means that the judge is persuaded that the juror cannot render a fair verdict and thus should not serve. Strikes for cause are therefore a good index of the effectiveness of different voir dire procedures in revealing prejudice. It was the major outcome variable in our research, as it was in Christie's analysis.

Our data were obtained from 13 capital cases tried in Kentucky between 1975 and 1980. They constituted approximately one third of similar cases tried in the state during this time and were representative of capital cases we have encountered in other states. The trials were classified by us and independently by the trial or appellate attorney into one of four categories describing the scope of the voir dire. These categories ranged from: (a) individual questions put to each potential juror under sequestration ($n = 4$); (b) en masse questioning followed by questions to sequestered individuals on selected topics ($n = 3$); (c) en masse questioning supplemented with individual questions to nonsequestered jurors ($n = 2$); and (d) en masse questioning of the panel in open court ($n = 4$).

The data indicate that, for defense-inspired challenges, significantly ($p < .05$) more sustained challenges for cause occurred under individual questioning with sequestration than under questioning en masse in open court (see Figure 2.1). That is, defense attorneys were better able to persuade the courts to dismiss potential jurors who appeared inimical to their case when the voir dire was conducted with individual, sequestered potential jurors. In contrast, cases for which there was sequestered interrogation on the death penalty (Groups 1 and 2) resulted in significantly ($p < .03$) fewer *Witherspoon* removals[3] than occurred in those cases in which all questioning was done in open court (Groups 3 and 4). Other analyses showed that these differences could not be accounted for by differential willingness on the part of judges to sustain the challenges for cause raised by attorneys.

We have completed a replication of these findings (Nietzel, Dillehay,

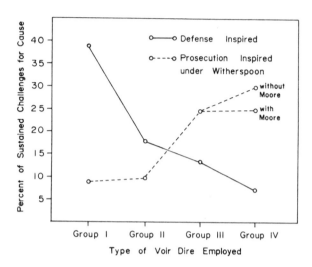

FIGURE 2.1. The Relationship Between Types of Voir Dire and Number of Sustained Challenges for Cause. *Note.* From ''The Effects of Variations in Voir Dire Procedures in Capital Murder Trials'' by M. Nietzel and R. Dillehay, 1982, *Law and Human Behavior, 6,* p. 7. Copyright 1982 by Plenum Publishing Co. Reprinted with permission.

& Himelein, 1984) with a sample of 18 capital cases tried in Kentucky ($n =$ 9), South Carolina ($n = 7$), and California ($n = 2$). Based on our original criteria, we assigned each trial to one of two groups. Group 1 ($n = 13$), consisting of trials in which judge and attorneys posed questions to individual jurors sequestered from one another, was identical in definition to Group 1 in our 1982 study. Group 2 ($n = 5$) consisted of trials using less enhanced forms of voir dire; it includes all trials that would have been classified as Group 2, 3, or 4 in the 1982 study.

The data replicated the finding that defense-inspired removals for cause were significantly more ($p < .02$) frequent under Group 1 voir dire conditions, and that this difference was robust enough to withstand interstate variability that approached significance. Table 2.2 summarizes the data for these 18 trials on five dependent measures: (a) number of persons examined, (b) percentage of potential jurors excused for illness, hardship, or other personal excuses; (c) percentage of potential jurors eliminated by prosecution challenges under *Witherspoon*; (d) or for other reasons of cause; and (e) percentage of jurors eliminated by defense-inspired challenges for cause. Only the last measure was significantly associated with type of voir dire.

With this sample of 18 trials, we also were able to analyze the effects associated with our presence (one or the other of us) as jury selection con-

Table 2.2. Dispositions of Potential Jurors in Eighteen Capital Murder Cases by Type of Voir Dire, State, and Presence of Jury Selection Consultants

TRIAL	No. Examined	Successful Excuses		Defense-inspired Causes (successful)		Witherspoon Causes (successful)		All Prosecution Causes (successful)	
		N	%	N	%	N	%	N	%
Group 1									
South Carolina Trials (N=7)									
Allen & Childers (C)	70	4	5.7	16	22.8	3	4.3	3	4.3
Arnold & Plath (C)	107	10	9.3	37	34.6	11	10.3	13	12.1
Gooslby (C)	51	8	15.7	10	19.6	5	9.8	7	13.7
Johnson (C)	43	5	11.6	3	7.0	3	7.0	3	7.0
McKelvie (C)	45	6	13.3	6	13.3	6	13.3	6	13.3
Tate (C)	59	14	23.7	9	15.2	6	10.2	6	10.2
Yates (C)	55	10	18.2	8	14.5	5	9.1	6	10.9
MEAN (South Carolina)	61.4	8.1	13.9	12.7	18.1	5.6	9.1	6.3	10.2)
Kentucky Trials (N=5)									
Ice (NC)	80	18	22.5	17	21.2	14	17.5	15	18.8
Kordenbrock & Kruse (C)	93	6	6.4	41	44.1	5	5.4	6	6.4
Smith (C)	53	3	5.7	7	13.2	14	26.4	15	28.3
White (NC)	76	32	42.1	27	35.5	16	21.0	17	22.4
Wiley (NC)	57	5	8.8	16	28.1	4	7.0	7	12.3
MEAN (Kentucky)	71.8	12.8	17.1	21.6	28.4	10.6	15.5	12	17.6
Nelson (California) (C)*	109	18	16.5	17	15.6	7	6.4	8	7.3
MEAN (All Group 1)	69.1	10.7	15.3	16.5	21.9	7.6	11.4	8.6	12.8
Group 2									
Ford (KY) (C)	59	11	18.6	9	15.2	7	11.9	7	11.9
O'Bryan (KY) (NC)	59	11	18.6	6	10.2	12	20.3	12	20.3
McQueen & Burnell (KY) (NC)	64	13	20.3	6	9.4	7	10.9	12	18.8
Odom (KY) (NC)	51	7	13.7	5	9.8	7	13.7	8	15.7
Wry (CA) (C)	47	1	2.1	2	4.2	1	2.1	1	2.1
MEAN (All Group 2)	56	8.6	14.7	5.6	9.8	6.8	11.8	8	13.8
Non-consultant Cases Mean (N=6)	64.5	14.3	21.0	12.8	19.0	10.0	15.1	11.8	18.0
Consultant Cases Mean (N=12)	65.9	8.0	12.2	13.8	18.3	6.1	9.7	6.8	10.6

*Two consultants were present: Beth Bonora of the National Jury Project and Ronald C. Dillehay.

C = Jury Consultant Present

NC = No Consultant Present

sultants. Our presence was not associated with an increased percentage of defense-inspired challenges for cause, but it was related to significantly fewer removals by the prosecution under *Witherspoon* (see Table 2.2) and to a significantly larger number of jurors successfully challenged by the defense on the grounds that they were automatically in favor of the death penalty (data not included in Table 2.2).[4]

Trial judges have been very responsive to these data when they have been presented in affidavits or expert testimony. Whenever we have reported these results in support of motions for enhanced voir dire, judges have granted a more extensive form of voir dire than they originally planned to grant. Although there are perils in the courts' use of social science data, these experiences have made us sanguine about the possibility that trial courts will consider data that shed light on voir dire procedures. However, individual, sequestered voir dire may not always be the preferred mode of jury selection (see Box 2.1).

Box 2.1. Enhanced Voir Dire: The Negative Effects

Individual, sequestered voir dire is not free of risk. Tradeoffs are involved in the concentrated inquiries of individual jurors and must be considered because they introduce negative influences. These influences are most obvious in that part of capital trial voir dire known as *death qualification*. Death qualification involves the process by which courts identify and exclude from capital juries those people who either would never consider voting to impose the death penalty in any case, regardless of the evidence or would not be fair and impartial in determining a capital defendant's guilt or innocence. These two criteria originated in the previously mentioned case of *Witherspoon v. Illinois*, and people who are not "death-qualified" are sometimes also called "Witherspoon excludables." In death qualification, those people who *automatically* favor the death penalty in all capital cases (called the ADP group) are also excluded by cause from the jury. In our experience, Witherspoon excludables are identified in voir dire much more frequently than are ADP excludables.

Because of death qualification, social scientists are interested in whether the removal of death-penalty opponents results in juries that are less representative of their communities and that are prone toward conviction at the guilt-or-innocence phase of the trial. (Capital trials are *bifurcated* or conducted in two phases: the *guilt-or-innocence phase* and the *penalty phase*, in which the jury decides the sentence if it has convicted the defendant at the first phase.) The weight of evidence gathered by different methods shows that death qualification of jurors results in more removals of blacks, women, people with certain beliefs (Jews, atheists, agnostics), and poor people (Bronson, 1970; Fitzgerald & Ellsworth, 1984; Zeisel, 1968); more removals of persons willing to accept certain legal defenses (e.g., insanity) and the importance of due process (Ellsworth, Bukaty,

---

(continued)

Cowan, & Thompson, 1984; Goldberg, 1970); more removals of less authoritarian persons (Jurow, 1971) and persons who interpret pro-prosecution evidence less favorably (Thompson, Cowan, Ellsworth & Harrington, 1984); and more removals of persons who are not conviction-prone (Cowan, Thompson, & Ellsworth, 1984; Ellsworth et al., 1984; Goldberg, 1970; Jurow, 1971; Zeisel, 1968).

A remedy must be sought if death qualification results in conviction-prone juries, and threatens due process. Two solutions have been proposed. The first solution calls for elimination of death qualification questions during voir dire. Prosecutors oppose this limitation for obvious reasons, but defense consultants may wish to recommend that in capital cases the best voir dire on death penalty attitudes is no voir dire at all. This constitutes an exception to the advice that expanded voir dire benefits the defense. The second solution to death qualification problems and the one that has a more promising future is the impaneling of two separate juries, one which deliberates at the guilt-and-innocence phase and is not questioned about the death penalty, and a second which deliberates at the penalty phase and is death qualified.

Whenever death qualification takes place, the process itself may change the beliefs and attitudes of qualified jurors. This issue has been the subject of a research program by Haney (1984a), who has investigated whether the death qualification process increases jurors' expectations and preconceptions that a defendant is guilty and that a death sentence is the preferable sentence.

Haney (1984a) randomly assigned 67 community volunteers (after removing all *Witherspoon* excludables) to watch one of two videotapes of a simulated capital voir dire conducted by experienced attorneys. The videotapes were identical except that in the 2-hour *experimental* tape, the venirepersons underwent 30 minutes of death qualification, which included removal of two confederates because of their death penalty opposition. The 90-minute *control* tape was identical to the experimental tape except that the 30 minutes of death qualification was edited out. After watching one of the two tapes in groups of 8 to 12, participants answered a 17-item questionnaire designed to assess their attitudes about the trial and its participants.

Results showed that participants exposed to death qualification were significantly more conviction-prone, more likely to believe that other trial participants (defense attorney, prosecutor, and judge) thought the defendant was guilty, more likely to believe that the judge and prosecutor favored the death penalty, and more likely themselves to prefer the death penalty in a hypothetical capital murder case. Haney (1984b) concluded that "exposure to death qualification may seriously compromise the fairness and impartiality of capital juries" and suggested that there are at least five psychological processes that may underlie the biasing effect: (a) using language in voir dire that suggests that defendants will be found guilty; (b) imagining a certain outcome (e.g., sentencing defendant to death) increases persons' expectations that the event will occur; (c) discussing the death penalty desensitizes or habituates persons to the emotional trauma involved in imposing it; (d) publically affirming one's willingness to consider imposing the death penalty increases commitment to that position; and (e) excluding death-penalty opponents suggests to jurors that the law disapproves of such people.

On the basis of his research, Haney recommended the biasing effects of death qualification may be minimized by conducting it individually with each juror

(continued)

sequestered from the others. We concur with Haney's recommendation for individual, sequestered voir dire, which resulted in the California Supreme Court requisition that in California the death qualification portion of any voir dire "be done individually and in sequestration" (*Hovey v. Superior Court**). (*Hovey* is also noteworthy for its sophisticated analysis of the research on the hypothesis that death qualification produces conviction-prone juries.)

Unfortunately, the advantages of individual, sequestered death qualification may not be as clear-cut as we or Haney have assumed. First, there are no data to show that it actually reduces the biasing effects. Second, as Haney (1984b) acknowledges, there are reasons to suspect that it may even intensify some of the problems and introduce new ones.

> Separated from the rest of the voir dire, death penalty questions become clearly distinguished from other topics in a way that underscores their importance. Prospective jurors are likely to infer that these special questions address . . . an issue ostensibly far more important than standard topics . . . that are merely addressed before the open jury panel. . . . (I)n the name of reducing repetitiveness of death qualification, the court may have inadvertently increased its symbolic significance and its emotional intensity. (Haney, 1984b, pp. 148–149)

In a capital case, defense consultants find themselves in a dilemma. Either they can recommend that attorneys "go easy" on death qualification, thereby risking the failure to rehabilitate some jurors with death-penalty scruples and to identify some ADP jurors, or they can advise attorneys to conduct vigorous death qualification, with the risk that the intensity of that process, possibly magnified by each juror's isolation, will, in turn, intensify the pro-death sentiments of the jurors. There is no immediate resolution of this dilemma except separate evaluation of each case; the defense consultant must then use the method that seems to have the fewer costs.

---

*28 Cal. 3dl, 168 Cal. Rptr. 128, 616 P. 2d 1301 (1980).

The selection of the voir dire procedures to be evaluated in any jurisdiction must be carefully considered in discussion with attorneys. Although it may be possible to conduct ad hoc investigations, the consultant's research is likely to be more complete and persuasive if it is programmatic and planned prior to any particular litigation.

Using the Struck System. The consultant may be asked for a recommendation with regard to the manner in which attorneys exercise their peremptory challenges in voir dire. There are two basic systems for using peremptory challenges. In the *"as you go"* system, each side is required to exercise its peremptories after the voir dire of each prospective juror. Usually the prosecutor is required to accept or strike a juror before the defense does, but at times the two sides may alternate the order of their strikes.

In the *struck system*, peremptories are not exercised until a certain number of jurors have been examined and qualified for cause. Several variations in the struck system are used in the federal and state courts; however, in most systems, the defense and the prosecution exercise their peremptories independently by striking the names of their challenged jurors from two identical lists of qualified jurors. The lists are then given to the judge or clerk, who announces the resulting jury.

Under the struck system, in a case in which the prosecution has six peremptory challenges, the defense has nine, and a jury of 12 is to be impaneled, 27 venirepersons are first qualified for cause; their names are then given to each side. If both sides use all their peremptories and if no venireperson is struck by both sides, 12 venirepersons are left to constitute the jury. If one side does not use all its peremptories or if both sides strike one or more of the same persons, resulting in more than 12 "survivors," the court will usually draw 12 names at random from the surviving group. Those 12 people will be sworn as the jury.

The struck system is the preferable method for exercising peremptories *in most cases*. The struck system permits both sides to weigh the use of its peremptories carefully by comparing all the jurors at the same time, after all the data have been gathered. Neither side is forced into a guessing game in which it must use peremptories without knowing whether it will encounter more objectionable jurors later. The struck system also fits nicely with the mechanics of individual, sequestered voir dire; after being interviewed and qualified for cause, a venireperson is admonished not to discuss the case and to return later when the peremptories will be exercised.

A consultant may prefer the "as you go" system only when opposing counsel is a relatively inexperienced trial attorney who, in addition, has fewer peremptories than the consultant's team. Such an attorney may "burn" (use up) too many peremptories at the beginning of voir dire. However, when a consultant works for a defense attorney, it is usually the prosecuting attorney who is more experienced. Judges are usually not opposed to a struck system, especially if they can be convinced of its efficiency.

Conducting Composition Challenges. The right of a defendant to jury panels or pools[5] that are representative of a cross-section of the community was enunciated in the 1946 case of *Thiel v. Southern Pacific Co.*[6] The cross-sectional rule is well established by case law and statute (Farmer, 1976), but the requirement of representativeness applies not to a given jury or jury panel but to a succession of panels over time in which there has been systematic under-representation. The desirability of cross-sectional jury pools is linked to two presumed advantages of cross-sectionality. First, it is assumed that the fact-finding ability of juries composed of people with diverse backgrounds and experience will be superior to that of more homogenous groups. Second, it is believed that jury verdicts will be respected more by defendants and the community if the integrity and apparent fairness of the jury are demonstrable. Representative composition of a jury reflects a commitment to fairness in the jury selection process.

Defendants may challenge jury composition in an attempt to show that grand or petit jury pools are not cross-sectionally representative. Because of their training in research design and data analysis, trial consultants can make important contributions to a composition challenge. Several strategies can be used to establish a prima facie case that a jury pool is nonrepresentative (Farmer, 1976; Kairys, 1972; Van Dyke, 1977), but the one in which behavioral scientists are most likely to be involved is a demonstration of a substantial disparity between the percentage of some "cognizable group" of people in the jury pools and that group's representation in the community. The definition of cognizable group is problematic; racial groups are cognizable (*Hernandez v. Texas*),[7] as is sex (*Taylor v. Louisiana*),[8] but age groups are less uniformly cognizable. One court has established that, in order to be cognizable, the group must "have a definite composition, must have members who share common attitudes or ideas or experience and must have a community of interest which cannot be adequately protected by the rest of the populace" (*United States v. Guzman*).[9]

Of the several methods by which jury pools can be assembled, the most common procedure is the drawing of names from voter registration lists, either randomly or through selection by appointed jury commissioners. In jurisdictions in which the method for selecting names can be shown to be discriminatory on its face, the procedure is faulty on constitutional grounds. Of more interest to the consultant are instances in which the selection procedure permits a possibility of discrimination, resulting in an under-representation of some cognizable group. The amount of under-representation that will be tolerated by the courts must then be determined.

The courts have not set an absolute standard for determining the degree of underrepresentation that is unconstitutional, but they have established some guidelines in recent decisions. One of the most important cases is *Castaneda v. Partida*[10] in which Rodrigo Partida, a defendant convicted of burglary, contended that Mexican-Americans were underrepresented on the grand juries of Hidalgo County (Texas). Although 79.1% of Hidalgo County's population was Mexican-American, over an 11-year period only 39% of Hidalgo County grand jurors had Spanish surnames.

Relying on the application of the binomial distribution (see Finkelstein, 1966) for its statistical analysis, the Supreme Court first determined the number of Mexican-Americans who would be selected over the years on a random basis. The expected number was 688 (79.1% of 870 grand jurors over the 11 years) as compared with the observed number of 339. The standard deviation in this case was 12, the square root of [870 (total n) × .791 (probability of selecting Mexican-Americans) × .209 (probability of selecting non-Mexican-Americans)]. Therefore, during the 11 years, the disparity ($n = 349$) between the expected and the obtained number of Mexican-American grand jurors was 29 standard deviations! In a footnote to the majority opinion, Justice Blackmun wrote, "As a general rule for such large samples, if the difference between the expected value and the observed number is greater than two or three standard deviations, then the hypothesis that the jury drawing was random would be suspect to a social scientist." Other statistical procedures can be used to evaluate the disparity between obtained and expected group representation (Sperlich & Jaspovice, 1979). Chi-square analysis can be used to analyze outcomes for several groups at the same time. Z scores can also be used.

Despite Justice Blackmun's reference to the criterion of 2 or 3 SD, some decisions have not found disparities exceeding 3 SD to be constitutionally defective (Swain v. Alabama[11]; People v. Powell[12]); in some decisions, an absolute rather than a relative under-representation has been found improper as in Duren v. Missouri,[13] which held that jury venires that averaged < 15% women were unacceptable.

Jury pools that are nonrepresentative tend to be so in certain directions. Ellison and Buckhout (1981, p. 186) summarize the typical venireperson as "more prestigeful, older, and most often from another socioeconomic class than the typical accused person in a criminal trial." For this reason, convincing demonstrations of a disparity can lead to the formation of a new pool whose greater heterogeneity will usually be beneficial to defendants.

The major problem with jury composition challenges is that their chances for success at the trial level are extremely low. The chance for an appellate victory is only slightly better. Composition challenges are enormously time-consuming and fraught with complications. It is not sufficient to show that a disparity exists for any specific year; the underrepresentation must be shown to have persisted for several years. Because the amount of missing data will usually increase in such time, the statistical comparisons will be jeopardized by data that are incomplete or biased. Frequently, it is difficult to determine ethnicity or other variables from a list of names; thus it is also very difficult to make accurate determinations of sample characteristics.

A composition challenge is best undertaken when the consultant has preliminary data that suggest a significant disproportion in the panels and when there are enough resources that the challenge is not a barrier to other activities that may be more effective.

Training Attorneys in Voir Dire Skills. Advising attorneys on how best to interview jurors during voir dire is related to improving the conditions of voir dire. Attorneys are very adroit in phrasing questions in a manner that encourages the desired answers. They are taught to control witnesses through the use of leading and closed-ended questions. They are also trained not to ask questions to which they do not know the answer; this technique is a cornerstone of effective cross-examination. In fact, a common experience in the education of all trial lawyers is their exposure to the following, presumably apocryphal, "war story."

A defense attorney was savoring his mounting victory over a witness who had previously testified that he knew the defendant had bitten off the victim's ear, but now admitted that he had not seen the defendant bite off the ear. In fact he had not even been present at the time the defendant might have bitten off the ear. A gloating attorney then went too far, asking the question (s)he never should have asked: "If you didn't see the defendant bite off the ear, and if you weren't even there when you think it was bitten off, how can you say that the defendant bit the ear off?" Came the famous, chilling reply: "Because I saw him spit it out." The message here is clear: The courtroom is not the place for attorneys to ask questions that might have surprising answers.

However propitious the previous lesson may be for examination of witnesses, it becomes a liability when an attorney seeks to discover what a juror really believes or feels about an issue. Such instances require open-ended questions that encourage the juror to talk more. Attorneys are often reluctant to pose open-ended questions to jurors because the group questioning format used in most voir dire insures that the entire panel may be exposed to prejudicial answers. No one wants to ask a juror how his past experience with the defendant has made him feel only to hear the juror announce to the rest of the venire, "It makes me feel that he's always been a crook." Open-ended questions and open-court questioning do not mix; without individual, sequestered voir dire, the consultant must be very cautious in urging attorneys to phrase questions in an open-ended manner.

Assuming that the structure of voir dire will permit open-ended interrogation, most attorneys will benefit greatly from a demonstration of good interviewing skills followed by some supervised practice on their part. The major technique to be developed is the phrasing of open-ended questions. Attorneys master this skill most easily when they learn to begin their questions with "who," "what" or "why."

The consultant should instruct the attorney in other important components of good interviewing, such as active listening and empathetic responding, and should demonstrate that a strategic return to closed-ended questions is most effective for the purposes of indoctrinating jurors and for "sewing up" challenges for cause. Attorneys usually show good instincts for these latter objectives; the consultant will not have to spend much time on them.

Attorneys can be best shown the value of open-ended questioning by engaging in some practice interviews with volunteer "jurors." With the attorney, we prepare a list of topics to be covered during voir dire. Attorneys often request that these questions be written for them so they can phrase them correctly. We have found that it is better not to write the questions verbatim because it detracts from the conversational tone the consultant wishes attorneys to use with jurors and distracts attorneys from listening carefully to jurors' answers. It is better to try to show attorneys the value of "just talking" with potential jurors about important topics in voir dire.

Juror Deselection

Trial attorneys are well acquainted with Clarence Darrow's (1936) "rules" of jury selection: never strike an Irishman from the jury; always remove Presbyterians for they are "cold as the grave" and will "contaminate" others; remove Baptists—the "sooner [Baptists] leave the better;" never take a wealthy man; retain Unitarians, Universalists, Congregationalists, and Jews; Methodists are worth considering because "they are nearer the soil." Finally, as to the presence of women on the jury, Darrow was characteristically direct: "They [are] absolutely dependable but I [do] not want them."

Darrow's recommendation competes with other advice of varying sagacity. For example, William J. Bryan (1971) quotes the following formula of a prosecutor: "Never accept any juror whose occupation begins with a P. This includes pimps, prostitutes, preachers, plumbers, procurers, psychologists, physicians, psychiatrists, printers, painters, philosophers, professors, phoneys, parachutists, pipe-smokers, or part-time anythings." We have heard of one attorney who uses a peremptory against any man who wears his hat indoors. Lawyers who read Shakespeare prefer to dismiss skinny men, convinced, as was Julius Caesar that men with a lean and hungry look are dangerous. Ward Wagner's (1981, p. 20) book *Art of Advocacy: Jury Selection* gives the most easily remembered advice: "If you don't like a juror's face, excuse him."

To their credit, most attorneys recognize the inadequacies of conducting jury selection through what might be called a strategy of prejudice. Nonetheless, they are often at a loss for a preferable substitute. Some attorneys accept the first 12 people called, abandoning any attempt to identify and deselect those jurors whose background and biases may taint their decision-making in a specific case. Attorneys justify this approach in various ways. Some believe that it is not possible to divine accurately the favorable and unfavorable members of the panel, and that it is therefore futile to try. Other attorneys prefer not to seem as though they are questioning the panel, presuming that they will convince jurors that they are all seen as fair, trustworthy persons who will decide the case correctly.

For attorneys who feel that the juror selection phase of voir dire is important, but who feel unprepared to conduct it, another strategy can be pursued. Someone else can be hired to do it. Over the past decade, the "someone else" has often been a psychologist who brings a particular theoretical system to bear on the use of the peremptory juror challenges to which attorneys are entitled. Suggs and Sales (1978) delineate several guiding theoretical systems for deselection. Jurors have been deselected on the basis of their physique, nonverbal behavior, level of moral reasoning, attitudes, authoritarianism, and demography.

Our model of juror deselection is tailored to the unique aspects of each case; in each case, we rate every prospective juror on the basis of a 4-variable composite. We have found that a 5-point scale ranging from 1 (least desirable) to 5 (most desirable) adequately distributes our judgments of jurors. In applying our 4-component model, we divide a jury trial into two phases. The first phase is the *opinion formation phase*, extending from the time a juror is called to serve on a specific case until the time jury deliberation begins. The second phase is the *social influence* phase, extending from the beginning of the jury deliberation until the time a final verdict is announced. The two phases differ from each other in several ways that have important implications for jury selection. Characteristics that recommend a juror on opinion formation grounds may be very distinct from those that are considered during the social influence stage.

The four components of our juror deselection model vary in the amount and type of evidence supporting their validity. They also differ in the means by which they can be assessed by the consultant. In describing each of the four components, we discuss the theory and research pertinent to their application and we describe the information sources that we consider most practical in evaluating jurors with regard to each component.

Sentiment

Sentiment is our most important selection factor. Sentiment refers to a collection of personality traits, attitudes, beliefs, and values that may influence a juror's decision. Jury verdicts are acts of discretion in which the "facts" are constructed in some degree by jurors who may cast either a merciful or a merciless eye on the evidence. Although some evidence may be so forceful that it resists any jury "revision," most disputes that go before a jury will contain sufficient ambiguities to make it reasonable to assume that sentiment will have its effect. Strong sentiment may dispose jurors to view certain crimes and defendants in a predetermined or jaundiced manner. Sentiment may make a juror unreasonably harsh or unrealistically accepting when sentencing a defendant. We seek jurors who we believe will have a favorable sentiment or at least not a negative sentiment about the party for whom we are consulting.

In juror profiling, as in many areas of applied psychology, the valid assessment of sentiment and the ensuing attempts to link it to overt behavior are the most difficult tasks the consultant will encounter. First, one must contend with problems of deception; many jurors do not want their true feelings about the case to be known and will try to ensure that these feelings are not discovered. (See Box 2.2 for a discussion of deception.)

Box 2.2. Detecting Deception

Attorneys and judges alike are concerned about deception—either in the form of misrepresentation, distortion, or of outright lying by prospective jurors. If jurors do not wish to serve they can indicate prejudice related to the issues at trial, and they will typically be dismissed by the judge for cause. However, that is not the sort of falsification that is of most concern. Rather, it is a distortion of one's beliefs, feelings, or accounts in an effort to get *on* the jury that is troublesome.

How is deception manifested during voir dire? It tends to be evinced in connection with factual issues, such as whether a potential juror has read a case or has formed an opinion of the guilt or innocence of the defendant. Deception may also occur in connection with potential jurors' expressed willingness to put aside what they know or believe about a case and base their conclusions only on evidence presented in court. It may occur also in the form of denial of an existing prejudice.

Interviews with jurors (Broeder, 1965) after their service suggest that a number of them may withhold information or distort what they say during questioning. Even infrequent deception can be serious. A single persuasive juror can influence jury deliberations. A holdout juror means the difference between a jury verdict and a hung jury, which may mean life or death to the defendant.

Can the deceptive prospective juror be identified during voir dire? What does basic research on deception imply for voir dire? First, research lends comfort to those who believe in the efficacy of voir dire, because experimental subjects usually detect deception above chance levels (see DePaulo & Rosenthal, 1979). Lies and lying behavior are evident in many cases (see Dillehay & Neises, 1984, for a more complete review).

Second, certain cues help the typical experimental observer to detect lies. Research in the last 15 years has been significantly influenced by the work of Ekman and Friesen (1969, 1974) concerning deception cues—behaviors by a communicator which indicate that what is being said is false, and a companion concept of leakage—the idea that the truth is evident in our expressive behaviors despite our words. The difference between these two is the difference between

(continued)

being able to detect that someone is lying (cues to deception) and discerning the truth about the sender's attitudes or dispositions (leakage).

Some kinds of behaviors by a deceiver appear to be better clues to the fact of deception than others. A review of literature through 1979 by DePaula, Zuckerman, and Rosenthal (1980), using effect size as a basis for comparing different channels, shows that the face is slightly better than the body as a source of deception cues.

Some experiments, however, have shown that cues to deception reside more in the body's expressive behaviors than in the face (Littlepage & Pineault, 1979). Presumably this is so because the face, which is normally used by observers in interaction as a rich source of nonverbal information, is more controlled than the body (Ekman & Friesen, 1969). Direct research on control of the face during deception (Fugita, Hogrebe, & Wexley, 1980; McClintock & Hunt, 1975) provides support for the idea that the face is indeed controllable in this way.

If the body were the best source of deception cues, assessors during voir dire might have to settle for second best because, in the typical voir dire, the body may not be visible to attorneys and consultants. Usually, the prospective juror is seated in a group in courtroom pews or on the witness stand; about all that can be seen of the juror is head and shoulders. Therefore it is fortunate that the voice is the best cue to deception (Ekman, Friesen, & Scherer, 1976, and Streeter, Krauss, Geller, Olson, & Apple, 1977, both cited in Edinger & Patterson, 1983, p. 42; see summary in DePaulo et al., 1980). Pitch becomes higher in deception. Vocal nervousness may be present (Hocking & Leathers, 1980), as may hesitation in response and lengthy answers (Harrison, Havalek, Raney, & Fritz, 1978), although the interpretation of latency of response and drawn out answers may depend on their verbal content.

Voir dire is a search for those people who, as jurors, would cause concern to the consultant. Connecting this theme to the question of deception, we can ask whether some people are more *inclined* to lie, thus requiring that others be on guard when dealing with them. It may also be asked whether some people are *better liars* than others.

The Machiavellian personality may be expected to be good at lying (Christie & Geis, 1970); such persons believe that if the truth will not serve their purposes, a lie will do. In addition, high Machs are generally better liars (see DePaulo & Rosenthal, 1979; Geis & Moon, 1981). High Machs may be better able to control the outward appearance of anxiety, even though their physiological arousal may not be different from that of low Machs (see Oksenberg, 1970, in Geis & Moon, p. 766). Knowing that a person is relatively Machiavellian may serve as a discriminative stimulus, alerting an observer to both the greater likelihood of lies and relatively more skill in lying. The observer will be more vigilant in detecting deception. Other research indicates that men are not better liars than women (DePaulo & Rosenthal, 1979).

It is not possible to be very specific as to the qualifications of the best detectors of deception. Women have a clear advantage over men in decoding nonverbal cues in general; however, when those cues involve the identification of liars, women apparently lose their advantage (e.g., Boice, 1983, p. 14; DePaulo & Rosenthal, 1979). The old adage, "It takes one to know one," does not apply: lying relatively well does not help one liar identify others (DePaulo & Rosenthal, 1979). High Machs are not relatively better than low Machs at identifying

(continued)

deceivers (DePaulo & Rosenthal, 1979). Furthermore, some evidence indicates that people who are good at detecting deception are not necessarily good at accurately decoding leakage (DePaulo & Rosenthal, 1979). This is not necessarily detrimental to accuracy of impressions in voir dire since other information is usually available to help in drawing inferences about jurors once deception is suspected.

We would feel remiss if we did not issue a caveat or two about the transportability to the courtroom of the research on detecting deception that we have been discussing. We have serious reservations about the unbridled application of experimental research to juror or jury behavior (Dillehay & Nietzel, 1980b). We raise here the question of external validity and call researchers to conduct supplementary research on lies and liars.

First, because much of the research on deception manipulates lying by having some subjects lie and some not, or by having subjects lie some of the time and sometimes not with either prepared lies or spontaneous lies, it is possible that we have not learned very much about detecting "spontaneous" liars. The cues given by liars when lying for their own purposes may be different from the cues given by nonliars or liars who are lying under instructions. In the absence of data to the contrary, we believe that lies in the laboratory will not differ from lies in the courtroom. The correspondences may depend in part on the similarity between anxiety that accompanies both nonexperimental and experimental lies.

It has been suggested that those high in Machiavellianism are better able to control the appearance of anxiety that accompanies lying and thereby reduce the incidence of detection. The cues used to identify lies also implicate the anxiety that accompanies lying as a basis for discovering lies. If manifestations of underlying anxiety are the cues to attempts to deceive, are these cues different from those caused by anxiety that is owing to factors other than lying? How can an observer distinguish between the prospective juror who is anxious because of the circumstances and the juror who is anxious because he or she is lying? Research has not yet provided an answer to this question (see Box 2.4).

Second, even if jurors intend to be candid, it is doubtful that they are accurate in describing influences on their own behavior or what their behavior will be in the future (Nisbett & Wilson, 1977). Third, assuming that valid indicators of sentiment are obtained, the problem that general attitudes may be poor predictors of specific behavior remains (see Fishbein & Ajzen, 1972, 1975; Wicker, 1969; but see Dillehay, 1973). In addition to the above fundamental problems, juristic consultants face other practical limitations. They must make their assessments without standardized instruments, they must predict a dichotomized rather than a graduated outcome, they must rely on a small sample, and they must do it all in a hurry. Little wonder that the assessment of sentiment is often a house of cards in juristic consultation—a shaky and undependable structure, but one in which the consultant must reside for a while, because sentiment will influence to some extent the way in which jurors perceive the evidence presented to them.

Several strategies have been proposed for assessing sentiment. One commentator (Emerson, 1968) has recommended personality testing of prospective jurors; another (Note, 1980) has proposed that jurors be assessed on their levels of authoritarianism, using Boehm's (1968) Legal Attitudes Questionnaire (LAQ) as the screening instrument; others have contended that graphoanalysis will reveal personality differences (Moore & Wood, 1980; Silas, 1983).

It is popular to predict sentiment on the basis of social and demographic variables. This strategy is advantageous in that it is not intrusive. It is also very economical and gives attorneys a system of deselection that is easily substituted in differing trials. Our own use of these indicators is limited either because we have not believed them to be powerful predictors of many verdict-relevant sentiments, or have believed that the direction of demographic-verdict relationships varies across trials. We do not depend on mock jury research to guide our use of social and demographic indicators; even if we were to do so, the data from such research are inconsistent (Davis, Bray, & Holt, 1977; Gerbasi, Zuckerman, & Reis, 1977; Mills & Bohannon, 1980; Saks & Hastie, 1978; Simon, 1967; Stephan, 1975) in regard to the predictive utility of jurors' sex, age, race, education, and occupation.

We use social and demographic indicators of sentiment selectively. The importance we attach to them depends on the nature of each trial and on characteristics of the litigant for whom we are consulting. We seldom use social and demographic variables as the decisive deselection indicator; however, we often use them as a starting point for constructing profiles of favorable and unfavorable jurors, keeping in mind that data gathered in voir dire may require either revision or abandonment of the initial viewpoint.

There is enough regularity in our use of *certain* indicators under *certain* fact situations to warrant the following list of ''rule-of-thumb'' principles about predicting sentiment:

1. If we have conducted a pre-trial survey of some kind, we include in our juror profiles the relationships between attitudes and social-demographic indicators that have been discovered in the survey.

2. With respect to sentencing dispositions, our consulting experience confirms results from national surveys that race, age, education, sex, and political affiliation are associated with death penalty attitudes (see Box 2.3). We extrapolate these findings to sentencing decisions that do not involve capital punishment and conclude that predispositions to punish severely or leniently are related to the above variables.

3. Among these indicators, occupation is one of the more robust correlates of verdict-relevant attitudes. For example, plaintiffs and criminal defendants usually should prefer not to have business proprietors and peo-

Box 2.3. Death Penalty Attitudes

Because of the frequent use of jury consultation in death penalty cases, it is important that consultants know the correlates of pro-death beliefs. The most reliable source for these data is national public opinion polls, whose results we summarize below. Although it is clear that the majority of Americans say they favor the death penalty for persons convicted of murder, a sizeable minority remains opposed to capital punishment. These data further indicate that although endorsements of capital punishment increased dramatically from the mid-1960s to the mid-1970s, the percentage of respondents favoring the death penalty has changed little from 1976 to the present (see Panel A).

Panel A. Favor Capital Punishment

	Harris Survey			*Gallup Poll*		
	Favor	Opposed	Not Sure	Yes	No	No Opinion
1965	38	47	15			
1969	48	38	14			
1970	47	42	11			
1973	59	31	10			
1976	67	25	8			
1983	68	27	5			
1978				62	27	11
1980				54	43	3
1981				66	25	9
1982				72	28	

Note. Respondents to the Harris Survey answered the question, "Do you believe in capital punishment (death penalty) or are you opposed to it?" Respondents to the Gallup Poll answered the question, "Are you in favor of the death penalty for persons convicted of murder?"

Panel B displays the relationships between death penalty attitudes and several personal characteristics. Proponents of capital punishment for murderers are more likely to be white, educated through high school, Republican, and male, although the sex difference has decreased between 1978 and 1981, the most recent years for which we found national figures.

Panel B. Death Penalty Preferences by Different Groups[G]

Factor	Year	Favor (%)	Opposed (%)	No Opinion (%)
Sex				
Males	1978	70	22	8
	1981	71	22	7
	1982	76	24	—
Females	1978	55	32	13
	1981	62	28	10
	1982	69	31	—

(continued)

Race				
White	1978	64	26	10
	1981	70	22	8
	1982	75	25	—
Nonwhite	1978	42	44	14
	1981	44	44	12
	1982	55	45	—
Education				
College	1978	61	31	8
	1981	62	32	6
	1982	67	33	—
High School	1978	65	26	9
	1981	72	20	8
	1982	75	25	—
Grade School	1978	53	29	18
	1981	55	30	15
	1982	72	28	—
Age (years)				
18–29	1978	57	35	8
	1981	62	31	7
	1982	70	30	—
30–49	1978	64	26	10
	1981	68	24	8
	1982	73	27	—
50+	1978	65	22	13
	1981	68	22	10
	1982	75	25	—
Politics				
Republican	1978	72	20	8
	1982	79	21	—
Democrat	1978	59	29	12
	1982	70	30	—
Independent	1978	61	30	9
	1982	70	30	—

[G] = Respondents to the Gallup Poll, answering the question: "Are you in favor of the death penalty for persons convicted of murder?"

Because of the death-qualification process used in capital trials, the consultant is forced to choose among venirepersons *of whom all* say that they would be willing to consider the death penalty. The task then becomes one of separating the staunch advocates of capital punishment from those who are more

(continued)

moderately disposed. For example, we have encountered staunch death penalty proponents who cite the Bible as the source of their convictions. People who hold such views are not necessarily quick to reveal them. National surveys are consistent with our own consulting experiences that stronger support of the death penalty is also associated with: (a) a belief that the death penalty deters others from committing murder; and (b) a belief that the courts are too lenient in dealing with criminals (according to Harris surveys, 49% of the people believed that courts were "too easy" on criminals in 1967 whereas 81% believed the same in 1982).

On the other hand, those people who oppose capital punishment are most likely to give the following justifications to their position: (a) their religion forbids it (the Bible states, "Thou shalt not kill.") and; (b) the death penalty is not a deterrent to crime.

ple involved in the so-called precision professions (engineering, accounting, etc.) selected as jurors. Occupation is probably linked to verdict tendencies because it forces daily associations with people who profess to have similar attitudes toward social issues and because it reinforces certain values that eventually are considered essential in one's occupation. Our favorite composite of "pro" and "con" occupations is provided by Wrightsman (1978, p. 149–150) who quotes Keith Mossman, an attorney, as follows:

As a young practicing attorney, I used to get advice from experienced trial lawyers who agreed that potential jurors could be chosen on the basis of occupation. Cabinetmakers and accountants, the adage went, should be avoided because they require everything in a case to fit together neatly. Carpenters, on the other hand, were said more likely to accept a defendant's case, since they were accustomed to making do with available materials. . . . Along with occupational criteria, some of the old men of the trade thought that nationality played a crucial role in jury selection. According to the maxim, jurors of Southern-European descent tended to be more sympathetic to a defendant than did more exacting jurors with German or Scandinavian blood. In all my years of practice in Iowa, however, I have yet to encounter the ideal juror—a Spanish carpenter.

4. Non-white male jurors are usually less prone to conviction than are white jurors, and they are more favorable to defenses of insanity and diminished capacity. These tendencies prevail even if race is not an issue in the trial.

5. Young, well-educated women tend to be favorable plaintiff jurors, especially in suits in which defendant represents conservative, "establishment" professions or institutions. Medical malpractice cases illustrate this principle nicely.

6. Young, upwardly mobile men are usually not sympathetic to plaintiffs or to the mitigating evidence presented by criminal defendants.

7. Middle-aged or older, traditionally socialized women are often good defense jurors in trials in which the defendant is charged with a crime of sexual assault.

Authoritarianism. The personality variable most often linked to verdict-relevant predispositions is authoritarianism, a syndrome of characteristics described by Fromm (1941) and later, by Adorno, Frenkel-Brunswik, Levinson, and Sanford (1950). The typical authoritarian personality manifests the following attributes:

> (He) accepts middle class conventionality because it has widespread acceptance and support, but he has not internalized the meaning of these social norms. He is hostile toward and aggresses against outgroups, especially ethnic minorities and relatively powerless, deviant groups, while at the same time glorifying his own moral authority figures. Being opposed generally to an examination of motives and of a highly practical bent, he is given to mystical explanations of phenomena and thinks in fixed and rigid ways, especially about people, who are ordered in his thinking by themes of strength–weakness, superiority–inferiority, dominance–submission. He asserts himself in a show of power and toughness and justifies hostile treatment of others as widespread and necessary. He tends to see others as unlike himself and in negative or pejorative terms—sometimes in a way that may psychologically purge himself of those characteristics; other times so as to explain his own sense of inadequacy. Sexual deviancy is a preoccupation and harsh punishments are advocated. (Dillehay, 1977, p. 238-239)

Because of these characteristics, combined with tendencies to be intolerant of ambiguities, to press for conformity to group norms, and to be closed-minded, the authoritarian personality will generally not be a good juror for the criminal defendant or the civil plaintiff. However, if the defendant resembles the authoritarian's preferred authority figures, as may occur if a police officer is on trial for assault or if a favorite political leader is charged with scandalous behavior, the authoritarian may make a good juror.

Assessment of authoritarianism should be based on multiple sources of information. Although jurors may sometimes be asked directly about their attitudes, they may censor or distort their answers for several reasons. The *F-scale* of Adorno et al. (1950), an early measure of authoritarianism, correlates negatively with education, intelligence, and social class. These variables are almost always discernible through juror information forms or voir dire. Items drawn from Boehm's LAQ that attempt to tap authoritarian attitudes can be posed to potential jurors during voir dire or may be included on juror information forms. However, we do not know of item analyses that would justify a preference for using any specific questions. Christie (personal communication, 1979) asserts that the single best discriminating item for authoritarianism from the F-scale is endorsement of the statement: "Obedience and respect for authority are the most important virtues children should learn." Other variables believed to be positively related to authoritarianism include frequency of church attendance, endorsement of arguments containing conspiratorial themes, attraction to politically conservative issues and candidates, and negative attitudes toward strangers or foreigners. It is obvious that some of these markers are more accessible during voir dire than others; frequency of church attendance may be the most easily gathered data, but in certain communities there may be a restricted range on this item due to the fact that most jurors are frequent church-goers.

Much controversy surrounds the validity of nonverbal cues to jurors'

Box 2.4. Nonverbal Cues in the Courtroom

Overt behavior existed before language, so it comes as no surprise that observation of nonverbal cues has been practiced across the centuries. In the *Iliad*, Homer discriminated courageousness on the basis of nonverbal information: "A coward changes color all the time; he cannot sit still for nervousness, but squats down, first on one heel, then on the other." (quoted in McReynolds, 1975). Solomon was wise on the matter of body language: "He winketh with his eyes, he speaketh with his feet, he teacheth with his fingers." (Proverbs 6:13). And Freud (1905) proclaimed, "He that has eyes to see and ears to hear may convince himself that no mortal can keep a secret. If the lips are silent, he chatters with his finger tips; betrayal oozes out of him at every pore."

Although interpretation of nonverbal behavior is one of the flashiest skills of jury consultants and the one that often sets them apart as wizards in the eyes of some attorneys, the importance of nonverbal indicators in jury deselection is often limited for three fundamental reasons. First, the average courtroom limits the consultant's opportunity to observe a full range of nonverbal cues. Jurors usually sit more than 15 feet away, in a group of 25 or more and behind varying barricades that generally allow no more than a "shoulders and above" view. We have seldom been in a courtroom arranged so that a consultant could observe a venireperson's pupil dilation, foot movements, leg-position asymmetry, or stomach sag. The consultant has only one chance to observe all channels. There are no videotapes, no instant replays, no split screens. These conditions contrast dramatically with the laboratory conditions under which most research on paralinguistics, facial expressions, and kinesics has been conducted.

Second, nonverbal cues are often redundant with information communicated more quickly and more precisely through verbal channels. Nonverbal cues are important in situations in which there are discrepancies between the messages

(continued)

conveyed verbally and nonverbally. When the messages are congruent, attention that is paid primarily to verbal content will result in valid decoding of the information being transmitted. Ekman and Friesen (1969) describe five roles that nonverbal behaviors can play in communication. Nonverbal behavior can *accent* what one says (leaning toward someone while speaking of feelings of affection); it can *complement* what one says (frowning while criticizing someone); it can *repeat* what one says (motioning someone closer while saying, "Come here."); it can *regulate* human interactions (making or not making eye contact with someone who is approaching); or it can *contradict* what one says (expressing criticism in a sweet voice). In voir dire, the consultant is concerned mainly with this last category, in which nonverbal behaviors contradict verbal ones, especially when what is being communicated involves emotional or evaluative behavior.

Finally, it must be remembered that voir dire imposes substantial environmental, social, and psychological influences on the participants. Because of these multiple determinants, it is difficult to interpret the meaning of any single nonverbal indicator or cluster of indicators. For example, do postural and paralinguistic signs of anxiety indicate a characterological trait or do they reflect a situational anxiety induced by an emotionally arousing question? The jury consultant will usually be more interested in differential responsiveness than in stable personality differences.

One of the most systematic systems for isolating the source of observed emotionality in jurors has been developed by Suggs and Sales (1978), who recommend the following procedure:

> During the initial questioning by the judge and the attorneys, the interviewers invariably start out by asking the prospective juror questions to elicit background information such as his occupation, marital status, and where he lives. These questions are unlikely to evoke emotional and deceptive responses, and thus, this phase of the questioning may be used to *obtain a baseline of the juror's repertoire* of kinesic, paralinguistic, and verbal behaviors in response to questioning by the particular interviewer. During this questioning, the observers rate the communicative behavior of the juror in terms of being positive or negative toward the interviewer. . . .
>
> The juror's responses on these same dimensions are again rated when the interviewer asks attitudinal questions which are relevant to the case. These questions will vary from case to case, but, in general, will deal with the prospective juror's dispositions toward the attorneys, litigants, and the legal and factual issues of the case.
>
> The observers compare the juror's responses within each interview in an attempt to determine whether the juror has positive or negative feelings toward the attitudinal issues which were discussed. In other words, the observers attempt to determine whether and at what point in the interview the juror becomes positively or negatively aroused in his communicative behavior by comparing his baseline responses with his later responses. (Suggs & Sales, 1978)

Harper, Wiens, and Matarazzo (1978) discuss five channels by which nonverbal phenomena can be communicated: (a) paralinguistics (nonverbal aspects and temporal patterning of speech); (b) facial expression; (c) kinesics (body movements, postural changes, gestures); (d) the eyes; and (e) proxemics (use of physical space in interactions). The physical arrangement of the courtroom as well as the judicial control of voir dire eliminate proxemics as an area in which sufficient variation in expression occurs to provide a useful channel. In addition, as we have already discussed in the topic of deception, some channels do not

(continued)

carry as much information as others about certain topics. These differences may be owing to the relative ease in censoring displays in the various channels or to interference between channels that masks information from an individual channel (Dittman, 1972).

Panel A summarizes some of the more valid paralinguistic, facial, kinesic, and eye cues to five characteristics with special significance in voir dire.

Panel A. Paralinguistic and Nonverbal Cues Observed During Voir Dire

Behavior	Paralinguistic	Face	Kinesics	Eye
Anxiety	Speech disturbance (especially Mahl's (1959) non-ah dysfluencies) Faster speech pace Inverted u function between productivity and anxiety Stilted speech Sighing, inhibited breathing Blocking, inappropriate laughter	More smiles in the anxious, but interpersonally skillful person Fewer smiles in the anxious, and interpersonally less skillful person	More nonpurposive body movements More postural shifts More body-forward hand movements (e.g., finger tapping)	More eye contact with a threatening stimulus More blinks
Deception	Slower speech pace Decreased productivity Higher voice pitch Longer response latencies	More smiles Attempts at pleasant facial expressions	Tense posture Less head nodding Less immediacy* Fewer gesticulations	Mixed findings on amount of contact depending on degree of vigilance in the respondent
Positive Affiliation	Increased productivity	More smiles	More immediacy* Open posture of arms and legs Arm position asymmetry Leg position asymmetry Higher rate of gesticulation More head nods	Pupil dilation More eye contact
Negative Affiliation	Decreased productivity	Fewest smiles	Extreme reclining position Arms crossed over chest Legs crossed	Less eye contact up to moderate levels of dislike At high levels of dislike, eye contact increases
Interpersonal influence and persuasiveness	Moderate to high productivity Fewer speech disturbances	More facial activity	Open posture More head nodding Fewer body-focused hand movements	Increased gaze at "audience"

---

*"Immediacy" refers to greater touching, forward body lean, eye contact, and direct shoulder orientation to addressee (Mehrabian, 1971).

sentiments and the ability of consultants to read "body language" in evaluating jurors (see Box 2.4). We pay attention to at least one paralinguistic indicator of authoritarianism—signs of deference shown by potential jurors in the courtroom. Authoritarians are likely to show deference toward persons whom they regard as trustworthy authority figures; they are less likely to defer to persons they regard as "below" them in power, status, or influence. Deference is revealed through use of formal means of address ("Yes, sir," "No, sir," rather than "Yes" or "No"), acquiescence to opinions expressed by authority despite earlier indications that the juror may have been more ambivalent, statement of opinions in a more cautious or polite manner than is common, solicitation of cues from authority about desirable behavior in a given situation, and avoidance of conflict with authority figures. Deference extended to the prosecutor and/or the judge but not to defense counsel may signal authoritarianism. The key to this judgment is that the deference is *differential*. Deference shown to all courtroom personnel is probably not revealing of authoritarianism as much as it is revealing of feelings of intimidation or anxiety inspired by the courtroom itself. The symbols and formality of the courtroom probably produce the appearance of more authoritarianism in jurors than may actually be the case. This artificial elevation often makes it difficult to separate "trait versus state" authoritarianism during voir dire.

Other Sentiments. Depending on the nature of the charges, the defendant, and the defense, we try to assess prospective jurors' attitudes about drug use, undercover police work, minority groups, welfare, and private enterprise as well as personal characteristics such as aggressiveness, psychological-mindedness, and a capacity for attentiveness.

Another dimension on which prospective jurors have been classified is *level of legal development* (Tapp & Levine, 1974) in which the "fair" juror is one who uses postconventional moral reasoning as conceptualized by Kohlberg (1969). Because attorneys approach voir dire as an adversarial process, they may show little interest in seeking the fair juror, although, according to Suggs and Sales (1978), Tapp's system may be most useful to those prosecutors who typically try to remove the postconventional types, leaving behind preconventional and conventional jurors who may be responsive to the authority associated with the prosecutor. *Internal locus of control* and the *belief in a just world* are two other characteristics that have been proposed as sentiments relevant to juror decision-making. Suggs and Sales (1978; citing Brodsky) speculate that *internals* may make less desirable jurors for civil and criminal defendants because they are less influenced by mitigating circumstances, and that persons who subscribe to a "just world" view of events may be unsympathetic to plaintiffs and crime victims.

Social Influence

Our second selection factor is social influence. Here we include the set of characteristics and behaviors that is evinced during a jury's deliberations. Jury deliberation is, of course, very distinct from the opinion formation stage that occurs during the trial proper. A juror's task is no longer solitary. Communication is not prohibited; it is encouraged. During deliberations, jurors are expected to influence one another; they are now obliged, not forbidden, to discuss the case and seek consensus.

We believe that jury selection methods tend to focus primarily on only the opinion formation stage, neglecting the personal qualities that may be important during social influence. Is a certain juror independent or conforming? Which jurors will generate social pressure? Which jurors will resist it? Will a given juror tolerate ambiguity or press hard for a decision?

Characteristics that suggest a pro-defense juror with respect to opinions may subsequently be associated with unfavorable behavior during deliberations. Consider this example: Some attorneys follow what we term a "superficial similarity" strategy: trying to retain jurors similar in race, age, and sex to the defendant on the assumption that these features dispose the juror to identify with and be sympathetic toward the defendant. Although such an attraction may exist, it does not insure that the juror will be a protagonist for the defendant during deliberations. We have seen black defendants convicted by juries with several black members (especially older blacks or women). We have learned that although these black jurors began the deliberation with pro-defense sentiments, they were unable to persuade other jurors to join them or even, during deliberation, to sustain their own inclination to acquit the defendant.

Superficial similarity also presumes that jurors with a background similar to that of the defendant will be lenient because of a "there but for the grace of God go I" mentality. However, common backgrounds may dispose jurors to adopt a more internal frame of reference in attributing responsibility to the criminal defendant. Jurors who have themselves overcome difficult problems may not sympathize with or excuse criminal behavior. Therefore, attempting to select jurors with backgrounds similar to that of the defendant is risky.

Social influence must be inferred from a pattern of indicators. Education and occupation may point to persons who are likely to have developed leadership habits. Administrators, managers, sales persons, and people who "live by their words" may be influential jurors. We look for indications of geographic or job mobility and other signs of turnover that may be associated with resistance to conformity.

We try to observe the informal interactions of the jury pool. This is best accomplished by having one member of the selection team sit among prospective jurors and observe the friendships, cliques, and patterns of deference that emerge. During voir dire, we also look for signs of impatience, impulsivity, and authoritarianism, all of which will be relevant to the quality of the ensuing deliberation. On occasion, we attempt to impanel a jury that will either tolerate a minority opinion of ''not guilty'' or will isolate or nullify a juror who holds pro-prosecution sentiments. A hung jury is rare, but at times may be the best verdict that can reasonably be expected. Obviously, this objective requires special sensitivity to the multiple indicators of social influence that are manifest in the courtroom.

Experience. Another factor we consider is juror experience. How often has an individual served as a juror? What are the decisions in which the person has participated? Was the defendant acquitted or convicted? Was the jury unable to reach a verdict? In civil cases, did the jury find for defendant or plaintiff? Other types of courtroom experiences are also considered. Has the potential juror ever testified in a criminal case or participated as plaintiff, defendant, or witness in a civil case? Has a family member participated in any of these ways? Attention to juror experience is based on the frequently documented principle that future behavior is reasonably well predicted by past behavior in similar situations. For this reason, we are most interested in a person's past behavior as a juror, but also consider as relevant any participation in a formal court proceeding.

We believe that experienced jurors tend to be less favorable toward civil plaintiffs and criminal defendants. If this is true, criminal defense attorneys should avoid experienced jurors. Prosecutors, however, should prefer them.

The data from surveys, archival research, and mock juror experiments are mixed as to whether there is a relationship between juror experience and jury verdicts. On the basis of post-trial interviews, Broeder (1965) concluded that juror experience had an impact on verdicts. Reed (1965) mailed questionnaires to former jurors and reported that experienced jurors were significantly more likely to have voted guilty than were novice jurors. Werner, Strube, Cole, and Kagehiro's (1985) examination of 201 criminal trials in Salt Lake City, Utah, revealed that the conviction rate for four-person juries with no experienced jurors was 50%, whereas that for juries with one or more repeaters was 73%, a difference that was not statistically significant. Kerr (1981) reported that the number of experienced jurors on 210 criminal trial juries in San Diego, California, did not predict jury verdicts (see also Kerr, Harmon, & Graves, 1982).

Faced with this conflicting evidence and the tendency for defense attorneys to prefer novice jurors (see Belli, 1954; Bailey & Rothblatt, 1971), we examined, through the use of extensive archives, whether experienced jurors are more likely to convict than are inexperienced jurors (see Dillehay & Nietzel, 1985 for a complete account of this research).

Our sample consisted of all the criminal trials ($n = 175$) in Fayette County (Kentucky) Circuit Court for 1973. All were felony cases except for 20 misdemeanors that came up on appeal from district court. Verdicts were gathered from court records and ordered into the following outcomes: (a) not guilty, (b) hung jury, (c) guilty of a lesser included charge, (d) guilty on some but not all charges, and (e) guilty as charged in the indictment. Twelve trials ended before a verdict was reached; the final sample consisted of 163 trials.

In Fayette County, the venire serves for a 30-day period. A member of the panel may be called for any number of trials during that time. We indexed juror experience by five variables: (a) *number of experienced jurors* (NEJ), which was derived by counting the number of jurors on each jury who had served on at least one previous jury in their term; and (b) *total juror experience* (TJE), which was computed by counting the number of previous trials for each juror and then summing over all jurors. The last three variables described forepersons: (c) *the prior jury experience of the foreperson*; (d) *the number of jurors who had previously served as a foreperson*; and (e) whether the *current foreperson had served as a foreperson*.

The means and standard deviations for the five experience measures by types of jury verdicts are shown in Table 2.3. Pearson product moment

Table 2.3. Means and Standard Deviations of Experience Factors for Trial Outcomes[a]

			Number of experienced jurors		Total juror experience		Number of previous forepersons		Juror experience of the foreperson		Forepersons previously a foreperson	
Verdict	N	%	M	SD	M	SD	M	SD	M	SD	M	SD
Not guilty	42	26	5.33	4.29	11.69	13.16	.60	.91	1.24	1.66	1.83	.38
Hung	26	16	6.66	4.17	14.92	14.07	1.04	1.00	—	—	—	—
Guilty, lesser charge	22	13	6.86	4.51	14.18	12.36	.50	.60	1.50	1.63	1.77	.43
Guilty, on some charges	9	6	7.00	4.85	16.67	15.42	1.11	1.17	1.56	1.88	1.78	.44
Guilty, on all charges	64	39	7.88	4.13	18.19	14.58	1.00	1.05	1.75	1.62	1.81	.39
Totals	163	100	6.83	4.34	15.37	13.99	.84	.98	1.54	1.65	1.81	.39

Note. From "Juror Experience and Jury Verdicts" by R. Dillehay and M. Nietzel, 1985, *Law and Human Behavior, 9*, p. 185. Copyright 1985 by Plenum Publishing Co. Used with permission.

[a]*Note.* Total juror experience is the sum of all prior service during the term for all jurors on the jury. $N = 137$ for Juror Experience of the Foreperson and for Foreperson Previously a Foreperson. The foreperson on hung trials was not identified. Scores for Foreperson Previously a Foreperson were 1 = yes, 2 = no.

correlations among verdict and experience variables showed that: (a) the experience measures intercorrelated moderately to substantially among themselves, a not too surprising result; (b) with increasing NEJ, there was an increased likelihood of a guilty verdict ($r = .23$, $p < .01$); (c) with increasing TJE, there was an increased likelihood of a conviction ($r = .18$, $p < .05$); and (d) no foreperson variable was related to verdict.

Stepwise multiple regression showed that NEJ was the best single predictor of juror verdicts, accounting for ~6% of the variance in trial outcomes. A graphic view of the percentages of not guilty, hung, and guilty verdicts (a combination of convictions on lesser charges, some but not all charges, and all charges) for juries with different levels of NEJ is shown in Figure 2.2. This figure shows that the deviation toward more guilty verdicts and fewer not guilty verdicts occurs when more than a majority of a jury are experienced. (Additional analyses in Dillehay and Nietzel, 1985, indicated that the above relationship could not be accounted for by hypothesizing that prosecutors in particular are selectively eliminating jurors who appear to be acquittal-prone, that is, voted not guilty at their initial trial.)

Although foreperson variables did not predict jury verdicts, we discovered the following characteristics of service as a foreperson: (a) seasoned jurors are picked more often than would be predicted by chance ($p < .05$); (b) jurors who have served once as a foreperson are more likely to serve in that capacity again ($p < .001$); and (c) 89% of forepersons were men,

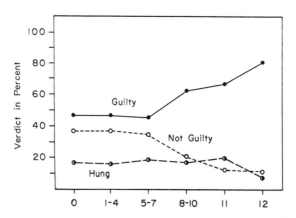

FIGURE 2.2. Verdict changes as a Function of the Number of Experienced Jurors. *Note.* Guilty Includes Guilty of a Lesser Charge, Guilty of Some but not All of the Charges, and Guilty as Charged. *Note.* From "Juror Experience and Jury Verdicts" by R. Dillehay and M. Nietzel, 1985, *Law and Human Behavior, 9*, p. 187. Copyright 1985 by the Plenum Publishing Co. Reprinted with permission.

whereas men comprised only 56% of the jurors in our sample (chi-square = 64.9 1 df, $p < .001$).

In addition to finding that juror experience exerts a small but significant effect on jury verdicts, a second study of 164 convictions in the same court between January 1973 and December 1974 (Himelein, Nietzel, & Dillehay, 1984) showed that NEJ, TJE, and the previous juror experience of the foreperson all correlated significantly with the severity of sentence recommended by the jury. (Kentucky is one of a few states that retains jury sentencing, although juries are given sentencing authority in capital cases in most of the states that have the death penalty.) NEJ showed the largest association with severity of sentence ($r = .20$, $p < .05$), although it was not significantly greater than the other two significant correlates.

Recently, we have completed a replication study of the association of juror experience with jury verdicts with a sample of 169 consecutive criminal trials in Fayette County between January 1974 and July 1975. In this sample, we failed to find an effect for juror experience on verdicts. Possible explanations for the discrepancy between this study and the initial investigation are that the strength of the experienced juror effect may depend on several other parameters including the overall level of juror experience and a careful index of any juror experiences on civil trials that may occur during a term (judges sometimes "borrow" jurors to fill out a civil jury panel).

We conclude that, under certain conditions, juror experience will influence jury verdicts and that the influence is one of increasing convictions. An exception to this rule may occur when the evidence against the consultant's side is weak, in which case experienced jurors may be better able to recognize the poor quality of the evidence.

There are several possible explanations for the finding that experienced jurors are more likely to convict. Based on other evidence (e.g., Kalven & Zeisel, 1966), we believe that most of the consequences of experience have their impact before jury deliberation (the social influence phase of the trial). Therefore, we would seek explanation of the phenomenon in the different ways in which jurors perceive the criminal justice system, the evidence, or the trial participants. The following considerations are possible explanations:

1. Judging the acts of another person and possibly causing that person to be punished can be a very upsetting experience that initially makes jurors cautious and tentative about their actions. However, with experience, people become more comfortable in making difficult decisions, especially if there is implicit and sometimes explicit feedback from the court that those decisions were right.
2. Jurors begin to redefine what reasonable doubt means, realizing that

it does not mean *any* doubt. Although the novice juror may let even a trace of indecision prevent a vote for conviction, the experienced juror becomes unwilling to suspend every judgment simply because he or she is unable to shed the fleeting misgivings that accompany almost any decision.

3. Jurors ultimately come to resolve conflicting testimony between defendants and the state by believing the state. Although at first it may be difficult to know which side of the story to believe, jurors find it very unlikely that in trial after trial it is the state, the police, or the prosecutor who lies. Whether or not it is justified, repeated exposure to defendants who directly dispute the state's evidence probably diminishes the believability of successive defendants.

4. In their term of service, jurors associate frequently with the same prosecutors and judges. These experiences are likely to culminate in a feeling of trust, familiarity, attraction, and comradeship (see Skolnick, 1966; Zajonc, 1968). The more sporadic appearances of defense attorneys cannot cultivate the same loyalty and sense of identification in jurors.

5. Jurors who may have acquitted a defendant early in their term may be subjected to an accumulating pressure from their neighbors, family, and friends to be less soft on crime, and to prevent the guilty from going free. Experience may mold jurors to believe that their duty is to convict the people brought before them.

Assessment of Juror Experience. Prior juror experience is easily assessed. Juror information forms completed in most courts routinely require information about the extent of previous jury duty. In-depth examination of this experience can then be pursued during either group or individual voir dire.

Intelligence

Our fourth selection factor is intelligence. In most cases, it is the least emphasized of the four factors. However, for trials in which the evidence is very technical, in which the judge's instructions are very complex, or in which there is complicated expert testimony, we give intelligence more weight. We consider intelligence to mean what psychologists conventionally consider it to mean, although we are most interested in what is termed fluid intelligence: the capacity to conceptualize, to integrate, and to abstract. Cognitive flexibility or complexity may be a better term. *In general, more intelligent jurors probably benefit criminal defendants; however, there may be exceptions.*

In some cases, the defendant may want jurors whose strong affective tendencies are ascendant over their cognitive abilities, a condition that might be described by a clinician as an "experience balance tipped toward the emotional pole." Intelligent jurors may also be less desirable if they find it challenging to play "devil's advocate" or to match wits with a consultant's expert witnesses, particularly when those experts may not be effectively rebutted by testimony from the opposition's witnesses. Therefore, professionals who share fields of experience with the consultant's experts are often peremptorily struck. For example, mental health professionals may not make good defense jurors in a case in which the insanity defense is used. Taking this principle one step further, highly intelligent jurors may be less desirable in cases in which the weight and prestige of the experts' opinions are on the consultant's side and in which less intelligent jurors may be likely to defer to these experts' opinions.

Assessment of Juror Intelligence. Jurors' intelligence can be assessed from such past achievements as education and, perhaps, by occupation. Courtroom indices of intelligence can include jurors' effectiveness and complexity of oral expression, vocabulary level, and apparent comprehension of the events that occur during voir dire.

HOW THE CONSULTANT SHOULD BE IDENTIFIED

Attorneys have always been concerned about whether—and how— to identify jury consultants to prospective jurors. Attorneys are hesitant to inform venirepersons that they are using consultants during the voir dire, fearing that people will react negatively.

We are convinced that this fear is not warranted in most cases. For several reasons, introducing consultants to the venire may have positive effects. First, we believe that it is ethically preferable to disclose the purpose of the consultant's presence at the voir dire. Second, it is usually best to observe prospective jurors from counsel's table. If consultants sit at the counsel table, some introduction and explanation must be given to the panel; deception is both unethical and a poor strategy. We prefer the following simple introduction: "This is (*name*), who is here today to help us in the selection of the jury." Third, those jurors who are included on the jury may feel as though they have passed some more stringent set of criteria established by "experts" and may therefore reflect positively on the selection process. Although it is possible that deselected venirepersons may feel negatively about their removal, they have no influence on the verdict. Fourth, in adversarial struggles, a psychological benefit may derive from letting the opponent know that your side has the advantage of special resources in the form of a jury consultant. (Although some lawyers denigrate the use of consultants, many of them tend to believe that consultants possess unique, useful abilities.) We make it a point to introduce ourselves and disclose our function to the prosecutor, the judge, and other court personnel[14]

In all of our posttrial interviews with former jurors, not one juror has indicated that use of a jury consultant was either improper, unfair, invasive, or offensive. This finding is corroborated by other experienced consultants (Suggs & Sales, 1978). The ex-jurors often stated that they would like to use a consultant if they ever were involved in a trial.

EVALUATION

We try to evaluate our jury selection strategy in two ways. First, we attempt to conduct posttrial interviews with jurors for the purpose of assessing the validity of our predictions. These interviews must be conducted with caution and sensitivity. It is best to wait until the term of the jurors has expired before talking to them to avoid any risk of influencing them on trials for which they may still serve. From these interviews, we have no quantitative estimate of our overall accuracy in juror deselection beyond the observation that we are right more often than we are wrong.

We have performed a more formal comparison on the 35 separate verdicts represented in the 31 death penalty cases reported in Nietzel and Dillehay (1982) and Nietzel et al. (1984). Juries recommended death sentences in 61.1% of the 17 verdicts in trials in which we did not consult as opposed to 33.3% of the 18 verdicts in trials in which we did. The phi coefficient for the relationship between our presence and type of sentence was .26. The low power associated with a sample of 35 prevents this value from being statistically significant, a limitation of little importance to defendants and attorneys.

Our presence as jury consultants cannot be disentangled from a host of confounds, such as the attorney's level of preparation and experience, making interpretations of any associations problematic. However, confounds can cut both ways; they do not always contribute to the dreaded Type 1 error. For instance, a confound may militate against a significant consultant effect because attorneys are more likely to recruit consultants for the trials they perceive as "losers."

NOTES

[1]"Voir dire" describes any preliminary examination that the court may make of someone presented as a witness when there are objections to that person's competency or qualifications. However, in this chapter, we restrict the meaning of the term to the examination of prospective jurors.

[2]604 F. 2d 121 (1979).

[3]For a decade and a half, *Witherspoon v. Illinois,* 391 U.S. 510, 88S. Ct. 1770, 20 L. Ed. 2d 776 (1968) has controlled the disposition of potential jurors who express reservations about the use of the death penalty. This important decision prevents the challenging for cause of jurors who hold general objections to the death penalty or who might refuse to recommend capital punishment in certain kinds of cases. The result of *Witherspoon* is that a venireperson can be excluded for cause only if the venireperson states unambiguously that he or she would automatically vote against the imposition of capital punishment regardless of the factors and circumstances in any proceeding. It is generally believed that a skillful defense attorney can, in the course of individual sequestered voir dire, rehabilitate or ''save'' most venirepersons who would be challenged by the prosecution because of their anti-death-penalty sentiments. As we completed this book, the U.S. Supreme Court decided an important case that modifies *Witherspoon's* criteria for excluding death penalty opponents. In *Wainwright v. Witt* (No. 83-1427, Slip Opinion, January 21, 1985) the court held that the appropriate standard for excluding a juror for cause because of his views on capital punishment was that the juror's beliefs would ''prevent or substantially impair the performance of his duties as a juror in accordance with his instructions and oath.'' Although this standard is likely to result in more frequent exclusion of death penalty opponents from capital juries, its full impact will take some time to assess.

[4]Jurors who indicate that they would automatically vote for the death penalty in all cases in which defendant is convicted of first-degree murder are also usually struck for cause from the panel. These jurors are sometimes known as the ADP group.

[5]A jury pool is a group of citizens who meet the statutory requirements for jury service and who are subject to being called to serve for a certain period of time. Members of the jury pool are usually drawn by specially appointed jury commissioners or other officials.

[6]328 U.S. 217 (1946).

[7]347 U.S. 475 (1954).

[8]419 U.S. 522 (1975).

[9]337 F. Supp. 140, 143 (S.D.Y. 1972).

[10]430 U.S. 482 (1977).

[11]380 U.S. 202 (1965).

[12]40 Cal. App. 3d 107 (1974).

[13]439 U.S. 357 (1979).

[14]One exception to this rule would be cases where your client is perceived to have an unfair advantage because of personal wealth, power, or other influence. In such cases, consultants may want to minimize their visibility so as not to contribute further to a negative perception of the client.

Chapter 3
Public Opinion Surveys and Change of Venue

Public opinion surveys are one of the most powerful tools available to the trial consultant. They are used frequently (Bonora & Krauss, 1984; Ginger, 1977; Kairys, 1975; Vinson & Anthony, 1985) by jury workers. In this chapter, we discuss three uses of opinion surveys, and we describe our use of surveys when applied to motions for change of venue.

THREE USES OF PUBLIC OPINION SURVEYS

Surveys as Evidence

The most traditional use of opinion surveys has been identification of the beliefs and/or attitudes of some large group of people. Surveys are used in copyright and trademark litigation in which an advocate seeks to assess the public's recognition of some symbol or name or the public's ability to distinguish between similar trademarks (for general discussions, see Cannito & Becker, 1979; Note, 1953; Zeisel, 1960). Surveys have been used in antitrust cases to establish whether two or more products compete with one another and in obscenity trials to establish community standards (Haller, 1982).

Using surveys in this manner usually involves social scientists as expert witnesses rather than as trial consultants, and for that reason falls outside the scope of this chapter. However, the methodology of these surveys is quite similar to those described below. The admissibility of surveys and their relationship to the hearsay rule is one area of case law that should be known by consultants who use surveys. Discussions of the evidentiary status of public opinion surveys can be found in Cannito and Becker, 1979; McElroy, 1976; and Zeisel, 1960.

Trial by Survey

Opinion surveys are also used in what we term trial by survey, in which a sample of respondents randomly selected from the venue answer questions about their opinions of the case and give their reactions to the litigation tactics planned by the attorneys with whom the consultant is working. In many instances, the survey conducted for the change of venue request can double for this purpose; however, a more detailed inquiry may be necessary when there are no data or reasonable hypotheses to predict the reaction of potential jurors to courtroom phenomena. A survey used in this manner allows attorneys to pretest the significant trial issues and to fine-tune their presentation of them to the impaneled jury. These data can also be used to construct a juror profile that links the relationships discovered in the survey to characteristics of the venire from which jurors will be selected. Our two experiences with the trial by survey technique proved it a valuable but very demanding effort in terms of time and money, one which is also limited by technical and methodological constraints (see Berk, Hennessy, & Swan, 1977).

Related in some of their purposes to the trial by survey are trial simulations, an often elaborate set of procedures used for case planning. Box 3.1 describes trial simulations in more detail.

Change of Venue Surveys

We have centered our use of public opinion surveys in support of motions to change venue. Venue surveys are especially potent tools for the trial consultant for two reasons. First, they provide data that permit informed jury selection and litigation strategies sufficiently in advance of trial. Second, although it is not frequently granted, a change of venue is the most effective technique available for improving the chances of selecting a favorable jury in a case with excessive publicity.

In the rest of this chapter we: (a) summarize the case law pertaining to change of venue and other remedies for pretrial prejudice; (b) describe the step-by-step methods we use in conducting and presenting the results of venue surveys; (c) present data from five surveys with special attention to ways in which the results reveal the effects of prejudicial pretrial material; (d) review the methodological and interpretive problems associated with venue surveys; and (e) discuss areas of cross-examination that a consultant testifying about a venue survey will usually encounter (see Nietzel & Dillehay, 1983, for a briefer account of this material).

LEGAL STATUS OF CHANGE
OF VENUE AND OTHER REMEDIES
FOR PRETRIAL PUBLICITY

Irvin v. Dowd[1] was the first case in which the U.S. Supreme Court struck down a state conviction on the grounds of prejudicial publicity before defendant's trial. Six murders had been committed in the vicinity of Evansville, Indiana, between December 1954 and March 1955. Leslie Irvin was arrested for these murders on April 8, 1955, convicted of the murder of Whitney Kerr, and sentenced to death.

Shortly after Irvin's arrest, the prosecutor and local police issued highly publicized press releases that contained information that Irvin had confessed to the present crimes and 24 burglaries with a similar modus operandi; that he had been previously convicted of arson, burglary, and AWOL charges; that he was a parole violator and a fraudulent check artist and was remorseless and without conscience. Irvin's attorney obtained a change of venue to adjoining Gibson County, which was found to have been saturated by the same publicity that tainted the original venue. Petitioner's motion that venue be moved a second time, to a more distant

---

Box 3.1. Trial Simulations

In prolonged, high-stakes litigation, trial consultants may abandon opinion surveys in favor of presenting the case to a "mock jury" recruited and compensated for listening to the case and providing direct feedback to the advocates on: (a) how evidence is being understood, (b) how arguments are being received and, (c) how litigants are being perceived (Dancoff, 1982). This procedure, known by such names as trial simulation (Cahn, 1983) or shadow juries (Vinson, 1982), usually takes one of two forms.

1. In the *pretrial simulation*, the mock jury is formed prior to the trial. The attorneys for one side present the core of the case to the jurors, whose deliberations are observed and video-taped and who then discuss the "trial" performance of the attorneys with the consultant and/or attorneys. In subsequent simulations, new mock juries deliberate on case presentations that have been refined on the basis of previous presentations. The consultant is responsible for: (a) forming the simulation juries so that they are representative of the venire, (b) helping stage the simulation in order to capture the reality of courtroom phenomena, (c) directing the inquiry of the "jurors" to maximize the information on how attorneys can best present the case, and (d) developing a jury selection strategy based on what he or she observes during the deliberations and questioning of the mock jury. A pretrial simulation conducted on three successive nights was used by the

(continued)

litigation team for MCI in their 1980 antitrust case against AT&T. The real jury found for MCI and awarded it a $600 million verdict (see Cahn, 1983 for a discussion of this simulation).

2. In the *simultaneous simulation*, a shadow jury is recruited which mirrors the demographics and characteristics of the impaneled jury. The surrogate jurors are paid to attend the trial and to assume the role of jurors. They observe everything the true jurors observe and receive the same admonitions. During the trial, the consultant conducts extensive interviews with the shadow jurors in order to obtain their reactions to the litigants, the evidence, and the conduct of the trial in general. The consultant then presents this information to the attorneys, who can use it to modify or solidify their trial strategy. An example of a simultaneous simulation is provided by Vinson (1982), who describes his consultation for IBM's defense team in the antitrust case brought against them by California Computer Products of Anaheim, a trial in which the judge directed a verdict for IBM.

Prior to our work as trial consultants, we developed a procedure for studying jury processes that resembled the shadow jury technique and yielded valuable information about jury deliberations that we have incorporated in our consultation work. Our method of the "alternative jury" (Nietzel, Dillehay, & Rogers, 1976) involved the impaneling of collegiate volunteers for the trials of criminal felons in circuit court. Our "juries" were exposed to the full trial simultaneously with the actual jury. Alternative jurors completed the same Juror Data Sheet as the actual jury and listened to a tape recording of the court's orientation instructions presented to the entire jury panel on the first day of each jury term. The alternative jurors were present at the voir dire of the actual panel.

Alternative juries had complete access to the following elements of the trial: (a) the judge's pretrial instructions; (b) attorneys' opening statements; (c) all testimony, evidence, and exhibits; (d) attorneys' opening statements; and (e) the judge's charge and instructions to the jury. The alternative jury was instructed to follow the judge's admonishments forbidding discussion of the case while it was in process. The alternative jury received a copy of the judge's written instructions as well as an official ballot on which to record its verdicts. A private deliberation room was provided in the courthouse and the alternative jury deliberated with no time limitations.

Alternative jurors indicated individual sentiments regarding the guilt of the defendant on a secret, written "first ballot" administered just before deliberations began. In addition to this first ballot and the recorded deliberation, a number of postdeliberation measures were collected. We asked jurors to describe the defendant on an Adjective Check List and a 15-item bipolar adjective scale. Each juror nominated in writing the "most powerful member of the jury," and each juror described the "most powerful juror" and the rest of the jury on the 15-item adjective scale. We impaneled juries for ten criminal trials involving 17 different criminal charges.

Originally, in using the alternative juries, we intended to develop a method with maximal external validity for the study of jury phenomena. A major benefit of this research was the acquisition of much knowledge about the ways in which jurors interact, including the knowledge that deliberation may be a more powerful influence process than was concluded by Kalven & Zeisel (1966) in their classic study of the American jury. Our work with alternative juries was

(continued)

also advantageous in that the juries proved to be an ideal vehicle for the inception of ideas about jury selection and courtroom dynamics. Our four-component model of jury selection (see chapter 2) was the product of studying these alternative juries, and our first, tentative theories about effective advocacy were fashioned out of this experience. As does any effective training environment, alternative juries provide the opportunity for detailed inquiry, immediate consensual feedback, and a relatively safe context in which to make mistakes.

Analogous to a series of dress rehearsals staged for the benefit of the director, alternative juries are such a valuable learning opportunity that we recommend them as one of the best initial preparations for trial consultants. As an introduction to courtroom procedure and dynamics, jury decision-making, litigation strategy, and consultation opportunities, they are invaluable.*

In contrast to surveys, trial simulations allow concentrated study of the most important issues that the jury will face. They permit more thorough discussion of the way in which evidence is perceived than do surveys which by their nature constrain the type of questions asked and the completeness of the answers given. Simulations encourage the creation of alternative strategies and give the litigation team an opportunity to see the effect of these innovations. One limit of simulations is representativeness—it is often difficult to assemble a "practice jury" that mirrors the characteristics of the venire. This problem is compounded when the decision to conduct a simulation is made at the last minute. Orchestrating a successful trial simulation demands much early planning and good organizational skills.

---

*Some judges have found simulated juries to be effective as a device for inducing attorneys to settle their litigation prior to trial. U.S. District Court Judge Thomas Lambros of Cleveland often impanels a six-member jury from the regular jury pool to listen to lawyers present their evidence. No witnesses are called, but summaries of their testimony are given to the jury. The jury reaches a decision and often discusses how it reached its "verdict" with the litigants. According to Lambros, of the 80 cases in which he has required a "make-believe" jury, approximately 43% have settled even before the simulated trial began, 51% settled after the simulation ended, and 3% went on to a formal trial (Finlay, 1984).

county, was denied. A venire of 430 persons was examined; 268 were excused by the court on finding that they had fixed opinions of Irvin's guilt; 90% of those jurors examined on the point admitted to some opinion of his guilt; eight of the final jury selected believed Irvin was guilty.

Since *Irvin*, the Supreme Court has identified several factors that must be considered in determining whether pretrial influences have resulted in a due process violation. In *Murphy v. Florida*[2] the court held that Murphy, the well-publicized "Murph the Surf," had not been denied a fair trial and that jurors need not be totally ignorant of a defendant's past, especially in light of jurors' assurances that such knowledge would not interfere with their impartiality in deciding the case. However, exposure to information in news accounts, which is strongly probative of defendant's guilt in the case at trial but which may not be admissable at trial, has been held to violate due process. Such was the case in *Rideau v. Louisiana*[3] in which a local TV station, at three different times, broadcast a 20-minute film of the petitioner, surrounded by the sheriff and state troopers, confessing in detail to several charges. Rideau was convicted and sentenced to death by a jury, at least three members of which had seen the televised confession. The Supreme Court reversed the conviction, stating that "due process . . . required a trial before a jury drawn from a community of people who had not seen and heard Rideau's 'interview'."

In a recent (June 27, 1984) change-of-venue case (*Patton v. Yount*),[4] the Supreme Court held that a trial court's findings of jurors' impartiality during voir dire was a question of fact entitled to a "presumption of correctness" by reviewing courts. Defendant sought a change of venue on the grounds that prejudicial publicity prevented impaneling an impartial jury at his second murder trial (defendant was convicted of murder and rape at his first trial, 4 years earlier). Although 77% of the venirepersons admitted "they would carry an opinion into the jury box," the court concluded that their testimony was ambiguous enough to protect the presumption of correctness owed to the trial judge.

Assuming the harmful effects of some pretrial, extraevidentiary material, it may be asked what procedures are available to restore a fair trial for the accused. Four alternatives can function to cure pretrial prejudice.

Continuance

The trial can be postponed until a later date with the expectation that the passage of time will dampen the effects of prejudicial material. Psychologists may be skeptical about the contention that harmful memories are eroded merely by the passage of time, but judges tend to believe that passage of time is a great healer. For example, in the majority opinion in *Patton v. Yount*, the court stated: "That time soothes and erases is a perfectly natural phenomenon, familiar to all."

Expanded Voir Dire

The preferred method for avoiding prejudice from pretrial influences is to conduct a searching voir dire of potential jurors. Standard 3–3.5 of the American Bar Association's (1978) *Fair Trial and Free Press* recommends that in cases in which jurors may have been exposed to prejudicial publicity (a) examination of jurors about such exposure should be conducted outside the presence of other chosen or prospective jurors; (b) the amount of exposure and the prospective juror's testimony as to state of mind are relevant in determining acceptability; and (c) when there is a "substantial likelihood" that the regular number of peremptory challenges is inadequate, the court shall permit additional challenges in order to allow the impanelling of an impartial jury. Our faith in a thorough voir dire as a valuable protection against partiality is tempered by the realization that jurors can hide their true feelings from an examiner if they so choose and that even when jurors are candid, attorneys and judges may fail to recognize a bias.

Imported Venires

A venire may be imported to the venue from another county whenever it is found that potentially prejudicial media coverage of a criminal matter has been intense and has been concentrated in a specific locality in a state (ABA, 1978). The use of a foreign venire avoids the disruption of a venue change yet affords a venire that is presumably less affected by prejudicial material than the local venire. Imported juries are allowed in several states, and several other states are considering amendments that would permit them. The best known imported jury was impaneled in the 1980 trial of mass murderer John Wayne Gacy; 12 jurors and four alternates were selected from Rockford and sequestered throughout the trial, which was held in Chicago, 80 miles to the southeast. For an imported venire to cure problems of pretrial prejudice, it must be far enough removed from the venue not to share sources of prejudicial information. This requirement may, however, strip the procedure of its major advantages as a solution/convenience.

Change of Venue

From an administrative view, changing venue is the most extreme remedy for the influence of prejudicial material. Moving a trial from a community infested with pretrial prejudice can be a very effective protection. Nonetheless, courts are reluctant to change venue because of the expense, the inconvenience, and the tradition that justice should be administered in the community where the crime occurred (Burgess, 1967).

According to the ABA (1978) Standards:

> A motion of change of venue or continuance shall be granted whenever it is determined that, because of the dissemination of potentially prejudicial material, there is a substantial likelihood that, in the absence of such relief, a fair trial by an impartial jury cannot be had. This determination may be based on such evidence as qualified public opinion surveys or opinion testimony offered by individuals, or on the court's own evaluation of the nature, frequency, and timing of the material involved. A showing of actual prejudice shall not be required.
>
> If a motion for change of venue or continuance is made prior to the im-

panelling of the jury, the court may defer ruling until the completion of voir dire. The fact that a jury satisfying prevailing standards of acceptability has been selected shall not be controlling if the record shows that the criterion for the granting of relief set forth has been met. (Standard 8-3.3 in *Fair Trial and Free Press*; ABA, 1978)

Beginning with a line of cases since 1959, the Supreme Court has adopted a "reasonable likelihood of prejudice" standard for the granting of new venue, which squares with ABA Standard 8-3.3 (*Sheppard v. Maxwell*)[5]; or a "probability" standard (*Estes v. Texas*)[6]; see also *Marshall v. United States*[7] and *Groppi v. Wisconsin*.[8] (This standard may be weakened by the recent *Patton v. Yount* decision.)

A number of factors can contribute to a reasonable likelihood that prejudice will endanger a defendant's right to a fair trial. The particular nature of the case, existing community values, the composition of the community, and community exposure to extraevidentiary material in the form of pretrial publicity can influence the degree of prejudgment.

In small homogeneous communities, the most potent source of influence usually involves pretrial publicity. Thus, the impact of even minimal amounts of pretrial publicity must be assessed in order to protect against a reasonable likelihood of prejudice. In cases that receive great publicity, the effects of the publicity must be analyzed, particularly if the content of the publicity is likely to generate a desire for vengeance.

The methods for showing a substantial likelihood of prejudice can include testimony or affidavits of individuals in the venue, qualified public opinion surveys, and other materials having probative value (ABA Standard 8-3.3(b)). When pretrial publicity is of major concern and if adequate resources are available, a public opinion survey is the preferred technique to show that a likelihood of prejudice exists. A survey can reach a large number of people in a fairly short time, and it can reveal not only the extent of pretrial publicity but the actual impact of it on a community. Such a showing is important in view of Supreme Court decisions that hold that mere exposure to prejudicial material or mere existence of any preconceived notion is not sufficient to rebut the presumption of a prospective juror's impartiality.

A venue survey is designed to ascertain whether so many people have preformed opinions about a case or are so biased against a particular defendant that the ability of the defendant to obtain a fair jury is threatened. Venue surveys include questions that gauge the number of people who have read or heard about a case, what they have read or heard about it, whether they have formed opinions and attitudes about it, what these opinions and attitudes are and how they affect the way the case is perceived. Venue surveys are usually more complex than surveys used as evidence because the former technique seeks to assess attitudes and knowledge whereas the latter method is usually concerned only with measuring knowledge.

In the next section, we discuss the step-by-step procedures of several venue surveys we have conducted.

HOW TO CONDUCT A VENUE SURVEY

Planning the Survey

The consultant must have as much "lead time" as possible (at least 2 months) for conducting the survey and coordinating it with other activities by the defense. In this initial stage, there are three important tasks.

Media Analysis. First, all publicity must be studied in order to identify the key phrases used by the media in describing the crime. This is the language most likely to be recognized by the public in survey questions. A related aim of this media analysis is discovery of a specific issue which is particularly sensitive and potentially biasing in the case at hand, such as inadmissible evidence (e.g., the existence of prior convictions). Phrasing and content of survey questions should be based on the information revealed by the media analysis.

Theory of Defense. As was stressed in chapter 1, consultants must know the theory of the case to be developed by their side as well as the nature of the opponent's case. We try to hold an extended conference with defense attorney(s) as early as possible to learn these perspectives, which then form the basis for survey questions concerning attitudes about the insanity defense, the credibility of witnesses, etc. The defendant's preference for a new venue is also decided at this meeting.

Recruitment of Personnel. The consultant should recruit the staff who will conduct the survey at as early a date as possible. The number of personnel required for the survey depends on the size of the sample to be selected. We have used as few as two and as many as six interviewers. Another social scientist with experience in survey methodology should review the survey instrument and comment on its adequacy, phrasing of questions, and response format.

Designing the Instrument

Our survey instruments are organized into four sections, three of which remain essentially the same across surveys; one section consists of questions designed uniquely for the case at hand. Our typical instrument can be completed over the telephone in 10–15 minutes.

Introduction. We use the following standard introduction:

> Hello. Is this Mr./Mrs. ____? My name is ____, and I work for [e.g., Kentucky Office of Public Advocacy or an opinion survey team]. We are doing a survey of _____ County voters to see how they feel about our criminal justice system, certain crimes, and ways of dealing with crime in our society. our society.
>
> There are no right or wrong answers to these questions. We are just interested in your personal opinions. All of your answers will be kept completely confidential. O.K.?

Standard Questions. We follow our introduction with a set of questions that appear in all of our surveys. These questions assess attitudes about crime and punishment and the respondent's ability to meet juror eligibility requirements. The call is terminated after the first question if the respondent is not eligible for jury service.

1. First of all, are you a registered voter? (If no, terminate call.) What party?
2. I'd like to talk a minute about different types of crime. How serious are the following types of crime in your area of the state?
   a. Burglaries and armed robberies: Would you say these are: Not at all serious? Somewhat serious? Very serious?
   b. Violent crimes—Assaults and murders: Would you say these are: Not at all serious? Somewhat serious? Very serious?
3. Now a few questions about law enforcement. How successful in fighting crime do you think each of the following actually is?
   a. Having harsh (long) sentences for convicted criminals: Would you say this is: Not at all successful? Somewhat successful? Very successful?
   b. Increasing the number of local police: Would you say this is: Not at all successful? Somewhat successful? Very successful?
4. Now, let me make some statements and see what you think.
   a. The death penalty is an effective deterrent to serious, violent crimes. Do you agree or disagree with that statement?
   b. Most of what you read in the newspaper about certain crimes turns out to be pretty much the truth. Do you agree or disagree with this?

In recent surveys, we have included additional standard questions that assess respondents' opinions about the state prison system and parole eligibility. Some survey data (Costantini & King, 1980) show that "law and order" attitudes toward crime and punishment are linked to a tendency to prejudge guilt of defendants.

Special Questions. The special questions section contains questions that are tailored to the case at trial. They assess how knowledgeable the public is about the case, what opinions the public has about the defendant, how much evidence the public is aware of in the case, what preferences the public would have for sentence if the defendant should be convicted, etc. We begin these questions by informing respondents: "We are now going to turn for a minute to the issue of pretrial publicity in newspapers and other sources." The first two questions assess whether the respondent has read or heard anything about the case. We provide minimal description of the crime in the first question and then add a few significant facts to the second question. The second question is asked only if the respondent answers "no" or "don't know" to the initial probe. An example:

5. Do you remember reading anything or hearing anything about the shooting of Bob Thomas and the killing of Frank Burns on February 10, 1979, in Daniel County?
6. (Ask only if respondent answers no or doesn't know.) Frank Burns was killed and Bob Thomas was wounded in an apparent holdup of their Convenient Mart on Baker Road in Simpson, Kentucky, last February. Do you remember reading or hearing anything about that case?

Knowledge and attitudes about the defendant are then assessed. The initial questions test recall and then recognition of defendant's identity. His (her) name is not mentioned until the recall questions have been completed.

7. Do you know who has been charged with the murder of Frank Burns and the attempted murder of Bob Thomas in this case?
8. What is (are) the name(s)?
9. In your own mind at this time, do you think that Rowdy Dan Lawless, a man arrested in the Convenient Mart case, is probably guilty or not guilty of murdering Frank Burns?
10. From what you know about the case, how much evidence is there that Rowdy Dan Lawless is guilty of that murder? A lot of evidence? Some evidence? A little evidence? No evidence?
11. If a jury finds him guilty of this murder, what sentence do you think he should receive? A prison sentence from 20 years to life? A life sentence? The death penalty?

Pretrial publicity is the topic of four more questions:

12. How many articles about Frank Burns' killing would you guess you have read?
13. How many stories on TV or radio have you heard about this case?
14. Thinking of your own opinions about this case, what do you think has most influenced you? What you have read in the paper? What you have seen or heard on TV and radio? Your own personal decisions? Conversations you have had with others?
15. Knowing your community the way you do, do you think that Rowdy Dan Lawless would receive a fair trial in ____ County?
16. Why or why not?

This section also includes several questions about one issue in the case which we, in consultation with the attorneys, have singled out as particularly prejudicial. These "key issue questions" usually cover material that would be inadmissible at trial but which has received extensive coverage in the media or is common knowledge in the venue county. In this particular example, the key issue was the degree to which the public was aware of the well-publicized fact that Lawless had been charged with the murders of two young gas station attendants in an adjacent county on the night before the Burns' slaying. The fact of this charge would not have been admissible at the trial. Key issue questions in this case were the following:

17. Do you remember ever reading anything or hearing anything about the killing of Ricky Minor and Tommy Young on February 9, 1979, in Simpson, Kentucky?
18. (Ask if respondent answers no or is not sure.) Ricky Minor and Tommy Young were shot to death at the U-Pump-It Station on the corner of First and Main Street last February. Do you remember reading anything or hearing anything about that case?
19. Do you know who has been charged with the murder of Minor and Young in that case?
20. What is (are) the name(s)?
21. Do you think there is some link between the Convenient Mart killing and the killings at the U-Pump-It Station?
22. [If yes] What is the link?
23. [Ask if answers to 20 and 21 are affirmative.] What has most caused you to believe there is this link between the killings at U-Pump-It and the Convenient Mart? What you have read in the paper? What you heard on TV or the radio? Your own personal decision? Conversations you have had with others?

Judges are interested in what they perceive as the "bottom-line" question on juror impartiality—regardless of what the juror has heard or what opinions the juror may have formed, will the juror be able to put those opinions aside and decide the case only on the evidence presented at trial? The demand characteristics for an affirmative answer to this question, particularly when asked by a judge in open court, are so strong that its utility as a screener of bias is dubious. Although consultants should try to educate judges about the problems people have in answering such a question (e.g., Nisbett & Wilson, 1977), they probably should include a similar question in their survey and then discuss the multiple determinants of answers to it and the resulting problems of interpretation.

We now are considering asking the bottom-line question in our survey in this form: "Regardless of what you have read or heard about this case, do you believe that if you were a juror you could decide the case solely on the basis of the evidence presented at the trial?" Another form of the question is given by Constantini and King (1980), who ask whether a respondent "[can] be an impartial juror" in the case at hand. However, their data also indicate that more than half of the respondents who believe the accused is guilty before the trial also believe that they could be impartial jurors.

Demographics and Other Identifying Questions. This section includes items about respondents' age, marital status, employment, religious preference and frequency of church attendance, education, income, race, favorite newspaper and TV station, and frequency of reading and viewing the news. These questions permit a comparison of the sample's demography with the county's registered voters. These data can also be used at a later date for the construction of juror profiles to aid in the selection of the jury. We conclude the questionnaire–interview by saying:

> O.K. That is really all I have to ask you, except for one thing. Thinking back over all that we've talked about earlier, is there anything you would like to tell me? Well, then. Thank you very much for taking the time to talk with me. You have been very helpful! Goodbye.

Following the first draft of the instrument, we review it with the defense attorneys. Another behavioral scientist with survey sophistication should critique the instrument for fairness of wording and choice of response categories. We have found this latter safeguard to be an effective mechanism for dealing with the inevitable line of cross-examination that attempts to suggest that the questions were loaded or leading.

Training the Interviewers

We have used psychology graduate students or law students as our interviewers. Our data do not indicate any basis for preferring either type of interviewer. There are individual differences in percentages of completed interviews and amount of information elicited, but they are not systematic and simply confirm the obvious conclusion that some people are better interviewers than others. The only basis for a preference would be to ward off one line of cross-examination. Use of psychology trainees prevents the question of whether the ethics of law students might require them to be advocates for "their client," thereby nullifying the claim that they were objective or "blind" interviewers. Adequate training of our interviewers requires several hours. We use the following sequence of training.

Orientation. Interviewers are told that they will be conducting a survey about the effects of pretrial publicity. They are not told anything about the case although it is unavoidable that they will gather some information simply from conducting the interviews. We do not discuss change of venue with them; every attempt is made to keep them "blind" to the venue.

Interview Training. The training of interviewers for the actual administration of the survey requires a 3-step process. First, we model several calls that include the most common problems to which interviewers must respond. These prototypes are discussed and the rationales for prescribed answers are reviewed. Second, interviewers are observed while they conduct practice calls with each other. Feedback is given, and practice calls are repeated if necessary. Third, we monitor two or three "real" calls for each interviewer and provide appropriate feedback.

Interviewers are given step-by-step instructions for the use of the random number sequence to be employed in contacting the sample (see Drawing the Sample section). Each interviewer is monitored for accuracy in the use of the random number system.

Detailed rules concerning callbacks, busy signals, scoring of and responses to common questions from respondents are given to the interviewers. Several instructions receive special emphasis in our training:

1. Survey questions and response alternatives are to be read verbatim.
2. Interviewers are to answer honestly all questions that a respondent may have about the ultimate purpose and uses of the interview.
3. Interviewers are told to say they are not permitted to answer any inquiries by respondents about whether an answer is right or wrong.
4. Interviewers are not to offer "don't know/not sure" as a response alternative to any questions, but they are to score such responses when they are given by a respondent in a "don't know/not sure" category.
5. Spontaneous comments and narrative answers are to be recorded verbatim.

Supervision of Interview. A number of phone interviews should be monitored and supervised. Monitoring is better done without advance notice to the interviewer. Supervision of calls is an important form of quality control. The expert testifying about the results of the survey can almost always expect cross-examination on extent and type of supervision.

Drawing the Sample

Before drawing the sample, the consultant should check local statutes about juror eligibility and acceptable juror source lists. Persons who are called but who would not be eligible for jury service cannot be included in the survey. We also exclude persons who will be witnesses or participants at the trial.

We draw our sample from phone books. Phone numbers are selected by use of random numbers that identify page of phone book and number of entries from the top or bottom of the page to be counted before the entry to be called is selected. Nonresidential numbers are omitted. We are aware of the nonrepresentativeness of a phone book sample but believe it to be negligible, particularly in identifying a jury-eligible sample.

There are no firm rules for sample size. Although the larger the better, with a sample of 100 per county an excellent size, we have found samples of $n = 30$ to $n = 60$ per county to be adequate in most cases. Judges are usually satisfied with samples of this size.

Because women are more likely than men to answer the phone, some procedure is necessary to try to approximate the population ratio of men to women. Albert Sindlinger describes the procedure he used in conducting a public opinion survey in the Watergate conspiracy trial (*United States v. Haldeman*,[9] pp. 177–178):

> If the person answering the telephone was female, the surveyor would determine whether there was a male over the age of 18 in the household who was available then or at some other convenient time. If the answer was no, the female was interviewed. If the answer was yes, the male was interviewed either then or by a later call back.

Another acceptable procedure is to predetermine on a random basis whether a man or a woman will be requested for each call and then to complete the call only if a respondent matching the schedule is available. In jurisdictions with a large proportion of unlisted phone numbers, it may be necessary to use random digit dialing to prevent a nonrepresentative sample.

We make calls only on the weekends or on weeknights between the hours of 6:30 and 10:00 p.m. Calls at any other times are likely to introduce major problems in the availability of respondents.

We conduct surveys in at least two jurisdictions—the original venue and a ''comparison county'' to which the trial might be moved. We prefer to survey several counties—the venue county, adjacent counties (which are usually preferred by judges but which are often contaminated by the same publicity as the venue), and the preferred county for venue, which is selected by consultation with defense counsel. This selection considers factors such as the nature of the case, demography of counties, and outcomes of previous trials in the counties under consideration. Such a strategy permits a comparison of responses that can show whether a venue change to a given county would in fact cure any problems of preformed opinion and bias. Data showing differences between jurisdictions can be presented to the court to determine the least prejudiced county for venue.

Presenting the Results

Results of venue surveys can be presented by expert's affidavits, testimony at an evidentiary hearing, or both. The most effective presentation requires testimony supplemented by charts and graphs that depict the crucial comparisons of counties. Close coordination with the attorney is important at this stage because some of the results may be included in the initial motion for change of venue and the request for an evidentiary hearing. The expert also can prepare an affidavit in support of the attorney's petitioning the court to provide funds for the survey work if defendant is indigent. A list of federal and state cases in which the courts have authorized payment for survey work is presented in an appendix of The National Jury Projects' *Jurywork: Systematic Techniques* (Bonora & Krauss, 1984).

We conduct our own scoring and analysis of survey results. Sophisticated analyses are seldom necessary for presenting the data; cross-tabulations and calculations of standard errors are usually the most complicated procedures we present at an evidentiary hearing. Nonetheless, the integrity of the surveys' results can be insulated against a heated cross-examination if the expert attests that all analyses were personally performed.

Some Illustrative Cases

The use of the public opinion survey can be illustrated by considering the results of surveys that we conducted in five capital murder cases tried in Kentucky between June 1980 and November 1981. The fact situations for the cases are summarized below. Attorneys in all cases were public defenders.

Case I. The defendant was a young black man charged with the murder of an elderly white woman and the burglary of her home. The victim was 77 years old and had been beaten to death. The defendant was charged with murder after three codefendants told police that they were with him in the victim's home and that he had murdered the old woman. The codefendants had been tried together and had been convicted of the burglary prior to defendant's murder trial. Murder charges against codefendants were dropped. The verdicts of the codefendant's burglary trial received repeated media coverage.

Case II. The defendant was a 52-year-old black man charged with the sodomy and murder of a young white woman at her apartment near the governor's mansion in the state capital. There were no witnesses, although a resident of the victim's apartment had heard the victim's screams during the attack. The victim had been stabbed 23 times. The defendant was a prison trusty who had been living and working in a dormitory along with 11 other trusties. The dormitory was on the grounds of the governor's mansion, across the street from the murder scene. The defendant was serving a prison term for conviction of armed robbery and assault. Following defendant's indictment, he and the other trusties were transferred to the Kentucky State Reformatory, and a grand jury which investigated the trusty program recommended that it be terminated. Extensive publicity focused on the defendant's past record and the security problems of the trusty program.

Case III. The important facts of Case III were illustrated in the previous section on special questions in the survey questionnaire. The defendant was charged with the murder of Frank Burns and the attempted murder of Bob Thomas, co-owners of a convenient food store. The news media had repeatedly reported that Thomas was an eyewitness to the murder of Burns, which had been characterized as an "execution-style" slaying. Even greater amounts of publicity were concerned with the fact that defendant was charged in an adjacent county with the murders of two young gas station attendants on the night before the killing of Burns. The fact of this charge was not admissible at the current trial.

Case IV. The defendant was charged with the murder for hire of a young man after the victim's wife and her lover solicited defendant to shoot the victim. The agreed-upon payment was the victim's gun collection. The defendant was convicted of first-degree murder, and the jury recommended a sentence of death. The conviction was appealed on the grounds that the trial judge failed to instruct the jury that defendant could not be found guilty on only the uncorroborated testimony of an accomplice (in this case, the wife's lover). The Supreme Court reversed the conviction, and the retrial was scheduled in the same venue as the initial trial. Considerable publicity was devoted to the Supreme Court's decision to overturn the first verdict on a "technicality."

Case V. The defendant was a 38-year-old man charged with beating to death and robbing a 65-year-old man. The victim was a somewhat notorius recluse who lived in a rural, secluded area of western Kentucky and was reputed to have hoarded a large sum of money in his home. He had been bludgeoned to death with a baseball bat in front of his home. Publicity focused on: (a) the anticipated testimony that two accomplices would offer against the defendant Riley McGrath in exchange for dismissal of charges against them; and (b) the fact that McGrath had an extensive prior history of felony convictions.

Case V is different from the first four cases because the defense attorneys did not seek a survey in support of a change of venue motion. Rather, they requested a survey of the venue county as a method of assessing whether a venue change needed to be requested. For this reason, data were not collected on alternative or preferred counties.

Survey Counties

Fourteen counties (five venue, six adjacent and three preferred) were surveyed across the five cases. Mean population for the venue counties was 39,682 (range: 17,910–61,310), for the adjacent counties 50,549 (range: 4,842–137,058), and for the preferred counties 97,919 (range: 17,765–204,165). According to 1980 Kentucky Vital Statistics for racial composition, the percentage of population that was nonwhite was 7.2% for venue counties (range: 0.6%–11.4%), 4.3% for adjacent counties (range: 0.9%–9.2%) and 11.5% for preferred counties (range: 9%–14.5%). Among all Kentucky counties the mean rank for per capita income was 26.8 for venues (range: 9–86), 29.7 for adjacent counties (range: 2–69) and 19.3 for preferred counties (range: 3–33).

Percentages of persons refusing to answer the survey were very stable across the counties, averaging 25.7% for both venue and adjacent counties and 29.4% for preferred counties.

RESULTS OF THE SURVEYS

Special Question Comparisons

Data for the "special questions" (5–15) are presented in Table 3.1 (Because of the special nature of the survey in Case V, its data are presented later in Table 3.7.)

Without exception, greater percentages of respondents in the venue counties had read or heard about the case than had residents of adjacent or preferred counties. This difference is more pronounced in the responses to question 5 (minimal description of the crime) than to the total recognition of the case measured by combining question 5 with the information-enriched question 6.

A more pronounced difference exists for questions that tap knowledge and attitudes about the defendants. In the average venue county, 44.0% of respondents recalled the defendant by name whereas only 9.3% in adjacent and 2.3% in preferred counties were able to do so. Of venue respondents, 33.5% believed before trial that defendant was probably guilty, as compared with 20.9% of adjacent county and 4.1% of preferred county respondents.

In those surveys in which we included questions about preferred sentence (question 11) and opinion of amount of evidence against defendant (question 10), venue respondents indicated they were more favorable toward the death penalty following conviction and believed that there was more evidence against the defendant than did respondents in the other types of county.

Asked to indicate the source of information that most influenced their

Table 3.1. Special Questions Comparison in Four Public Opinion Surveys

Survey Question	Case I[a] Ven. Co. (n=50) %	Case I[a] Pref. Co. (n=50) %	Case II[b] Ven. Co. (n=33) %	Case II[b] Adj. Co. (n=30) %	Case II[b] Ven. Co. (n=40) %	Case II[b] Adj. Co. (1) (n=41) %	Case III Adj. Co. (2) (n=30) %	Case III Adj. Co. (3) (n=37) %	Case III Pref. Co. (n=35) %	Case III Ven. Co. (n=60) %	Case IV Adj. Co. (1) (n=58) %	Case IV Adj. Co. (2) (n=60) %	Case IV Pref. Co. (n=59) %
5. Read or heard anything about case (minimal description)													
Yes	100	10	97	50	65	22	20	32.4	22.9	60	5.2	1.7	8.5
No	0	90	3	43.3	30	75.6	60.0	62.2	77.1	33.3	87.9	91.7	88.1
Don't know	0	0	0	6.7	5.0	2.4	20.0	5.4	0.0	6.7	6.9	6.7	3.4
5 & 6. (Total) Read or heard anything about case (additional information)													
Yes	100	12	97	60	90	90.2	83.8	86.5	40	85	31.0	28.3	27.1
No	0	88	3	33.3	10.0	9.8	13.3	10.8	60.0	10	62.1	56.7	69.5
Don't know	0	0	0	6.7	0.0	0.0	0.0	5.4	0.0	5	6.9	15.0	3.4
7 & 8. Able to name defendant(s)													
Yes	70	4	30.3	0	37.5	24.3	13.3	16.2	2.9	38.3	0	1.7	0
No	30	96	69.7	100	62.5	75.6	86.7	83.8	97.1	61.7	100	98.3	100
9. Personal opinion about guilt													
Guilty	18	2	40.6	10	48.8	43.9	48.3	16.2	8.6	26.7	1.7	5	1.7
Not guilty	6	0	0	0	2.5	0	0	2.7	5.7	0	1.7	0	3.4
No opinion/Don't know	76	98	59.4	90	48.8	56.1	51.7	81.1	85.7	73.3	96.6	95	94.9
10. How much evidence against defendant													
A lot	—	—	21.4	3.3	44.7	32.5	41.4	9.1	5.7	—	—	—	—
Some	—	—	50.0	13.3	21.1	40.0	13.8	18.2	11.4	—	—	—	—
A little	—	—	10.7	3.3	2.6	10.0	0	0	14.3	—	—	—	—

80

None	—	0	3.3	2.6	2.5	0	0	0	—	—	—	—
Don't know	—	17.9	76.7	28.9	15.0	44.8	72.7	68.6	—	—	—	—
11. Preferred sentence												
Death penalty	—	45.2	33.3	57.5	45.0	53.4	34.7	20.0	10	3.4	0.8	0
Life in prison	—	25.8	30	17.5	25.0	19.0	20.8	34.3	8.3	1.7	4.2	0
20 yrs. to life	—	6.5	13.3	15.0	2.5	10.3	11.1	17.1	1.7	0	1.7	0
Don't know	—	22.6	23.3	15.0	27.5	17.2	33.3	28.6	80	94.9	93.3	100
12 No. of Articles read	1.58 (n=4)	5.45 (n=28)	4.19 (n=17)	5.89 (n=34)	4.44 (n=31)	4.47 (n=24)	4.03 (n=22)	1.95 (n=13)	2.76 (n=38)	2.43 (n=7)	1.87 (n=15)	1.70 (n=5)
13. No. of TV/radio stories heard	1.75 (n=4)	3.64 (n=18)	4.41 (n=19)	5.83 (n=36)	5.10 (n=36)	3.44 (n=23)	3.63 (n=23)	3.45 (n=11)	2.38 (n=12)	2.42 (n=6)	1.73 (n=15)	1.29 (n=7)
14. Source of most influence												
Newspaper	50	40	22.8	27.5	11.5	44.3	25.0	11.4	21.7	8.7	12.2	6.3
TV/radio	33	3.3	22.8	27.5	19.6	24.2	22.2	22.9	1.7	30.0	9.8	8.3
Personal decision	0	6.7	6.7	6.3	27.7	9.7	11.1	0	25.0	0	0	14.6
Conversation with others	17	30.0	4.4	18.8	16.9	4.5	2.8	8.6	25.0	8.7	4.9	0
Don't know	0	20.0	43.3	20.0	24.3	17.3	38.9	57.1	26.7	52.2	73.2	70.8
15. Receive fair trial in county												
Yes	87	71	56.7	72.5	73.2	63.3	64.9	57.1	38.3	82	85	58.3
No	8	6.5	13.3	12.5	9.8	16.7	8.1	22.9	15.0	7.7	3.3	10.7
Don't know	5	22.6	30.0	15.0	17.1	20.0	27.0	20.0	46.7	10.3	11.7	31.2

Note. Tables 3.1–3.7 are from "Psychologists as Consultants for Changes of Venue" by M. Nietzel and R. Dillehay, 1983, *Law and Human Behavior, 7*, pp. 322–323, 324, 326, 327, 328, 329, and 330–331. Copyright 1983 by the Plenum Publishing Co. Used with permission.

Note. Ven. Co. = venue county; Adj. Co. = adjacent county; Pref. Co. = preferred county.

[a]Lack of resources and lead time prevented inclusion of adjacent counties in this survey.

[b]The judge had indicated that he would be very unlikely to consider a change of venue to any county other than the adjacent county which was subsequently surveyed. In addition, defense attorneys had some preference for a venue change to this adjacent county. For this reason, a separate "preferred county" was not included in the survey.

opinions, respondents across all counties cited newspapers as the prime source (23.3%), followed by TV/radio (17.5%), conversations with others (14.0%), and personal decision (9.8%); 35.4% of respondents were unwilling or unable to specify a most influential source of information. The most obvious difference between types of counties on this question was that only in venue counties was conversation with others the most frequent source of major influence; 28.5% of venue respondents named conversation as their leading influence as compared with 7.0% of adjacent county, and 8.5% of preferred county respondents. We have discovered this same difference in every public opinion survey we have conducted; conversation with others is the most frequently cited major influence only in venue counties. The importance of conversation with others also appears to be inversely related to the population of the venue county.

The question of whether defendant would receive a fair trial in respondents' counties has proven to be a relatively poor discriminator in our surveys, perhaps because of the high social desirability of a positive answer. An average of 58.5% of venue, 70.9% of adjacent, and 67.5% of preferred county participants answered yes to this question.

Table 3.2 presents chi-squares for the between-county differences in Cases I through IV. The following results are noteworthy:

1. With rare exceptions, venue versus preferred comparisons were significant and in the predicted direction. Preferred versus adjacent county comparisons were also frequently significant, with respondents from adjacent counties revealing more negativity toward defendants.
2. Significant differences between adjacent counties were rare, occurring on only two questions in Case III. In this case, the defendant was charged with a multiple homicide in adjacent county # (2).
3. On question 14, the significant chi-square is best explained by the greater endorsement of "no opinion/don't know" by respondents from adjacent versus venue counties and by preferred versus venue and adjacent counties.
4. We are aware that the large number of contrasts reported in Table 3.2 increases the "error rate per family." However, we believe that the results are sufficiently protected against Type I errors for two reasons: (a) almost all differences between venue and other counties remain significant even if we practice the stringent corrective of dividing alpha level by the number of contrasts per case or per question and, (b) the significant differences are conceptually predictable and consistent in a manner unlikely to arise from an inflated Type I error rate.

Key Issue Comparisons

Results for the Key Issue questions in each case are summarized in Tables 3.3 through 3.6.

Table 3.2. Chi-Square Values for Differences between Venue, Adjacent, and Preferred Counties in Cases I-IV

Question No.[a]	5	5 & 6 (combined)	8	9	10	11	14	15
Case 1								
Ven. vs. Pref.	78.2*****[b]	75.0****	43.9****	5.4**	—	—	18.6****	13.8****
Case II								
Ven. vs. Adj.	15.9****	11.0****	8.7***	6.1**	15.5****	<1	8.3**	<1
Case III								
Ven. vs. Pref.	11.7****	18.8****	11.4****	12.5****	14.8****	9.4***	11.0****	1.3
Ven. vs. Adj. (1)	13.6****	<1	1.1	<1	<1	<1	<1	<1
Ven. vs. Adj. (2)	12.2****	<1	3.9*	<1	<1	<1	3.2	<1
Ven. vs. Adj. (3)	6.9****	<1	3.4	7.8***	8.3***	3.1	8.2**	<1
Pref. vs. Adj. (1)	<1	19.4****	5.4**	10.1****	20.8****	4.2*	8.3***	1.5
Pref. vs. Adj. (2)	<1	10.9****	1.2	10.9****	8.6****	6.4**	11.8****	<1
Pref. vs. Adj. (3)	<1	14.9****	2.3	<1	<1	1.3	4.5	<1
Adj. (1) vs. Adj. (2)	<1	<1	<1	<1	1.5	<1	2.9	<1
Adj. (1) vs. Adj. (3)	<1	<1	<1	5.8**	13.1****	<1	4.9	<1
Adj. (2) vs. Adj. (3)	<1	<1	<1	6.5**	3.9*	1.6	3.3	<1
Case IV								
Ven. vs. Pref.	32.7****	38.2****	22.7****	13.1****	—	4.3*	25.7****	3.5
Ven. vs. Adj. (1)	37.6****	33.2****	22.4****	12.9****	—	1.1	5.7	16.6****
Ven. vs. Adj. (2)	45.1****	37.0****	17.4****	9.0****	—	3.3	22.1****	25.7****
Pref. vs. Adj. (1)	<1	<1	<1	<1	—	<1	5.5	4.6*
Pref. vs. Adj. (2)	1.6	<1	<1	<1	—	<1	2.8	8.3***
Adj. (1) vs. Adj. (2)	<1	<1	<1	<1	—	<1	2.9	<1

[a]For questions 5, 5 and 6 (combined), 8 and 15, chi-squares were calculated for the "yes" category vs. a category collapsed across "no" and "don't know" responses. For question 9, the contrast was between the "guilty" category vs. a category collapsed across "not guilty" and "no opinion/don't know" responses. For question 10, "a lot" and "some" were collapsed into one category and contrasted with a category collapsed across "a little," "none," and "don't know" responses. For question 11, the contrast was between "death penalty" and a category collapsed across all other response options. For question 14, "conversation with others" was contrasted with two other categories: "don't know/no opinion" and a category collapsed across the "newspaper," "TV/radio," and "personal decision" options. There is one degree of freedom for all contrasts except for question 14 where df = 2.

[b]*p < .05; **p < .02; ***p < .01; ****p < .001.

Table 3.3. Key Issue Comparisons: Case I

Question	Venue county ($n=50$) (%)	Preferred county ($n=50$) (%)
1. Elderly people are more often victims of violent crime than any other type of person.		
Agree	82	60
Disagree	12	28
No opinion/not sure	6	12
2. Have you read that three other people accused of the burglary of Ms. Roach's home have gone to trial?		
Yes	94	4
No	6	96
3. Do you know whether these defendants were found guilty or not guilty?		
Guilty	66	2
Not guilty	0	0
Don't know/not sure	34	98
4. Do you agree with those verdicts?	($n=33$)	($n=1$)
Yes	61	100
No	12	0
Don't know/not sure	27	0
5. Do you think the sentences they received were	($n=33$)	($n=1$)
Too severe	3	0
Too lenient	43	0
Just about right	24	0
Don't know/not sure	30	100
6. Do you believe that since these men were found guilty of this burglary it is likely that Jerry White is guilty of murdering Ms. Roach?	($n=33$)	($n=1$)
Yes	24	0
No	12	0
Don't know/not sure	64	100

Case I. In contrast with residents of the preferred county, venue residents were significantly more likely ($\chi^2(1)=94.0$, $p<.001$) to have read about the burglary trial and to know that defendants were convicted ($\chi^2(1)=46.7$, $p<.001$). Venue residents were far more likely to agree with the convictions and to believe that the sentences were too lenient. Twenty-four percent of venue respondents admitted that the burglary convictions made it more likely that White was guilty of murder. No respondent from the preferred county endorsed such a belief. Differences between the venue and preferred samples emerged on an item that tapped a collateral but much broader belief: 82% of venue respondents versus 60% of the pre-

Table 3.4. Key Issue Comparisons: Case II

Question	Venue county (n=33) (%)	Adjacent county (n=30) (%)
1. What was Martin Lewis doing for a living at the time the murder of Ms. Parker took place?		
Working as "trusty"	73	17
Any incorrect answer	6	0
Don't know/not sure	21	83
2. What effect would the fact that Martin Lewis worked as a "trusty" at the time of the murder have on your opinion of his guilt or innocence on this charge?		
More likely to be guilty	18	17
More likely to be not guilty	0	7
No effect	42	50
Don't know/not sure	39	27

ferred sample believed that the elderly were more often victims of violent crimes than other persons ($\chi^2(1)=4.9$, $p<.05$). Venue was changed to the preferred county in this case.

Case II. More than 4 times as many respondents from the venue county as the adjacent county knew that Martin Lewis was working as a prison trusty at the time of Parker's murder ($\chi^2(1)=17.7$, $p<.001$). However, when all respondents were apprised of the fact that Lewis had in fact been a trusty at the time of the murder, only 18% of the venue and 17% of the adjacent sample indicated that this status made it more likely that he was guilty of the murder. Of the adjacent county sample, 57% said either that the status of trusty would have no effect or would make it more likely that Lewis was not guilty; 42% of the venue sample responded with one of these two alternatives. This difference was not significant. Venue was changed to the adjacent county in this case.

Case III. Case III provides an unusual opportunity to examine the validity of survey data. The key issue in this case was the degree to which respondents would be aware of the additional (but inadmissible) murder charges against defendant in connection with the killings of Minor and Young. One would expect that awareness and knowledge of the Minor and Young episode would be greatest in the county of its occurrence which was adjacent county # (2).

On the basis of the first question, which used only minimal description, venue respondents were more likely to report having read or heard about

Table 3.5. Key Issue Comparisons: Case III

Question	Ven. Co. (n = 40) %	Adj. Co. (1) (n = 41) %	Adj. Co. (2) (n = 30) %	Adj. Co. (3) (n = 37) %	Pref. Co. (n = 35) %
1. Read or heard anything about killing of Minor & Young					
Yes	52.5	19.5	46.7	37.8	22.9
No	40.0	80.5	43.3	54.1	77.1
Don't know	7.5	0.0	10.0	8.1	0.0
2. (Total) read or heard anything about case (additional information)					
Yes	80.0	68.3	93.3	73.0	34.3
No	17.5	31.7	6.7	24.3	65.7
Don't know	2.5	0.0	0.0	2.7	0.0
3. Able to name defendant					
Yes	30.0	15.0	16.7	10.8	2.9
No	60.0	85.0	66.7	78.4	97.1
Don't know	10.0	0.0	16.7	10.8	0.0
4. Is there a link between Convenient killing and these killings?					
Yes	50.0	22.0	34.5	24.3	8.6
No	10.0	7.3	17.2	2.7	28.6
Don't know	40.0	70.7	48.3	73.0	62.9
5. [If yes to no. 4] What is the link?	(n = 20)	(n = 9)	(n = 10)	(n = 9)	(n = 3)
Same defendants	70.0	22.2	50.0	44.4	0.0
Other similarity	20.0	66.7	30.0	33.3	0.0
Don't know	10.0	11.1	20.0	22.2	100.0
6. [If yes to no. 4] What has most caused you to believe there is a link?	(n = 20)	(n = 8)	(n = 10)	(n = 8)	(n = 3)
Newspaper	61.7	21.9	55.0	31.3	0.0
TV/radio	21.7	21.9	25.0	56.3	66.7
Personal decision	9.2	3.1	15.0	0.0	0.0
Conversation with others	7.5	28.1	0.0	0.0	33.3
No/don't know	0.0	25.0	0.0	12.5	0.0

the case than were respondents from adjacent county # (1) ($\chi^2(1) = 8.2$, $p < .01$) or the preferred county ($\chi^2(1) = 5.7$, $p < .02$). Adjacent county # (2) respondents were also more likely to report knowledge of the case to this question than were adjacent county # (1) respondents ($\chi^2(1) = 4.8$, $p < .05$).

On the total recognition elicited by combining question 1 and the information-enriched question 2, preferred county residents were significantly less likely (all p values $< .01$) than residents from any other county to report knowledge of the case. In addition, adjacent county # (2) re-

Table 3.6. Key Issue Comparisons: Case IV

Question	Venue county (n=60) %	Adjacent county (1) (n=58) %	Adjacent county (2) (n=60) %	Preferred county (n=59) %
1. Verdict of Smith's first trial				
Guilty	28.3	3.4	3.3	0.0
Not guilty	0.0	0.0	0.0	0.0
Don't know	71.7	96.6	96.7	100.0
2. Did you agree or disagree with that verdict?	(n=17)	(n=2)	(n=2)	(n=0)
Agree	58.8	0.0	50.0	—
Disagree	0.0	0.0	0.0	—
Don't know	41.2	100.0	50.0	—
3. Know that Supreme Court had ordered a new trial for Smith				
Yes	11.7	1.7	1.7	0.0
No	88.3	98.3	98.3	100.0
Don't know	0.0	0.0	0.0	0.0
4. What is your opinion of the Supreme Court's decision?	(n=7)	(n=1)	(n=1)	(n=0)
Good decision	14.3	0.0	100.0	—
Bad decision	85.7	0.0	0.0	—
Don't know	0.0	100.0	0.0	—

spondents were more likely than adjacent county # (1) respondents to report knowledge of the case in response to the combination of questions 1 and 2 ($\chi^2(1)=5.1$, $p<.05$).

Venue respondents were able to name defendant significantly more often than were preferred county respondents ($\chi^2(1)=7.80$, $p<.01$) and were also more likely to believe a link existed between the Convenient Mart Trial and these killings than respondents from the preferred county ($\chi^2(1)=13.2$, $p<.001$), adjacent county # (1) ($\chi^2(1)=5.8$, $p<.02$) and adjacent county # (3) ($\chi^2(1)=4.4$, $p<.05$). Adjacent county # (2) respondents were also more likely than preferred county respondents to believe that a link existed between the trial and the killings in adjacent county # (2) ($\chi^2(1)=5.1$, $p<.05$).

Chi-squares were not calculated for the differences obtained to question 5 because of small and unequal sample sizes. However, the results were consistent with the pattern established for the first four questions. Venue and adjacent county # (2) respondents were the most likely to define the link assessed in question 4 to be the identicalness of the culprit. Change of venue was denied.

Case IV. Key issue comparisons in Case IV were consistent with the data obtained in the first three cases. Although the absolute number of respondents holding beliefs potentially harmful to the defendant was small, venue respondents were significantly more likely than residents of all other counties (all p values < 0.001) to know that Smith was convicted at his first trial. Venue respondents were also more likely to agree with that verdict, to know that a new trial had been ordered by the Kentucky Supreme Court, and to believe that the decision was a bad one. Change of venue was denied.

Dispositions of Cases I through IV

Following the venue change in Case I, all charges were dropped against defendant. In Case II, a trial for capital murder was conducted in the adjacent county, and the jury returned a conviction and a sentence of life imprisonment. In Case III, following a trial on capital murder conducted in the venue, the jury convicted defendant and sentenced him to death. Following the denial of the motion to change venue in Case IV, defendant pleaded guilty in exchange for a sentence of life imprisonment.

Case V

Attorneys in this case were more interested in whether they needed to seek a change of venue rather than which county would make the most favorable new venue. With the exception of the key issue questions, the same questionnaire was used as in previous cases. However, comparisons in this case were made between the intended venue and the initial norms for venue, adjacent, and preferred counties that were derived from the first four cases. Table 3.7 presents comparisons between the Case V venue and the mean values for venue, adjacent and preferred counties for Cases I through IV.

In most of the comparisons in Table 3.7, values of the Case V venue fall between the means for the venues and preferred counties in Cases I through IV. For some comparisons, venue V has a more defendant-favorable value than has the average preferred county. For example on question 11, venue V respondents favored the minimum sentence much more frequently than did respondents in any other type of county. Venue V was markedly more favorable to the defendant than the average venue on the percentages of people who believed there was a lot of evidence against the defendant and who indicated that conversation with others was the most important source of influence on their opinion (question 14). With the above exceptions, the venue county in Case V was most similar to the average adjacent county. Based on these results, we recommended

Table 3.7. Special Questions and Key Issue Comparisons in Case V Compared with Means of Other Types of Counties in Cases I–IV

Survey question: special questions	Ven. Co. (n = 36) %	Other Ven.[a] (Cases I–IV) %	Adj. Co. (Cases II–IV) %	Pref. Co. (Cases I, III, IV) %
5. Read or heard anything about case (minimal description)				
Yes	50.0	80.5	26.1	13.8
No	36.1	16.6	66.3	85.1
Don't know	13.9	2.9	7.6	1.1
5 & 6. (Total) Read or heard anything about case (additional information)				
Yes	80.6	93.0	58.8	26.4
No	19.4	5.8	34.7	72.5
Don't know	0	1.2	6.5	1.1
7 & 8. Able to name defendant(s)				
Yes	13.9	44.0	6.2	2.3
No	86.1	56.0	93.8	97.7
9. Personal opinion about guilt				
Guilty	25.0	33.5	16.5	4.1
Not guilty	0	2.1	.6	3.0
Don't know	75.0	64.4	82.9	92.9
10. How much evidence against defendant[b]				
A lot	13.9	33.1	15.5	5.7
Some	33.3	35.6	18.7	11.4
A little	8.3	6.7	3.3	14.3
None	0	1.3	2.1	0
Don't know	44.4	23.4	60.5	68.6
11. Preferred sentence[c]				
Death penalty	36.1	37.6	26.6	10.0
Life	19.4	17.2	18.2	17.2
20 Yrs.–life	36.1	6.1	7.4	8.6
Don't know	8.3	39.2	47.8	64.3
12. No. of Articles read	2.47 (n = 18)	4.40	3.56	1.74
13. No. of TV/radio stories heard	3.00 (n = 16)	3.91	3.52	2.16
14. Source of most influence				
Newspaper	20.8	27.8	20.1	22.6
TV/radio	25.0	8.6	21.6	21.4
Personal decision	12.5	14.5	7.6	4.9
Conversation with other	11.1	28.5	6.4	8.5
Don't know	30.6	20.7	44.3	42.6
15. Receive fair trial in county				
Yes	75.0	58.5	69.1	67.5
No	13.9	15.0	10.1	13.9
Don't know	11.1	26.6	20.8	18.7

(continued)

Table 3.7. (*Continued*)

Survey question: special questions	Ven. Co. (*n* = 36) %	Other Ven.[a] (Cases I–IV) %	Adj. Co. (Cases II–IV) %	Pref. Co. (Cases I, III, IV) %
Key comparisons for Case V				
1. Is this McGrath's first criminal offense				
Yes	0			
No	44.4			
Don't know	55.6			
2. How describe his past?				
(a) Just minor and juven- ile offenses	10.0			
(b) History of misde- meanors	5.0			
(c) History of felonies	30.0			
(d) Is a persistent felony offender	25.0			
(e) Don't know	30.0			

[a]The means for other venue counties were derived by unweighted mean procedures based on the Cases I–IV. Means for preferred counties were derived by unweighted mean procedures based on Cases I, III, and IV. Adjacent county means were computed using an unweighted mean procedure because of the unequal number of adjacent counties across cases. A mean score was computed for the three adjacent counties in Case III and for the two adjacent counties in Case IV; these means were then averaged with the Case II adjacent county values to arrive at a mean Adjacent County score based on an *n* of 3.

[b]Venue and adjacent county data based on Cases II and III; preferred county data based on Case III.

[c]Venue and adjacent county data based on Cases II, III, and IV; preferred county data based on Cases III and IV.

that the attorneys not seek a change of venue. They agreed. Defendant's trial for capital murder was held in the venue county and ended in a conviction for complicity to first-degree manslaughter, a lesser included charge to murder. The jury returned a sentence of 20 years in prison, a sentence consistent with the results in Table 3.7.

METHODOLOGICAL AND INTERPRETIVE ISSUES

Despite their current popularity, change of venue surveys have been infrequently evaluated empirically in the professional literature. Woodward (1952) published what we believe to be the first empirical article on a venue survey. McConahay, Mullin, and Frederick (1977) reported data from their multicounty survey in support of Joan Little's motion to change the venue of her murder trial, and Horowitz and Willging (1984) report briefly on a venue survey that they conducted in a rural Ohio county. In a Canadian case, Arnold and Gold (1978/1979) assessed attitudes and affect of residents in the venue toward a defendant charged with kidnapping and then contrasted these values with ones obtained for other famous and infamous figures. Vidmar and Judson (1981) reported survey data for another Canadian case involving business fraud and misrepresentation. An admirable innovation in their methodology was the inclusion of several within-subjects comparisons that allowed conclusions about the harmful effects of defendant's specific record independent of the effects associated with prior convictions in general.

Constantini and King's (1980) analysis of their survey data for three criminal cases in California was particularly sophisticated and showed that respondents' increased knowledge about a given crime was correlated with greater pretrial, prejudicial opinions on their part. Consultants will discover that a publicity–prejudgment relationship is regarded very skeptically by many judges who appear to believe that the effects of pretrial publicity can be dismissed by a wave of the judicial hand. In fact, Constantini and King's discriminant function analysis indicated that, in comparison to general attitudes about crime, gender, and educational level (all of which were significantly related to prejudgment in their data), pretrial knowledge about a specific case was a more powerful predictor of prejudgments of guilt than were the other three predictors combined.

Our experience with requests for changes of venue confirms Pollock's (1977) warning that they are difficult to obtain. Nonetheless, we believe public opinion surveys can be a persuasive method of demonstrating the harmful effects of pretrial publicity. We suspect that the 50% "success rate" of the four cases described here will shrink as our sample increases; however, even a moderate increase in success over traditionally low levels will be important to trial lawyers. When venue is not moved, attorneys will still be able to use the survey data to support their arguments that more extensive voir dire should be allowed. This "side effect" is important in light of the relationship between enhanced forms of voir dire and more challenges for cause of biased venirepersons (discussed in chapter 2).

Repeated use of venue surveys allows the consultant to develop norms that make possible special types of comparisons. Our analysis of Case V illustrates the potential of constructing tentative norms or profiles for venue, adjacent, and preferred counties derived from other cases against which newly obtained data can be compared. Although the more typical contrast of a venue with concurrent control counties yields a necessary comparison, it can be supplemented by comparisons of the instant counties with profiles of venue, adjacent, and preferred counties derived from similar cases.

Because such profiles will be influenced by several community variables, the development of local norms will be required. For example, the venue counties in this study were small, rural, and politically conservative, and were composed of a largely Protestant, white population. The local media resources were confined to one newspaper, one radio station, and no local TV station. With few exceptions, these characteristics are typical of most counties in Kentucky and are also descriptive of conditions likely to exacerbate the harm of pretrial publicity. Adjacent counties were very similar in quality to the venues, whereas preferred counties were more populated and more heterogeneous with respect to demography and media resources. Such characteristics are part of the basis for preferring these counties as new venues. However, the characteristics of preferred counties in other parts of the country and/or with different types of cases may differ greatly from those encountered in Kentucky.

Obviously, the small sample sizes require that we view our norms as initial norms subject to the revisions that additional cases will necessitate. Nonetheless, the comparisons across cases that normative data permit constitute a practical innovation and research goal that may enhance the impact of venue surveys. Questions about the legal relevance of such data may limit the purposes for which they are admitted as evidence. These questions will have to be addressed by those seeking to use normative data in this manner.

Topics for Cross-examination

Hans and Vidmar (1982) identified four problems that undermine venue surveys and contribute to the low success rate of the technique. The first problem is ''judicial conservatism,'' or the general tendency of judges to be skeptical of the validity and admissibility of survey data. Judicial acceptance of survey data has increased in recent years, a trend that should be sustained by improvements in survey methodology.

A second problem is termed ''inherent weaknesses in survey methodology'' by Hans and Vidmar (1982). This criticism refers to the differences in conditions which impinge on survey respondents and venirepersons (anonymous versus public disclosures, unsworn responses versus responses under oath, hypothetical versus concrete inquiries) and to the methodological limitations of surveys (see Zeisel, 1960). The additional problem of attitude–behavior inconsistencies (Fishbein & Ajzen, 1975) applies to both survey respondents and venirepersons. These problems are best handled by experts' frank acknowledgment of them followed by balanced explanations of the limitations they impose on survey evidence as well as on the in-court testimony of venirepersons (see Vidmar and Judson, 1981 for a summary of expert testimony on these issues).

Methodological weaknesses pertaining to sampling and survey item construction are a third problem (see also Pollock, 1977). Sample size is a crucial consideration in survey research because it determines the accuracy of a sample's estimates. By conventional standards, our samples are very small, forcing us to confront the problem that the confidence intervals for the values obtained are quite large. It should be remembered, however, that accuracy of population estimates and representativeness of a sample are different concepts. McConahay et al. (1977, p. 210) argue: "The size of a sample has no effect upon its representativeness. . . . A random sample of fifty is superior to a non-random sample of five hundred from the standpoint of representativeness." Given the limits of time and other resources, small sample sizes are a frequent result that the consultant will encounter. However, there are some reassuring and mitigating aspects of our methods. First, reinspection of Table 3.1 shows a stability of values and a consistency of order for the different types of counties across the surveys. Second, the magnitude of differences between counties within separate surveys is usually of a size that would not be compromised even by wide confidence intervals. Finally and most important, the logic of our approach lies in demonstrating how unlikely the obtained difference between types of counties would be by chance rather than in claiming the high likelihood that a certain estimate falls within a narrow confidence interval. Of course, the relationship of small sample sizes to significance testing is a lessening of, not an increase in, the power to detect significance effects.

We try to eliminate leading questions by having the one of us who is not involved in construction of the instrument review all the items. Because identical questions are asked of all counties, significant differences are obtained in spite of, not because of, question form.

The relevance of the survey items is a different issue, one that concerns the best questions to ask. Probably it is best to ask the judge in advance what questions he or she will regard as the most useful for reaching a decision. Consultants should not confuse those questions that assess the qualifications of venirepersons to sit as jurors (presence of actual or implied bias) with those aimed at the less stringent post-*Sheppard* standard of showing a reasonable likelihood of prejudice for venue to be changed.

The final problem plaguing venue surveys is the "criterion problem" of how much prejudice is too much. As Hans and Vidmar (1982) suggest, absolute standards in answering this question are not possible or appropriate. However, we believe our practice of developing norms for different types of counties can provide criteria that, although not absolute, yield reasonable standards for comparison beyond those implied by concurrent data from adjacent and preferred counties. For example, knowing that a given venue's survey results exceed those obtained in 25%, 50%, or 80% of surveys conducted in similar venues provides judges with a standard that should be very informative to them. Confidence about the meaning of this standard can be increased by calibrating as many features of the normative group as possible (e.g., demography, amount of publicity, political values) and comparing them with the specimen case. In order to enhance the impact of normative comparisons, we recommend that surveys of venue and other counties be conducted as often as possible for similar types of cases whether or not venue changes are being sought. In this way, more adequate norms will become available, and the effects of important variables such as differing amounts of publicity can be assessed.

In addition to the problems discussed in the text, the expert testifying about the results of a venue survey may expect to encounter several other lines of cross-examination. In Table 3.8, in *column A*, we present the most

Table 3.8. Common Topics for Cross-Examination of Experts Testifying About Venue Surveys

Areas of Attacks	Strategies for Response
Leading Questions: "Isn't it true that the way questions are asked will determine to a great extent the answers you get?"	This is true and it is the reason the consultant (a) had another expert review the wording of the questions and (b) insisted that interviewers read the questions *verbatim*. Also, the consultant should point out that the inter-county differences are found *in spite of* the wording of items rather than *because of* it since the questions are the same for all counties.
Representativeness of Sample: "Isn't it true that a telephone survey will result in a biased sample that invalidates these results?"	The bias of a telephone sample is relatively small particularly when generalizing to jury pools rather than the entire county. Phone surveys are an accepted technique in polling research. Random digit dialing may be necessary in larger cities to insure a representative sample.
Differences between respondents and venirepersons: "Respondents aren't under oath, and aren't admonished against bias; are you saying that answers to a survey are as meaningful as a potential juror's answers in a courtroom?"	The consultant should acknowledge differences but try to educate judges on how these differences might make anonymous surveys more trustworthy than voir dire examination—demand characteristics, conformity, and social desirability are influences to be discussed.
Sample Size: "Isn't it the case that you are basing all your opinions on phone calls to 50 people out of a county with a population of 100,000 people?"	In as simple terms as possible, the consultant should present the standard error or confidence interval for results and explain that it depends on absolute, not relative sample size when the population is large. If a discussion of relative sample size is forced, the consultant can favorably contrast venue survey samples with those of national polls.

(continued)

Table 3.8. (*Continued*)

Areas of Attacks	Strategies for Response
Relationship between survey answers and actual bias: "Isn't it true that the research in psychology shows large inconsistencies between attitudes and behavior, making it difficult to predict one from the other?"	This problem must be acknowledged. However, it is not unique to surveys; it applies to voir dire as well. Vidmar and Judson (1981) point out that the discrepancies are more likely to occur with people who deny prejudicial attitudes but act in biased ways than vice versa.
Large county allows impaneling of impartial jury: "Even if we accept your survey's findings that 50% of the people are biased against the defendant, with 100,000 people in this county, that means 50,000 have no such bias. Don't you agree we could find 12 impartial people out of 50,000?"	Here, correlations between prejudgment and demographic characteristics will allow you to show how that strategy, while sounding logical, will likely result in a venire that is nonrepresentative of the county in various predictable ways.
Other alternatives: "Isn't it true that a continuance or extensive voir dire will cure these problems more easily than a change of venue."	This is often a question that the consultant will not be able to answer, but each of the alternative remedies have problems (see pp. 67–68 of this chapter) that the consultant should discuss.
Nuisance questions intended to make the witness anxious, angry, defensive and inarticulate.	The consultant should remain calm, understanding that the prosecutor is just doing a job in arousing emotions; the consultant is also just doing a job and should not become ego-involved in a contest. Remember: An expert is permitted to explain his or her opinion.
"How much have you been paid for your testimony here today?"	The consultant should state his or her fee without hesitation or apology (experts deserve to be paid for their work) and should point out that the fee is *not* paid for *testimony* but for the survey conducted by the consultant.
"It is true, is it not, that you have not spoken to a single resident of this county yourself?"	The consultant should answer that it is correct because to have done so may have biased the consultant's opinions and should stress the nonrandomness of such conversations and how they could therefore be misleading.
"It's true, is it not, that you have conducted surveys like this one only for the defense and never for the state?"	The consultant should answer: "That is true. I have never been asked by the state to perform one."
"Will you please turn over to the court the names of all the respondents to this survey?"	The consultant should maintain that this information is confidential. If purpose is to make sure that no respondent appears as a juror at the trial, the consultant can prepare a notarized affidavit indicating whether any respondents are among the jury pool when it is drawn.

(continued)

Table 3.8. (*Continued*)

Areas of Attacks	Strategies for Response
"Did you determine whether any of the respondents had been summoned for jury duty on this case?"	Consultants should beware this question. A consultant must not contact any potential jurors in the survey, but either should conduct the survey before the pool is drawn or eliminate the names of potential jurors from the phone book before random selection of phone numbers is performed.

common cross-examination tactics; in *column B*, we suggest strategies and responses that may be useful in coping with each line of attack. Some of this material is drawn from Vidmar and Judson (1981, see pp. 87–96) who thoroughly discuss the lengthy examination of an expert testifying on the result of a venue survey.

NOTES

[1]366 U.S. 717, 81 S.Ct. 1639, 6 L. Ed. 751 (1961).

[2]421 U.S. 794, 95 S.Ct. 2031, 44 L. Ed. 2d 589 (1965).

[3]373 U.S. 723, 83 S.Ct. 1417, 10 L. Ed. 2d 663 (1963).

[4]35 CrL 3152-3160 (June 27, 1984).

[5]384 U.S. 333, 86 S.Ct. 1507, 16 L. Ed. 2d 600 (1966).

[6]381 U.S. 532, 85 S.Ct. 1628, 14 L. Ed. 2d 543 (1965).

[7]360 U.S. 310, 79 S.Ct. 1171, 3 L. Ed. 2d 1250 (1959).

[8]400 U.S. 505, 91 S.Ct. 490, 27 L. Ed. 2d 571 (1971).

[9]559 F. 2d 31, 59-71 (D.C. Cir. 1976)

Chapter 4
Psychologists as Expert Witnesses

In the opinion of Judge David T. Bazelon (1974), "psychiatry . . . is the ultimate wizardry . . . in no case is it more difficult to elicit productive and reliable testimony than in cases that call on the knowledge and practice of psychiatry." Bazelon's criticism applies equally well to psychologists; in fact, data suggest that trial judges prefer the testimony of psychiatrists over other mental health experts on topics such as insanity, competency, and diminished capacity, although the preference for psychiatrists versus clinical psychologists is not a significant one (Poythress, 1983).[1]

Bazelon's impatience with psychological/psychiatric expert testimony is not an isolated reaction. Attorneys are often highly critical of such testimony. Jay Ziskin, best known for his guidebook on how to cross-examine (or "Ziskinize") psychiatric and psychological experts, argues that "there are no principles of psychiatry which have been adequately validated," (p. 5), "the status of clinicians' testimony as 'expert' is highly dubious" (p. 6), and "the continued participation of members of these professions in the legal process is a travesty and is well recognized as such by the public and media . . . " (Ziskin, 1981). Warren Burger, Chief Justice of the U.S. Supreme Court, once complained about the "uncertainties of psychiatric diagnosis" and "the tentativeness of professional (psychiatric) judgment" (Burger, 1975). Gass (1979) argues that the scientific bases for psychological opinions are unsound, and that such testimony is no more helpful "to the trier of fact than the thoughtful opinion of an ordinary layperson." Sharply worded critiques of psychologists' expert testimony can be found in several well-known legal sources, including Ennis and Litwack (1974), Dixon and Blondis (1976), and Bonnie and Slobogin (1980).

Psychologists and psychiatrists have been no less concerned about the propriety of their testimony. For example, Thomas Szasz has made a career of criticizing psychiatry's "overreach" into moral and legal matters. Morse (1978a) has argued that most of the questions posed to the psychologist-expert in insanity and commitment cases involve social judgments and morally evaluative answers that should be answered by jurors. Poythress (1982) describes the negative reactions he received from a trial judge when he attempted to limit his expert testimony to Morse's (1978a, b) recommended: (a) description of a person's psychopathology; (b) probability statements about the occurrence of legally relevant behavior in persons like the person in question; and (c) avoidance of conclusions on ultimate legal questions such as responsibility and causation. Of course, Ziskin was also trained as a clinical psychologist, making his litany of pointed objections all the more galling to his colleagues who testify as experts. On an entirely different topic, McCloskey and Egeth (1983) ask whether psychologists should be offering expert testimony on the unreliability of eyewitness identification, questioning the scientific support for such unreliability and doubting whether psychologists' testimony improves jurors' ability to evaluate eyewitness testimony (see Loftus, 1979, 1980, 1983 for an opposing view).

The irony of all this criticism and uneasiness is that it coexists with an unprecedented expansion of expert psychological testimony on a panorama of issues at litigation. Although psychologists testified as experts before 1900, it was not until the middle of this century after three important appellate decisions that the status of psychologists as expert witnesses was solidified. The first case was *People v. Hawthorne*,[2] in which the Michigan Supreme Court held that the trial court had erred in not permitting a psychologist to offer expert opinion on a defendant's sanity. The 5–3 majority opinion held that the standard for qualifying as an expert was not possession of any specific degree, but the extent of a witness' knowledge. A federal case, *Hidden v. Mutual Life Insurance Company*,[3] extended *Hawthorne's* logic to a civil case and held that a psychologist should have been allowed to testify about the mental condition of a plaintiff who claimed that a mental condition prevented him from working. The most important case on the admissibility of expert psychological testimony is *Jenkins v. United States*,[4] in which, writing for the majority, Judge David T. Bazelon stated:

> . . . the lack of a medical degree, and the lesser degree of responsibility for patient care which mental hospitals usually assign to psychologists, are not automatic disqualifications. . . . *The critical factor in respect to admissibility is the actual experience of the witness and the probable probative value of his opinion.*

The logic of *Jenkins* has been adopted by most federal and state jurisdictions. In these courts, the testimony of a properly trained clinical psychologist will be accepted and treated equivalently to that of a psychiatrist provided that the testimony is probative (having the effect of proving or tending to prove some assertion) and that the testimony presents information beyond the experience of the common person. In the next section, we discuss the most common examples of expert testimony by psychologists. Each of those examples occurs frequently enough in litigation to have stimulated a professional literature and to have attracted a cadre of experts willing and presumably qualified to offer expert opinions.

TOPICS FOR EXPERT
PSYCHOLOGICAL TESTIMONY

Table 4.1 summarizes 16 areas of expert testimony frequently offered by psychologists. For each category of testimony, the ultimate question(s) that the expert is usually asked to answer are identified, and some of the more authoritative/comprehensive references describing the particular testimonial topic are listed. These references were selected because of their relevance to the practicing psychologist; they include original empirical studies as well as review and discussion papers that support or discourage psychological testimony. The list of topics in Table 4.1 is not exhaustive. Expert psychological testimony is constantly in flux. Today's list will be outdated tomorrow. Supported by decisions like *Jenkins* and subject to the broad discretion of the judiciary, the domain of psychologists' expert testimony has expanded dramatically, bounded only by the creativity of the trial advocates who request our participation and by our own ethical obligations not to testify on matters that exceed the boundaries of our competence. Psychological expert testimony has become a growth industry, the fruition of a rather long history of discussing possible uses in court of psychologists as experts (Blau, 1984; Gaines, 1956; Lassen, 1964; Levitt, 1964; Louisell, 1955; Lower, 1978; Nash, 1974; Pacht, Kuehn, Bassett, & Nash, 1973; Rice, 1961; Schulman, 1966; Shapiro, 1984; Smith, 1967). Conferences on methods of expert testimony in court are increasingly popular. One of the more surprising presentations, as a workshop led by Jay Ziskin, is described as follows:

> Mental health professionals who provide psychiatric and psychological testimony are often challenged by well-prepared attorneys as to their evidence, opinions and expert status. This workshop is designed to acquaint mental health professionals with various types of challenges and how to best defend against attack in psychiatric and psychological testimony.

Criminal Law

Insanity. The area of testimony with the greatest public visibility is psychologists' opinions in support or rebuttal of a defendant's claim to being criminally insane and therefore not legally responsible for the crime charged. The legal standards for insanity vary across jurisdictions, but one of three famous cases will be controlling in almost all U.S. courts.

Table 4.1. Topics of Expert Testimony by Psychologists

Area of Expert Testimony	Questions Addressed in the Testimony	Cases and References
Insanity defense/criminal responsibility	What is the relationship between the defendant's mental condition at the time of the alleged offense and the defendant's responsibility for the crime with which the defendant is charged? What sort of "personality profile" does the defendant have, and is it consistent with the crimes charged?	M'Naghten (1843)[5]; Durham v. United States (1954)[6]; U.S. v. Brawner (1982)[7]; Rogers, Wasyliw, & Cavanaugh (1984); Slobogin, Melton, & Showalter (1984)
Competence to stand trial	Does the defendant have an adequate understanding of the legal proceedings?	Dusky v. United States (1960)[8]; Lipsitt, Lelos, & McGarry (1971); Roesch & Golding (1980); McGarry et al. (1973)
Sentencing	What are the prospects for the defendant's rehabilitation? What deterrent effects do certain sentences have?	Estelle v. Smith (1981)[9]; Wolfgang (1974)
Eyewitness identification	What are the factors that affect the accuracy of eyewitness identification? How is witness confidence related to witness accuracy?	United States v. Amaral (1973)[10], Law and Human Behavior (1980, Vol. 4, No. 4); Loftus (1983); McCloskey & Egeth (1983); Yarmey (1979); Wells & Loftus (1983)
Trial procedure	What effects are associated with variations in pretrial and/or trial procedures?	Hovey v. Superior Court of Alameda County (1980)[11]; Haney (1984); Grisso (1981)
Civil commitment	Does a mentally ill person present an immediate danger or threat of danger to self or others which requires treatment no less restrictive than hospitalization?	Lessard v. Schmidt (1972)[12]; Addington v. Texas (1979)[13]; Monahan (1981); Robinson (1980)
Psychological damages in civil cases	What psychological consequences has an individual suffered as a result of tortious conduct? How treatable are these consequences? To what extent are the psychological problems attributable to a preexisting condition?	Hidden v. Mutual Life Insurance Co. (1954)[14]; Reese v. Naylor (1969)[15]; Gaines (1956)

Topic	Question	Cases/References
Psychological autopsies	In equivocal cases, do the personality and circumstances under which a person died indicate a likely mode of death?	*Biro v. Prudential Insurance Co.* (1970)[16]; Widman (1980); Selkin & Loya (1979)
Negligence and product liability	How do environmental factors and human perceptual abilities affect an individual's use of a product or ability to take certain precautions in its use?	*Seaboard Coastline R.R. v. Hill* (1971)[17]; Gass (1979; pp. 544–550); Levitt (1969)
Trademark litigation	Is a certain product name or trademark confusingly similar to a competitor's? Are advertising claims likely to mislead consumers?	*Anti-Monopoly, Inc. v. General Mills Fun Group, Inc.* (1982)[18]; Zeisel (1983)
Class action suits	What psychological evidence is there that effective treatment is being denied or that certain testing procedures are discriminatory against minorities in the schools or in the workplace?	*Larry P. v. Riles* (1979)[19]; *Griggs v. Duke Power Co.* (1971)[20]; *Wyatt v. Stickney* (1972)[21]; Bersoff (1981); Loh (1984; pp. 107–191)
Guardianship and conservatorship	Does an individual possess the necessary mental ability to make decisions concerning living conditions, financial matters, health, etc.?	Hafemeister & Sales (1984); Sales, Powell & Van Duizend (1982)
Child custody	What psychological factors will affect the best interests of the child whose custody is in dispute? What consequences are these factors likely to have on the family?	*Painter v. Bannister* (1966)[22]; Okpaku (1976); Litwack, Gerber & Fenster (1979–1980); Swenson, Nash, & Roos (1984)
Adoption and termination of parental rights	What psychological factors affect the best interests of a child whose parents' disabilities may render them unfit to raise and care for the child?	*In re David B.* (1979)[23]; Shapiro (1984; pp. 108–118)
Professional malpractice	Did defendant's professional conduct fail to meet the standard of care owed to plaintiff?	*Hammer v. Rosen* (1960)[24]; Deleon & Borreliz (1978)
Social issues in litigation	What are the effects of pornography, televised aggression, spouse abuse, etc. on the behavior of a defendant who claims that his or her misconduct was due in part to one of these influences?	*Hawthorne v. Florida* (1982)[25]; Fiora-Gormally (1978); Walker (1984)

The traditional test for insanity in U.S. courts has been the *M'Naghten* rule, established by a British Court in 1843, which held that a defendant was insane and not morally responsible if it could be shown that she or he suffered such "a defect of reason, from disease of the mind, as not to know the nature and the quality of the act he was doing, or, if he did know it, that he did not know he was doing what was wrong."

M'Naghten's emphasis on cognitive reasoning was criticized by psychiatrists as inadequate, moralistic, and too restrictive, and it was replaced at the Federal level by Judge Bazelon's decision in the 1954 case of *Durham v. United States. Durham* held that a defendant was not criminally responsible if it could be shown that his or her conduct was the product of a mental disease or defect.

Durham's "product test" was intended to broaden the criteria by which psychologists evaluated defendants and testified about their findings; however, it had the unwanted consequence of leaving them adrift on a sea of professional jargon, subjective judgments, and confused testimony. Recognizing the deficiencies of *Durham*, Judge Bazelon set it aside and replaced it in 1972 with a new rule adopted from the American Law Institute's Model Penal Code. In *U.S. v. Brawner*, the new test for insanity became one in which "a person is not responsible for criminal conduct if at the time of such conduct as a result of mental disease or defect he lacks substantial capacity either to appreciate the wrongfulness of his conduct or to conform his conduct to the requirements of the law."

Paralleling developments in the assessment of competence (see below), criterion-based assessment instruments for the evaluation of legal insanity have recently been developed (see Rogers et al., 1984; Slobogin et al., 1984). These instruments reflect attempts to standardize the assessment of criminal responsibility, to improve the reliability and content and construct validity of the diagnostic judgments and to make our assessment methods more relevant to the legal standards that will be applied.

Although a defendant's mental disease or defect may not reach the standard set for insanity it may still be relevant to lessening the severity of the charge against the defendant. Various terms exist for mitigating mental conditions. "Diminished capacity" refers to a mental condition which reduces a defendant's ability to act with the intent necessary for a certain crime, such as murder in the first degree. Some courts permit a defendant to try to show that the act was committed under an "extreme emotional disturbance" which has received several definitions; e.g., the New York Supreme Court said that an action influenced by extreme emotional disturbance could be one in which "a significant mental trauma has affected a defendant's mind for a substantial period of time, simmering in the unknowing subconscious and then inexplicably coming to the fore."[26]

Competence to Stand Trial. The question of insanity pertains to the mental condition of the defendant at the time the alleged crime was committed. The issue of competence concerns the defendant's mental condition at the time of trial. The two concepts must be distinguished in the testimony of experts because they have distinct criteria and are not necessarily interrelated. The standard test for competence to stand trial was established in *Dusky v. United States* which stated that "the test must be whether (defendant) has sufficient present ability to consult with his lawyer with a reasonable degree of understanding—and whether he has a rational as well as factual understanding of the proceedings against him." Incompetence to stand trial is a very specific disability. A person may be mentally ill, even psychotic, and still be competent to stand trial.

In recent years, a number of specialized assessment instruments have been developed which attempt to measure the characteristics which the law requires of competent defendants. Table 4.1 identifies the three best known instruments of this type; Roesch and Golding's (1980) IFI appears to possess the greatest number of psychometric virtues (see Golding, Roesch, & Schreiber, 1984).

Sentencing. Psychologists may testify about a defendant's mental condition or psychological history for the purpose of acquainting a jury with factors that may be relevant to a sentencing decision following a conviction. This testimony occurs most often in the bifurcated death-penalty trial when the jury has convicted defendant during the guilt and innocence phase and additional testimony is considered at the sentencing phase to determine what sentence to impose. Expert testimony may be offered to show the deterrence or nondeterrence effect of capital punishment (e.g., Wolfgang, 1974), to mitigate the sentence, or more rarely, it may be introduced to show aggravation and to provide a reason for the jury to sentence the defendant to death. The most controversial figure in this later connection is James Grigson, a Texas psychiatrist, who has frequently testified in death-penalty trials about the high probability that a given defendant will continue to behave dangerously in the future. In *Estelle v. Smith,* (a capital case in which Grigson testified for the state that the defendant, Ernest Smith, would pose a continuing threat to society), the APA filed an *amicus curiae* brief which stated that mental health professionals are unable to predict an individual's future capacity for dangerous behavior accurately enough to justify expert testimony on the topic. The Supreme Court ultimately reversed Smith's death sentence on the grounds that a defendant must be warned that the material collected in a psychiatric interview can later be used against him.

Eyewitness Identification. Eyewitness identification and testimony is a persuasive piece of evidence in many criminal trials. Despite the confidence that eyewitnesses have in their testimony, psychologists who have studied human memory and perceptual abilities have raised serious questions about the presumed accuracy of eyewitness identification; they also question the legal system's assumption that the confidence of witnesses about the accuracy of their perceptions is a valid indicator of such accuracy. Experimental psychologists have conducted extensive research on the factors that limit the accuracy of eyewitness identification, and defense attorneys have frequently attempted to have expert testimony about the fallibility of eyewitness testimony introduced for the purpose of helping the jury critically appraise such testimony. Specifically, this testimony is used to correct what some experts (Loftus, 1983) believe is jurors' tendencies to "overbelieve" the reports of eyewitnesses.

Admissibility of this testimony is uncertain because *U. S. v. Amaral*, the leading opinion on the use of psychological experts in this regard, held that a trial judge has broad discretion in determining whether the content of an expert's opinions is within the knowledge and experience of the average juror and therefore should not be admitted. In *Amaral*, the court reasoned that the expert's testimony would not be of "appreciable help" to the jury and would consume too much time; the court reasoned further that such testimony might confuse jurors and therefore need not be admitted. Horowitz and Willging (1984) point out the irony in the courts' refusal to accept such testimony with its extensive experimental literature conjoined with the courts' acceptance of the often purely conjectural opinions of psychologists about criminal responsibility.

Trial Procedure. Psychologists may be asked to testify about research that assesses the consequences of variations in trial procedure. Some of our research has concentrated on the effects of conducting voir dire in alternative ways (see also Haney, 1984a) and on venue changes; chapters 2 and 3 summarize the type of testimony that can be given. Other examples of this type of testimony involve Grisso's (1981) research on the ability of juveniles to comprehend the language used in the typical *Miranda* warnings to criminal suspects, and Buckhout's (see Ellison & Buckhout, 1981; pp. 114–128) research on biased line-ups.

Civil Law

Civil Commitment. In most jurisdictions, the involuntary commitment of an individual to a mental institution requires the opinions of two qualified mental health professionals (states vary greatly in their definitions of who are qualified mental health professionals) that (a) the person is mentally ill, (b) the person presents an immediate danger or immediate threat of danger to self or others, (c) treatment that will reasonably benefit the individual is available at the institution to which the individual has been committed, and (d) hospitalization is the least restrictive alternative form of treatment. For lengthy periods of commitment, the court must hold a formal hearing that is conducted according to the rules of criminal procedure and that is tried before a jury unless respondent waives the right to a jury. Although these hearings are usually brief in comparison to the typical criminal trial, they require psychologists and psychiatrists to testify about one of the thorniest questions they encounter on the witness stand: the prediction of future dangerous behavior. The literature which pertains to predicting future dangerous behavior (e.g., Monahan, 1981; Mulvey & Lidz, 1985) is essential material for the expert who testifies at commitment hearings.

Psychological Damages. When civil plaintiffs allege that they have been injured or damaged by the tortious conduct of a defendant, they may seek damages for pain and suffering, traumatic neurosis, or mental distress. A psychologist may testify about the degree to which plaintiff's injury involves neurological damage, the extent to which personality or intellectual changes have occurred, whether plaintiff has developed a diagnosible clinical condition, and/or the consequences of the mental distress on plaintiff's personal, family, and occupational adjustment. Chances for rehabilitation and even issues of proximate cause may be included in the psychologist's testimony. In workmen's compensation cases, the psychologist often testifies about employment-caused psychological damage. In many states, the expert will be asked to determine what percentage of the damage is owing to the work stress and what percentage is attributable to some ''preexisting condition.'' That portion of the damage resulting from the preexisting condition is not compensable in many states (see Shapiro, 1984; especially chapter 6).

Psychological Autopsies. Because some life insurance policies exclude the beneficiaries from receiving policy benefits if the insured committed suicide, psychologists have testified about the likelihood that a given death was a suicide. The psychologist is asked to construct a psychological profile of the deceased using whatever data can be collected and then to compare this ''autopsy'' to the empirical research on the high-risk variables for suicide. This type of testimony appears especially hazardous in light of the large number of false positives rendered by even the most accurate actuarial/clinical prediction systems of suicide (Garfield, 1978).

Negligence and Product Liability. Experimental psychologists, particularly those with expertise in sensation, perception, and learning may be asked to testify about the effectiveness of product design, warning labels, or safety signs in insuring that products are safely used in the manner intended. This testimony may be used to support or to rebut a plaintiff's claim that a given environmental condition is likely to affect the average person's perceptual processes adversely. For some product liability issues there may be existing experimental research on the question; however, it is more likely that the psychologist will design a special experiment and collect original data to present in court. The psychologist who testifies about his or her own research in such cases may be surprised at the sophistication in research design demonstrated by attorneys during cross-examination.

Trademark Litigation. Trademark suits also often call for original empirical studies. One company sues another because the second company uses a name for its product that is so similar to the name used by the first company that it is likely to cause consumer confusion or to deceive the consumer. When companies sue for trademark infringement, they often hire experts to conduct public opinion polls to prove that a certain name has acquired special meanings or that a competitor's trademark is confusingly similar. Surveys of this type also have been conducted in trials alleging fraudulant advertising.

Class Action Suits. In class action suits, many people are mutually interested in a single concern. One or more of the group sue or are sued as representatives of the class without being joined by all of the group members. Psychologists have been retained as expert witnesses in cases involving the reform of prisons and hospitals and the right to effective treatment (*Wyatt v. Stickney*), the right to education (*Mills v. Board of Education*[27]), and post-*Brown v. Board of Education*[28] cases which claim that standardized intelligence tests are discriminatory against minority children who are being assessed for possible special education placements (*Larry P. v. Riles*).

Psychologists have been required to give detailed testimony (usually at the appellate level) on the construction and psychometric qualities of tests used in personnel selection and promotion. *Griggs v. Duke Power Company* was the first Supreme Court case to consider an employer's possible discriminatory use of psychological testing of employees. In *Griggs*, the court agreed with 13 black employees that the Duke Power Company's use of the Wonderlic Personnel Test and Bennet Mechanical Comprehension Test was discriminatory because it could not be shown that the tests were job-related and because the tests had a disproportionately negative effect on blacks. In another North Carolina case, (*Albemarle Paper Co. v. Moody*[29]), the court specified several guidelines for demonstrating job-relatedness, relying in large part on APA's *Standards for Educational and Psychological Tests and Manuals.*

Guardianship and Conservatorship. Several important legal determinations make judgments on whether an individual has the requisite mental capacity to make certain decisions regarding his or her life. The question of physical or mental disability to care for oneself is raised in legal proceedings known as guardianship and/or conservatorship hearings. All states provide some form of these laws. Hafemeister and Sales (1984) define guardianship as the formal appointment by the court of a person to make decisions for the disabled person in the areas of shelter, nutrition, health, etc. A conservator is a person or entity appointed by the court to manage the finances of a person judged to be civilly incompetent. In the past, these hearings were perfunctory and often abusive to the ward. Recently, the American Bar Association has drafted model legislation calling for evaluations in this area to be conducted by multidisciplinary teams that would include a physician, a social worker with expertise in working with the disabled, and "a psychiatrist, licensed clinical psychologist, and/or other appropriate experts" (Sales, Powell, & Van Duizend, 1982).

Psychologists are sometimes asked to examine persons for the purpose of giving expert opinion on whether the individual can competently make a specific decision in his or her life. The psychologist may testify about whether a person has the testamentary capacity to draw a valid will, whether a confession was obtained coercively, whether a patient can make a competent decision to accept or refuse a certain treatment, and whether a child is competent to give testimony of a certain type.

Domestic Law

Child Custody. Legal disputes over which parent should receive custody of the children following a divorce are often among the most hotly contested courtroom disputes. Psychologists are retained in such cases to evaluate a number of factors which may contribute to the "best interests of the child," the standard for custody decisions reflected in the laws of many states. Michigan's statute, described by Lowery (1984) as one of the country's clearest, specifies ten criteria in determining "best interests," many of which would be the subject of a comprehensive psychological evaluation. For example, the "capacity and disposition of competing parties to give the child love, affection and guidance and continuation of educating and raising of the child in its religion or creed" should be considered. "The mental and physical health of the competing parties" and the "permanence, as a family unit, of the existing or proposed custodial home" are other considerations.

Adoption. Many of the factors to be considered in custody evaluations are also taken into account when experts are asked to testify about the ability of a proposed adoptive family to satisfy "the best interests" of a child to be adopted (Shapiro, 1984). Parental fitness is also the subject of professional evaluation when the courts must decide whether to terminate the custodial rights of mentally disabled parents. Shapiro (1984) lists the following five criteria that the expert must assess in evaluating the significance of parent's mental disability to termination of parental rights: (a) the probability that the illness will continue, (b) the chance for a substantial remission, (c) the parent's motivation for treatment, (d) the type of treatment that will be followed by the parent, and (e) the parent's compliance with prior treatments.

Other Areas

Malpractice. Normative treatment strategies and interventions are incorporated into a *standard of care* by a relatively informal process involving written debate, analysis of research data, expert testimony by professionals, and the development of guidelines by professional organizations. In most medical specialties, the standard of care (usually defined as the minimum common skill of practitioners in good professional standing in the relevant specialty area) is often well articulated through sworn expert testimony offered when a patient has brought a malpractice suit against a physician alleging that harm has been suffered because of the physician's negligent care.

If a client in psychotherapy does not receive treatment which meets minimal standards of care, and if harm comes to the patient or to a third party as a result of the negligent treatment, a professional tort liability (malpractice suit) may be brought against the therapist. In the practice of psychology, as in medicine, the standard of care is usually determined by the court through the use of expert testimony. Other psychologists or mental health professionals are called to testify regarding the minimum common skills expected of a psychologist in a specific circumstance. Although expert testimony concerning the standard of care is usually the criterion against which claims of negligence are judged, in some cases the courts have ruled that the standard of care provided in the community is too low and have imposed a standard of care more stringent than that defined by experts (Deleon & Borreliz, 1978).

Social Issues in Litigation. Psychologists who conduct research on currently relevant social topics such as child abuse, spouse abuse, the effects of pornography on sexual behavior, or the effects of televised violence on aggression may find themselves in demand as expert witnesses. In a notorious case of this type, Ronny Zamora, a 15-year-old boy, was charged with murdering his elderly neighbor while burglarizing her home. Zamora's attorney contended that the boy was not guilty by reason of insanity owing to "voluntary subliminal television intoxication." A psychiatrist testified before the jury that Zamora had been "conditioned" by television, but a psychologist was not permitted to testify about the general effects of TV violence on viewers. The jury convicted Zamora of first-degree murder and several lesser charges.

Psychologists have often been called as experts in cases in which battered women have killed their abusers and have then asserted that they killed in self-defense (Walker, 1984 indicates that such testimony has been admitted in at least 22 states and one federal court). Testimony in these cases focuses on the ways in which repeated abuse affects the woman's state of mind, her perception of the abuser, and her understanding of alternative solutions to the danger she faces.

COPING ON THE WITNESS STAND

Few psychologists would choose the witness stand as their favorite place to relax. The prospect of testifying in court as an expert causes anxiety and self-doubts among all but our most courageous colleagues. The expert's plight on the witness stand was reflected well by Ben Franklin's observation that "a countryman between two lawyers is like a fish between two cats." Many experts also would endorse James Haneker's claim that "lawyers earn their bread in the sweat of their browbeating."

Expert testimony need not be an Iliad of woes; however, it is an activity that requires several abilities that are not always developed in the average psychologist. Limited materials are available to potential expert witnesses who seek to prepare themselves for the rigors of the witness stand. Brodsky and Robey (1972) outline the attitudes, roles, and behavior that typify an effective, "courtroom-oriented witness." Their successful witness: (a) obtains some relevant legal training or experience; (b) consults extensively with attorneys prior to trial; (c) is knowledgeable about specific legal issues; (d) maintains exact professional records; (e) presents clear, jargon-free reports and testimony; (f) directs testimony to the judge or jury in a persuasive manner; (g) anticipates cross-examination tactics and reacts to them without emotion; (h) assists the attorney in preparing rebuttal evidence; and (i) follows up results of the trial in order to improve the quality of future appearances. Brodsky's (1977) "survival guide" for expert witnesses concentrates on how to cope with several of the better known cross-examination gambits that will be encountered (see also Blau, 1984).

Poythress (1980) describes the "learned treatise" tactic of cross-examination and provides numerous citations which can be used to rebut such an assault. In the learned treatise approach opposing counsel asks whether the witness is aware of a given article or empirical study and regards the article as authoritative. The witness is now in a dilemma. A witness who is unfamiliar with the study or denies its authority can be made to look uninformed or poorly trained particularly by refusing to recognize a series of articles. Conversely, an expert who acknowledges the study can be maneuvered into a position in which his or her professional opinion appears to conflict with the written judgment of another expert he or she has just admitted is an authority. Poythress (1980) has gathered "learned responses" that rebut some of the favorite cross-examination claims such as the unreliability of psychodiagnosis, the inability to predict future dangerous behavior, and the failure of professionals to discriminate between sane and insane persons.

Shapiro (1984) has written a practical guide on psychological evaluation and expert testimony, concentrating on the areas of competence to stand trial, criminal responsibility, personal injury suits, civil commitment, family law, and professional malpractice. He makes extensive use of case histories to illustrate ways to prepare expert testimony, ways to respond to common cross-examination questions, and ways to work effectively with attorneys.

In the remainder of this chapter we elaborate on some of the most important steps of preparation and coping processes that can be used by psychologists before and while giving testimony as an expert, both to enhance the impact of expert's opinions on jurys' decision-making and to minimize the damage that can be done to the testimony (and the expert) through vigorous cross-examination.

Preparation and Attitude

Proper preparation and the right attitude are the two most important ingredients for successful expert testimony. Proper preparation requires several steps, many of which should occur far in advance of a request to testify as an expert in a given trial. First, experts should restrict their testimony to areas in which their expertise is clear. Not only is it unethical to misrepresent oneself as an expert, but such a practice will usually be uncovered by thorough cross-examination and will ultimately lead to a devaluation of expert testimony in general. There is no substitute for a thorough, long-standing knowledge of one's area; a consultant who lacks such knowledge should avoid the expert witness role until it is obtained.

Familiarity with courtroom procedure on testimony by experts is the second necessity of advance preparation. The witness stand is not the place to learn about the differences between direct and cross-examination or between what is and what is not permissible testimony by an expert. These matters can be clarified through observation of other experts testifying at various trials and through rehearsal with attorneys who can practice direct and cross-examination techniques with the expert. Practice sessions should be video-taped so that the expert and attorney can review their performance critically and modify it where necessary. It is particularly important in such practice sessions that experts understand that they may always explain their answers if they wish and that these explanations are often the key to coping with difficult, close-ended questions asked by the cross-examiner. They must also experience the pressure, aggressiveness, and emotional conflict generated by heated cross-examination and discover how to remain calm and effective in the face of such an attack.

As a final ingredient in advance preparation, Ziskin's (1981) handbook on how to cross-examine mental health experts is recommended—for several reasons. The consultant should be prepared for a Ziskin-based attack since trial attorneys regard it as *the authority* on the topic. The attorney who relies on Ziskin will usually attack the consultant in one of six areas, claiming that: (a) psychology lacks a systematic, agreed-upon theoretical framework; (b) the current diagnostic-classification scheme of psychology is faulty, and insufficient data have been collected to evaluate DSM-III adequately; (c) most assessment instruments used by psychologists suffer from psychometric weaknesses; (d) examiner effects can distort the data obtained by psychologists; (e) there are specific errors, omissions, biases contained in the investigation and report conducted by the psychologist; and (f) the consultant's credentials are inadequate. There are competent, persuasive rebuttals available for all of these attacks except the last one, which depends on the individual witness. A consultant with weak credentials should probably not be testifying. Ziskin's book (1981) should be respected as a very penetrating adversarial tool, but one that need not be feared as a comprehensive source of objective scholarship. Experts should consult Ziskin because this foreknowledge will allow them to respond effectively to cross-examiners and thereby undercut the confidence that Ziskin's tactics may have inspired in opposing counsel. No amount of studying Ziskin's methods will help an attorney know more about psychology than does a well-trained psychologist. In fact, a little Ziskin may be a dangerous thing for those attorneys who rely on it, believing it to represent a fail-safe means of cross-examination. Experts may also take comfort in data which show that attorneys are not necessarily more vigorous in their cross-examination of experts even when they have been specially trained with Ziskin-like materials (Poythress, 1978).

In preparing for a specific appearance in court, the expert should make sure that the following steps have been taken. (Each of these activities, primarily concerning the evaluation of a defendant's mental condition, can strengthen some of the traditionally weak portions of psychological expert testimony.) First, it is wise to interview the defendant on several occasions. Repeated interviews indicate thoroughness, help to establish the reliability of one's observations, and provide a means for determining whether the interviewee is managing impressions in some way. Second, the psychologist should interview persons who observed the defendant at the time the incident in question occurred or those who have observed the defendant since the incident. Confronting experts with the observations of such "lay witnesses," who often contradict the observations of the expert, is a favorite cross-examination strategy. Experts may prevent this problem by gathering data from lay witnesses and then either incorporating it into their testimony or explaining why it is inconsistent with professional opinion. Police officers, eye witnesses, relatives of the defendant, and jailers are especially important sources of information because of their opportunities to observe the person in critical, naturalistic settings.

The expert should keep detailed records of interviews with the defendant or any other interviewees upon which the expert's testimony is based, including the time, location, and duration of the interview and the name(s) of any other person(s) present. Cross-examiners delight in exposing these kinds of factual gaps in an expert's testimony because they suggest carelessness or imprecision in the expert's work. Experts should also minimize consultation with the attorneys until they have formed their professional opinion on the question they are addressing in order to avoid the possibility and appearance that their opinion was influenced by the attorneys. Documentation of the sequence with which such contacts took place will be useful to the expert.

The consultant must school the lawyer who will conduct direct examination on the strengths and weaknesses of the consultant's testimony. In general, the consultant can take some of the sting out of cross-examination by admitting on direct examination to the problem areas in testimony while at the same time discussing what was done to minimize those problems. Preparing the attorney also has the benefit of strengthening the consultant's opportunities for rebuttal testimony.

A well-prepared expert is in the best position to project the proper attitude and demeanor for expert testimony, and the right attitude and demeanor are critical to an effective performance. Knowledgeable witnesses who are unduly humble, hostile, or anxious will so distract the jury from listening to their testimony that their opinions will carry less weight. The psychologist who testifies in court must learn how to be alert, persuasive, and credible without becoming so ego-involved in the process that objectivity is lost or that an emotional battle with opposing counsel develops. Because psychologists are not accustomed to the adversarial system, neither are they accustomed to the tactical use of emotions—and, on occasion, of personal attacks—that lawyers take for granted. Psychologists as experts must desensitize themselves to the sometimes nasty treatment they will experience on the witness stand. During such assaults, the consultant should remember that: (a) an attorney who attacks the consultant personally, with innuendo, sarcasm, or ridicule probably does so because the consultant's testimony has been effective and is difficult to rebut; (b) juries do not like experts to be treated unkindly unless the expert has somehow "asked for it"; the jurors may be sympathizing with the consultant; and (c) the lawyer is behaving in a way that is consistent with the expectations of everyone in the courtroom and with the lawyer's own expectations of the best way to do the job at hand.

The expert must not feel as though her or his testimony is the difference between winning and losing a case; as an expert, the consultant is paid for time and expertise—nothing else. Therefore, the consultant should avoid conceptualizing a performance in terms of winning or losing the litigation. A "win some, lose some" attitude coupled with a willingness to learn from past mistakes will enable the expert to survive almost any unpleasantness suffered on the witness stand.

Reframing Questions and Responding to Standard Cross-Examination

The skillful cross-examiner will pose controlling questions that make it difficult for the expert to answer in any way other than the one desired by the examiner. Experts cannot rephrase every question to their liking because it would make them appear evasive and biased to jurors. They can, however, pick their spots to reframe critical questions in ways that better suit their opinions. For example, when testifying about the mental condition of a defendant, the psychologist is often asked a series of questions concerning whether some conventional, nonpsychiatric motivation such as jealousy or greed or anger could have motivated the crime rather than the psychotic condition which the expert claims is responsible. The expert may attempt to respond to such a question by saying: "The answer to the hypothetical question you are asking me is, 'Yes, it is possible that anger could have motivated such an act.' However, if you are asking me whether anger motivated this defendant's act, the answer is 'no' and here are my reasons for saying that. . . . " In general, the expert should anticipate nontechnical, nonpsychological explanations that fit the facts of a given case and should then be able to show why these explanations are insufficient to account for the behavior in question.

Brodsky (1977) recommends the "push–pull" technique for countering cross-examination that focuses on realistic and well-known problems in clinical assessment. The expert who uses the "push–pull" does not deny the existence of such problems; in fact, the expert may even exaggerate their severity and then proceed to describe all the precautions that were taken in the specific case to prevent such problems from invalidating the results. Such a response shows the expert to be candid, knowledgeable, and careful in creating the conditions best suited to reliable and valid judgments. Such an expert, when asked, "Isn't it the case that in response to a clinical interview the respondent may lie or try to create an impression of disturbance that really isn't there?" would reply affirmatively: "Absolutely, deception and malingering are common and serious problems that can be expected in interviews with persons charged with serious crimes. Therefore, I took the following precautions in evaluating the honesty of the answers. . . . "

The expert must also know when to say, "I don't know" and be comfortable with that answer. Jurors respect this answer provided it is not given too frequently. It is also likely to be the correct answer in many instances. Novice witnesses are tempted to speculate on the stand rather than to admit an inability to answer a question. This tactic will usually backfire, leaving the witness with a bad case of "foot-in-mouth" disease.

Issues of Partisanship

Jurors are likely to be careful in evaluating the opinions of the expert who answers "yes" to the following question: "Doctor, isn't it true that you have testified in more than 45 criminal trials in which the defense of insanity has been raised? And, doctor, isn't it also true that you testified on behalf of the defendant in every one of those trials?" An expert who can be made to look like a "rent-a-witness" is seriously compromised before the jury. This is not likely to occur if the consultant has testified in the past on behalf of both sides in civil and criminal cases and a thorough, objective professional will usually have had opportunities to do so.

Experts are usually asked, "Doctor, how much have you been paid for your testimony today?" The expert should answer by saying that any reimbursement is received for time and expertise and not for the content of testimony. The amount of fees should be addressed directly by stating the usual hourly rate received by the expert. An amount commensurate with the prevailing fee for a private practitioner's therapy hour can serve as a standard for setting the fee.

NOTES

[1]Psychologists can take some satisfaction from Petrella and Poythress' (1983) data that demonstrate that actual forensic reports written by psychologists or social workers were rated

as more thorough and of higher quality than those written by psychiatrists. These differences occurred for both competency reports and reports on criminal responsibility.

[2]293 Michigan 15, 291 N.W. 205 (1940).

[3]217 F. 2d 818 (4th Cir. 1954).

[4]307 F. 2d 637 (D.C. Cir. 1962).

[5]M'Naghten's Case, 8 Eng. Rep. 718 (1843).

[6]214 F. 2d 862 (D.C. Cir. 1954).

[7]471 F. 2d 969 (D.C. Cir. 1972).

[8]362 U.S. 402 (1960).

[9]451 U.S. 454 (1981).

[10]488 F. 2d 1148 (9th Cir. 1973).

[11]28 Cal. 3dI, 168 Cal. Rptr. 128, 616 P. 2d 1301 (1980).

[12]349 F. Supp. 1078 (E.D. Wis. 1972).

[13]441 U.S. 418 (1979).

[14]217 F. 2d 818 (4th Cir. 1954).

[15]222 So. 2d 487 (Fla. Dist. Ct. App. 1969).

[16]110 N.J. Super 391, 265 Azd 830 (Super. Ct. App. Div. 1970).

[17]250 So. 2d 311, 314-315 (Fla. Dist. Ct. App. 1971).

[18]684 F. 2d 1316 (9th Cir. 1982).

[19]495 F. Supp. 926 (N.D. Ca. 1979).

[20]401 U.S. 424 (1971).

[21]344 F. Supp. 387 (M.D. Ala. 1972) aff'd in part 503 F. 2d 1305 (5th Cir. 1974).

[22]258 Iowa 1390, 140 N.W. 2d 152 (1966).

[23]5 Fam. L. Rep. 2531 (Cal. 5th Dist. Ct. of Appeals, March 28, 1979).

[24]198 N.Y.S. 2d 803, 165 N.E. 2d 756 (New York Court of Appeals 1960).

[25]408 So. 2d 801 (Fla. 1st DCA), Cert. Denied, 415 So. 2d 1361 (Fla. 1982).

[26]People v. Shelton, 385 N.Y.S. 2d 708 (June 16, 1976).

[27]348 F. Supp. 866 (D.C. 1972).

[28]347 U.S. 483 (1954).

[29]422 U.S. 405 (1975).

Chapter 5
Witness Preparation
in Civil Cases

Except in unusual circumstances, the parties to a civil case—in which the plaintiff brings the action against the defendant—are unprepared for what will happen to them during the suit and what they must do as witnesses. The same problem applies to other key witnesses. As a consequence of this situational novelty, the usual plaintiff or defendant must be prepared for the procedures that are followed in the trial, centered mostly but not entirely in the courtroom. Preparation must also be made concerning the facts and allegations of the matters being litigated. Furthermore, some of the preparation invariably concerns the strong feelings associated with being a party to or testifying in a case. Because the prospect of a trial is in itself an emotional experience, none of the important witnesses approach the action with indifference. Typically, they harbor emotions such as anger, resentment, fear, and uncertainty, all strong emotions that affect their ability to relate to attorneys and others in the case and to deal with the information on their side of the controversy. The testimony of the parties to the case is vital, although experts are usually essential as well. The testimonial prominence of lay witnesses increases anxieties, particularly because of the high stakes involved, such as professional reputations, self-worth, correction of an injustice to oneself or a loved one, the ability to earn one's living, revenge, or a combination of these and other strong motives.

This chapter pertains to witness preparation in civil cases only; we do not engage in witness preparation that involves the rehearsal of testimony with either prosecution or defendant witnesses in criminal proceedings. Reasons for this position are described more fully in chapter 7. In criminal cases, we make suggestions regarding appearance or deportment if defendants are likely to injure their chances for a fair trial because of such extralegal influences on the jury. In rare instances in which the prosecutor attempts to exploit a defendant's physical or psychological liabilities, we attempt to counter those efforts.

WHO IS BEING PREPARED
FOR TRIAL?

In most of the civil cases in which we have consulted, the witnesses who were being prepared were parties to the case—defendants or plaintiffs. Only occasionally have we had to prepare an expert to testify. Experts are often selected for their experience and their effectiveness on the stand and do not need extensive preparation. Although interest is focused necessarily on the witness, testimonial effectiveness also depends on the interaction between the attorney who asks the questions and the witness who answers them. This is true both in direct testimony when the attorney is on the witness's side, and in cross-examination by the opposing counsel. The consultant therefore must be attentive both to the relationship issues and to individual performance. In every instance, the consultant should remember that the contest is always for the mind of the juror. Winning that contest can be jeopardized if jurors are distracted by the chemistry between witnesses and attorneys that arises in the courtroom.

In one trial, part of our consultation entailed working with an attorney and his woman client, who was suing a psychiatrist for sexual involvement initiated in the guise of therapy. The woman appeared highly attractive, guileless, submissive, compliant, and self-deprecating. During lengthy and emotional testimony, there was some danger that she and the male attorney who was scheduled to conduct the direct questioning might well be perceived as a "couple," in part because of the attorney's general demeanor. There was too great a chance that her contribution to that relationship would not only divert jurors from the importance of her statements but provoke inappropriate attributions about her relationships with men in general. We suggested that another attorney in the firm do the questioning.

Because both the attorney and the consultant are usually present, preparation of the witness is preparation for the attorney as well: Attorneys benefit by accumulating the facts of the case, by learning about the witness, and by coordinating their role behavior with that of witnesses during testimony. Someone who is a key witness in the case and on whom the attorney must rely for information used in making legal and strategic decisions is of sufficient importance to warrant the time and expense spent on preparation. The witness and the attorney may spend ample time reviewing relevant facts, but new information or new perceptions of information may be derived during witness preparation, facts and understandings that have material implications for the case. Such events, often with the consultant as catalyst, have obvious importance for case development.

Preparation also develops the attorney's knowledge about and feelings toward the witness as a person and aids attorneys in the coordination of their respective responsibilities during testimony. The attorney develops a set of expectations for and a sense of timing with the witness; the witness learns about the attorney in turn. Ground covered by the consultant with the witness in the absence of the attorney can be valuable but lacks these important trial preparation ingredients.

IS THERE A LITERATURE ON WITNESS PREPARATION?

No literature in psychology deals directly with witness preparation. In other applications of psychology to law, such as eyewitness accuracy, jury decision-making, and expert testimony on competence and insanity, research and conceptual accounts can be found. The absence of research on witness preparation may result from psychologists' lack of familiarity with the extent and importance of this activity, coupled with the fact that behavioral consultants who often do it (such as members of the Association of Trial Behavioral Consultants) typically are not researchers. Research in this area may be forthcoming, however, and despite the lack of research specifically relating to witness preparation, relevant literature on communication and persuasion, interpersonal processes, self-presentation, etc., can be effectively used by the psychologist in this important area of consultation.

Attorneys have a limited literature on readying witnesses for trial but a wealth of personal experience on the topic. It is found in texts on trial diplomacy (e.g., Bergman, 1979, 378ff; Mauet, 1980, p. 11ff), typically used in law school courses on trial practice; the psychological consultant would do well to read this material. As primers for the attorney, these sources contain advice on familiarizing the witness with the procedures to be followed in court, on exposure to the courtroom itself, and on methods of clarifying content of the testimony to be given.

THE CONSULTANT'S OWN PREPARATION ON FACTS OF CASE

Multiple strategies can be adopted by the consultant in becoming familiar with a case prior to the development of witness testimony. We have used several: extensive preparation on the alleged facts of the case; limited exposure to the alleged facts; and "cold turkey," in which almost no information is revealed before working with the witness. Each method has advantages and disadvantages.

Broad knowledge of the case, including the witness's view of the issues and likely testimony, allows the consultant to be maximally useful in developing witness testimony. Under such circumstances, the consultant reacts to not only what is said, but also to what is not said by the witness. The missing content in witnesses' statements may occasionally be overlooked by the witnesses themselves and attorneys. At other times, the absent information or effect has new relevance that is made salient by something another witness has said or done, which the consultant could never know without his or her own extensive preparation. Furthermore, knowing the likely testimony of other witnesses permits the consultant to participate more fully in the development of attorney questions aimed at cultivating the most significant aspects of a witness's testimony. The chief disadvantage of this approach is the amount of consultant time it requires. Consultant preparation not only entails discussion with attorneys, but considerable other effort in accumulating information as well, largely through reading of depositions, a superb source of the substantive testimony of parties and witnesses in the case.

A consultant's more limited prior familiarization with a case dictates a slightly different role. Knowledge of the principal facts—usually derived through discussion with the attorney—of the witness's testimony readies the consultant to deal more narrowly with a witness's behavior, which by design may be the consultant's role in a given preparation. The restriction in role changes the consultant's contribution but does not necessarily diminish its value. With both the limited knowledge and the "cold turkey" method, however, all parties should recognize that role coordination among the attorney, witness, and consultant will suffer if the scope of consultant responsibility for case preparation broadens inadvertently during work sessions. Too much time may be spent in apprising the consultant of the facts of the case, perhaps precipitated by consultant comments on witness statements and behavior. Given these caveats, however, limiting background development has potential for reducing consultant time.

In cold turkey efforts, the consultant has almost no familiarity with the case. The terms of initial participation may simply be: "We want you to hear this testimony, and let's go from there." Valuable contributions can result from this introduction to the witness and issues, with subsequent escalated involvement.

Obviously, various factors—time, money, attorney–consultant relationship, apparent witness problems, consultant philosophy, etc.—dictate the strategy to be followed. We suggest that the attorney and consultant be well aware of the advantages and disadvantages of each option so that expectations are clear and compatible.

INTRODUCING THE CONSULTANT
TO THE WITNESS

Most people still think that a psychologist is a clinician whose work delves into one's innermost feelings and strives to facilitate adjustment, and that psychologists are needed only when a person is in psychological distress. Consequently, when a psychological consultant is brought in to help on a case, the witness may conclude that he or she has been judged in need of at least a psychological evaluation, if not counseling, with the result that the witness becomes self-conscious, defensive, or shaken. These potential, detrimental effects may be forestalled by some straightforward and simple steps entailing a nonthreatening introduction of the witness to the consultant.

We have used introductions that emphasize the expertise of the consultant in the areas of juror perception, attitudes, and behavior. Witnesses are prepared so that the clearest, most favorable presentation of the evidence to jurors, within the bounds of the facts, can be made, and so that the conclusions of one's side in the litigation can be fostered. Witness preparation is an attempt to develop testimony in light of jurors' perceptions, biases, and judgments. This introduction of a consultant to a witness is not a distortion by commission or omission; it is an honest focus of the consultant's role on the jury as an audience first, with the evidence and the witness as secondary considerations. Any functionally equivalent strategy will also succeed in putting the witness more at ease.

Such an effort may seem unnecessarily cautious or excessively protective. The reader should recognize, however, that witnesses, either as plaintiffs or defendants, are susceptible to overinterpretation of the motives or behaviors of their attorneys; this susceptibility can lead to an undermining of self-confidence that may have already been rocked by the events prompting the litigation. A smooth and interpersonally constructive introduction helps to build a relationship that is important to effective witness preparation. With thoughtful interventions from the consultant and reassurances for the witness, the relationship typically can be readily established.

MAJOR AREAS OF
WITNESS PREPARATION

In witness preparation, the consultant is both an advisor to the client-attorney and a change agent—largely a facilitator—who is intent on producing an effective presentation within the realities of the case. Accomplishing this overall objective requires attention to the following five areas of concern: the facts to which the witness will testify; feelings associated with the issues in the case, including the act of testifying; the courtroom environment; direct testimony; and cross-examination.

The Witness's Facts

All of the facts of the matter at hand are derived from the witness's account of the issues addressed and, however helpful or harmful those facts are to one's side of the litigation, the consultant is not present to alter the facts. Presentational style is fair game for intervention, however. Clarity, forcefulness, apparent confidence, and other features of a witness's performance can be improved with proper intervention.

Factual clarity is essential. Witnesses must be clear about what they know or believe to be true, what the facts are from their perspective. This is no mean accomplishment. As all of us are aware, recall of past events is not simply a matter of replaying the cognitive record. How soon did the physician get to the emergency room after the call was made? What was the nurse's report to the physician over the phone? What was the physician doing at the time? In some instances, existing records may help to reconstruct the critical events of the past, records that help with dates, times, and existing conditions surrounding the incident. Important facts may have to be testified to from the record rather than from recall, in which case witness confidence in the record is a prime concern.

Serious recall problems are sometimes avoided because of the unusual nature of the incident prompting the suit. A remarkable event may at the time of its occurrence trigger attention to both its features and context, facilitating acquisition and recall of essential facts. The omnipresence of litigation in dispute resolution may in itself prompt attention to detail and even to note-taking at the time of an especially unusual event. However, the consultant soon realizes that such aids to determining facts are seldom available, and that neither the defendant nor the plaintiff often had any idea at the time that a civil suit might result from the incident.

A witness must be able to admit ignorance if that is indeed the case. This simple truth is either not recognized or is misunderstood by many lay witnesses, at least at first, and there are good reasons for their state of mind. The adversary process in a lawsuit imbues participants with a sense of contest that permeates most of what is done. Both sides are there to win, after all. In this combative mental set, one tries to do one's best to fully develop one's own case; the more supporting facts, the better. Not having the answer to a question can be seen as a weakness to be shorn up by some responsive affirmation. In keeping with the fear of the witness at such a time, not being able to answer the question may prove in fact to be an opportunity relinquished. However, in the crucible of the court-room, that opportunity should seldom be seized by supplying shaky information. In addition, jurors may be surprised, and witness credibility may be endangered, if recall for some facts is abnormally complete. The witness must become comfortable with saying "I do not know" when there is no other truthful response.

Feelings About the Issues

Closely associated with information the witness has about the case are the feelings associated with that information and the affect generated by the case in general. Witnesses who are being readied for trial are usually plaintiffs or defendants, and their feelings run high. The consultant, working with the facts of the case, frequently finds such feeling intrusive, inimical, and pervasive. Also, aspects of the case may threaten the self-esteem and self-concept of the witness.

We have found that defendants often have surprising and pervasive self-doubt as a result of the incident that provoked the litigation in civil cases in which we have consulted. They seem to blame themselves unreasonably. Realistic judgment and objective evaluation were unjustly victimized by emotion. We have seen the self-abasement common to conscientious physician-defendants intensify into the projection of an apparent sense of personal guilt, culminating in testimony during role-playing that would appear in actual trial as directly incriminating. It is paradoxical that this has occurred when it seemed least warranted by the facts of the case. Such feelings obviously need careful consultant attention. A defendant beset by such doubts must see the situation as nearly as possible as it existed at the time the decisions at issue were made, not in retrospect, with the judgment of time and new information.

Attitudes toward the other side involve strong emotional currents for both plaintiffs and defendants. In many cases, the issues are cast in moral terms: the behaviors of defendants considered legally actionable are judged by plaintiffs as evil in their effects and in their underlying motives; plaintiffs in their turn are viewed as unfair and unreasonable, as judging *post hoc propter hoc*. In some ways, perception and evaluation across the lines of litigation show the mirror-image characteristics found in the views of enemies across the lines of battle in territorial disputes (White, 1966).

It is not the business of the consultant to disabuse the witness of these views. At times, it has seemed to us that the judgments have been warranted. Rather, the consultant must strive to eliminate detrimental effects of such emotion so that testimony may be given and received as desired.

Appropriate feeling should be the standard. Furthermore, truly affect-free testimony is probably neither attainable nor desirable. Concern with emotion may focus not only on affect attached to the witness's own testimony. The consultant may have to take into account emotion that arises over testimony anticipated from another witness; although the usual instance involves testimony from someone on the other side of the litigation, this is not what one invariably finds. Our experience shows that attention to spousal feelings may be essential to avert sympathetic distortion of testimony when a husband or wife is part of the audience. In one instance, the solution seemed to be to keep the husband out of the courtroom during some or all of his wife's testimony; part of the intervention was to persuade the husband to accept the view that his absence would not be seen by jurors as a lack of support or lack of caring for his wife, or worse.

In The Courtroom

The courtroom is a formidable setting for all but its habitual occupants. Its formality, order, and absolute judicial authority combine to inspire awe. This is true even in rural, "down-home" communities, in which one may still see counsel table liberties afforded to legal cronies of an earlier era. The impact of the judge is itself powerful even when idiosyncratic, and in some cases is not far from the following fictionalized account:

> Judge Taylor was on the bench, looking like a sleepy old shark, his pilot fish writing rapidly below in front of him. Judge Taylor looked like most judges I had ever seen: amiable, white-haired, slightly ruddy-faced, he was a man who ran his court with an alarming informality—he sometimes propped his feet up, he often cleaned his fingernails with his pocket knife. In long equity hearings, especially after dinner, he gave the impression of dozing, an impression dispelled forever when a lawyer once deliberately pushed a pile of books to the floor in a desperate effort to wake him up. Without opening his eyes, Judge Taylor murmured, "Mr. Whitley, do that again and it'll cost you one hundred dollars." (Lee, 1962, p. 167)

Familiarity with the courtroom is best attained by arranging to conduct some witness practice there, for example, a portion of the direct testimony. An introduction to the environment through private, individual access is preferable to a visit to a trial in progress, which is another method that may be used. When one is exposed to the courtroom first as a spectator, its imposing nature is unnecessarily overemphasized and a visitor to another trial gains no sense of the personal control and adequacy that can be experienced when the incursion is wholly of one's own making.

It is usually best not to telegraph your preparation to the other side, and it may be difficult to arrange for witness practice in the courtroom in which the testimony will be given while maintaining control over what people know about your preparation. If such a problem exits, it may be possible to visit the courtroom when no trial is in session, but to eliminate the preparation session. Some testimony and role play can then take place from a witness chair in another courtroom, even a moot courtroom in a law school, as part of witness readiness for the trial. The exposure to the courtroom in which the testimony will be given should include attention to the logistics of addressing the jurors directly from the stand, establishing and maintaining eye contact, becoming aware of the relative positioning of the attorney who will do the questioning, managing the placement of charts and other visual aids, if any, etc. A little familiarity with these matters may greatly ease or improve the day in court.

Direct Testimony

Whether the witness being readied for trial is the plaintiff or the defendant, direct testimony affords the opportunity for the witness to tell his or her side of the case, under the close control of both the witness and counsel. In the well-prepared case there should be no confusion about either the questions that will be asked or the answers to be given. Typically the direct testimony will be the witness's first testimony, although there is an important exception, which must be both anticipated and adequately prepared for: A defendant in a civil suit may be called by the plaintiff as if on cross-examination during the plaintiff's case-in-chief, which occurs before the defense gives its evidence.

Practice for direct testimony is both the practice of lines, and the organization and refinement of ideas. For several reasons, we have never found it advisable to approach the presentation of testimony as would an actor learning a script. First, there is insufficient time for that tack. Second, only partly owing to time limitations, a script for testimony is never written. Neither the attorneys nor the parties get far enough ahead of events to orchestrate matters to that degree. As a case develops on its way to trial, depositions are taken from the parties on both sides by the opposing attorneys; the deposition becomes part of the record that may be used at trial. There is seldom much preparation of witnesses for depositions; however depositions are an important factor in the development of testimony for direct and cross-examination. Scripts would have to be written very early in the development of a case therefore, because they would have to serve at both the deposition and testimony stage. More important, scripts would probably do more harm than good because of the nature of trial preparation and conduct and the psychological requirements for the presentation of evidence. Evidence evolves almost up to the moment of testimony no matter how thoroughly preparation is done. Unless the performance in court were flawless—akin to an impeccable live performance by an actor—a script would surely backfire with a jury, who would perceive the evidence as fabricated and the testimony as a sham. All of these problems can be avoided by preparation that focuses on essential ideas and their clear expression.

Videotaping is a beneficial adjunct during preparation. Initially somewhat self-conscious, witnesses quickly adapt to the taping, and it is valuable if visible behavior illustrates the consultant's points. The chance to compare testimony at different stages of preparation is useful with some witnesses, and the camera serves a surrogate audience function, which intensifies the sessions and, if used successfully, builds witness confidence.

Any visual aids (photographs, charts, physical evidence, mechanical models, etc.) to be used at trial require rehearsal. The use of a chalkboard, flip chart, flannel board, or other similar device that may be used to facilitate communication with jurors should be practiced with care during preparation for the direct examination. These visual communication methods should be seriously considered whenever physical or temporal relationships are testimonial ingredients; time taken in their development is well spent.

Cross-examination

Contrary to the popular movie or television depiction of examination by opposing counsel, the consultant can anticipate and prepare for nearly all of the topics and the substance of most of the questions to be asked during cross-examination. Each side knows the important points of law and, through the legal process of discovery, both sides are aware of most of the strengths and weaknesses of the case. Adversary counsel take depositions not only from the parties but also from expert witnesses. The approach and questions of the opposing side's cross-examination cannot be completely ascertained, but enough can be learned so that correct anticipation is likely and preparation will be fruitful. Both preparation on substance and on the style of cross-examination are important.

One can prepare for cross-examination by explaining in advance the legally permissible differences between direct and cross-examination and describing the likely behavior the attorneys on the other side will exhibit. Thus, the witness may be told that opposing counsel is permitted under the law to ask leading questions, that the judge may direct the witness to answer the specific questions asked, that the attorney may be aggressive and abrasive, etc. We instead let the witness know that we always practice cross-examination before the trial, and that we have asked one of the other attorneys in the firm to play the role of the opposing attorney, whose style is at least generally known as are the facts to be introduced in the case. We advise the witness that the questioning may be intense, and that we propose to videotape the session as we have the practice on direct questioning and will discuss it as before. To this point in the preparation, we will have been more supportive of the witness than challenging.

We prefer that the first session on cross-examination run through some of the more difficult issues to be confronted in the trial. We permit the session to continue for several minutes without interruption. The witness should stay in role, as if in the courtroom. Typically, the witness finds it difficult to avoid serious trouble, despite the fact that strengths and weaknesses of the case have been discussed, as have general ideas about the issues that are likely to be covered on cross-examination.

At some point in practice for cross-examination, the examiner should ask whether the attorneys have instructed the witness about what to say and whether the witness has rehearsed the answers. This question may be asked in court. It usually catches the witness off guard in practice, often leading to stumbling that jurors would interpret as evasive answers, raising real issues of credibility.

Witness difficulty in this session varies widely with the person and the case and with the attack of the attorney, but the session provides much material to discuss. Invariably there are preconceptions about such matters as admission of ignorance, latitudes of response allowed in the courtroom, permissible attorney behavior (theirs and yours) and the amount of detail to include in answers. Witnesses must be told that they will have opportunity to correct or to clarify issues on redirect examination. If questioned about rehearsing lines, a witness can honestly say that in discussion of the case with the attorneys, the witness told them of personal perceptions of the true facts of the case. If asked whether a psychologist(s) was present (we have never seen this happen, but it should be anticipated), the witness should answer affirmatively.

The witness should understand that answers on cross-examination should be brief, honest, and phrased as well as they can be. The natural tendency to be on guard and suspicious should not cause the witness to distort or fabricate the response; such distortion or fabrication is harmful. Attorneys are truly concerned that a witness may falsify a response on a trivial issue to make it consistent with some apparently important point. Bergman (1979, p. 383) supplies an example:

> In a child custody case, a neighbor is asked if she ever saw the father take a drink. The neighbor, trying to help the father as much as possible, responds haughtily, "No, of course not." Meanwhile, while the neighbor was out in the courthouse corridor, the father's priest has testified that he often visits the father to discuss theology over a few beers.

When the witness is shown by other evidence presented to the jury to have lied on a trivial point, all of the witness's testimony is undermined.

Some preparation should be devoted to the circumstance in which witness/defendants are called by the plaintiff as though on cross-examination. Such witnesses will not have had a chance previously to tell their side of the case from the stand. Defendant's counsel normally will have presented an overview of the case in the opening statement, however.

APPEARANCE

One's physical appearance undeniably affects the impressions formed by observers in almost any setting; the courtroom is no exception. Dress, grooming, and behavior in the courtroom are companion concerns of style and content of testimony. The image projected by the witness is important not only during testimony, when jurors' attention focuses particularly on the witness, but throughout the trial.

Actions and nonverbal cues such as posture can affect the judgment of the jurors of one's self-assurance and confidence in the issues litigated. Jurors notice facial cues, hand movements, and actions on the part of witnesses and some may use inferences based on these observations to reach conclusions about the case. Although witnesses present in the courtroom but not testifying are not "communicators" in the usual sense, their appearance creates impressions in the jurors that must be anticipated during witness preparation.

The question of attire always arises during witness preparation. In this and other matters we try to rely on existing witness inclinations. How does the witness normally dress on official or formal occasions? Will this manner of dress seem to the jurors to fit the courtroom situation? Even if the answer to the latter question is no, is it still advantageous not to change the witness's appearance? A plaintiff who is poor and of borderline intelligence should not be groomed or dressed as might a speaker at a business banquet. Within the framework described, we have no formal rules about colors, although some consultants do. We prefer that attire be understated or conservative. Although a witness is wealthy or is thought to be wealthy, the appearance of conspicuous wealth should almost always be avoided. Except in special circumstances, a defendant who has 15 suits appropriate to the season may do well to wear no more than two during a 2-week trial.

For good reasons, we prefer that witnesses be as natural in demeanor as possible in the courtroom, assuming that the predispositions of a witness are not injurious to the case. There is neither time nor ethical justification for attempting to make witnesses be something they are not. Even if there were, the new character might appear artificial in the stress of the courtroom. Newly acquired and consequently less well learned behaviors may be awkward or ill-fitting in the stream of behavior induced by the courtroom. In fact, theory and research on social facilitation (Green & Grange, 1977) indicate that under conditions of arousal dominant behaviors are favored and underlearned behaviors are impeded. It is our cardinal principle that a consultant should avoid complicating the performance of a witness at trial.

Witnesses should understand that jurors and prospective jurors form impressions based on behavior they observe in and about the courthouse, in restaurants, on the sidewalks, or anywhere else. People in the elevator, at the next table in the cafeteria, or at the bar down the street may be jurors. Attorneys will probably caution witnesses on such matters, aware that witnesses may think that areas other than the courtroom are "safe" territory. Once a jury is sworn, witnesses should be careful never to give the appearance of interaction with jurors. This applies to family members of the plaintiff or defendant as well. One of our cases was declared a mistrial because the wife and sister of a defendant exchanged pleasantries about the weather with two of the elderly women on the jury. We had a jury we thought was favorable for us; apparently the plaintiff's attorney, who complained to the judge, thought so too.

THREATS TO CREDIBILITY

It accomplishes little for a witness to be clear, organized, and effective in communicating ideas if the witness is not perceived by jurors to be credible. The jurors must decide what the facts are if the facts or their interpretations are contested. Credibility, defined as expertness and trustworthiness, is thus vital to the effectiveness of testimony.

Internal inconsistency in testimony can undermine credibility, but this is largely a matter of getting the facts straight—a line cannot be both straight and crooked. By improving the logical content of communication, and thus clarifying meaning, inconsistencies can often be removed. Other threats to credibility concern style of presentation, misplaced efforts to strengthen one's case by distortion or falsification of statements on secondary issues (including exaggeration), and paralinguistic or nonverbal behavior that is often perceived as signaling deception.

Extreme cases of particularly undesirable behavior on the part of a witness will present a great challenge to the consultant bent on improving testimonial style. The consultant may have to judge whether the witness is better off in character, exhibiting the unwanted behavior, or imbued with other and somewhat ill-fitting characteristics. Witnesses coached to behave out of character, in a way that conflicts with their customary and comfortable usual communication style, may appear artificial and produce incredulity in jurors. Sometimes the consultant can use an alternative to changing the witness's behavior. Such strategies to minimize losses or to eliminate them, include raising the issues during voir dire, clarifying the matter for jurors by asking questions which allow an explanation while the witness is on the stand, or by presenting the issue to the jury during the opening statement. These techniques can also be used to correct false impressions formed by jurors because of some physical or psychological disability of the witness. For example, a witness who has an eye problem may be unable to maintain eye contact with jurors and may therefore be perceived as "shifty."

The witness must know, both by being told and through the experience of feeling pressure to use distortion in an effort to avoid a seemingly damaging response on an ancillary issue, that an honest response is the best way to avoid serious issues of credibility. All of what a witness says can be jeopardized if distortion or falsification is uncovered for the jury on a side issue. The earlier example of Bergman illustrates the worst example of this problem because falsification on an issue that contradicts another witness on your side damages both witnesses' statements.

Communication Channels: Paralinguistics and Nonverbal Behavior

Research (Miller & Burgoon, 1982; DePaulo, Zuckerman, & Rosenthal, 1980) has shown that certain kinds of nonverbal and paralinguistic behavior are used by experimental subjects to form judgments of communicator honesty. Among these are anxiety, voice pitch, excessive or exaggerated behavior, uncertainty, and contradictions among communication cues. The validity of these signals of dishonesty is supported by experimental findings, which show that subjects instructed to lie exhibit similar behaviors. Thus, when a witness exhibits such behavior, observers may decide that the witness is lying (see Box 2.2). These issues should be addressed carefully during readiness for testifying. Other research (Wells, Lindsay, & Ferguson, 1979) shows plainly the extreme importance of communicator confidence in affecting audience acceptance of testimony. These investigators found that although communicator confidence and factual accuracy were unrelated, impressions of confidence nonetheless accounted for 50% of the variance in decisions to accept what was said as true. Again, the implications for witness preparation are clear: It is an accomplishment even if one does not teach good habits so much as eliminate bad ones that detract from the testimony or mislead an audience.

THE ASSESSMENT–
INTERVENTION–EVALUATION
SEQUENCE

In an abstract sense, the steps in witness preparation are assessment, intervention, and evaluation, repeated continuously as a cycle. In practice, these elements may occur in almost any order and combination, although intervention should be withheld until circumstances are assessed and a plan is formulated.

Assessment

Assessment of testimonial effectiveness of witnesses begins almost at first contact with the attorneys. Attorneys usually have formed judgments of the ability of the individual or the expert as a witness; although ultimately the consultant may disagree with the attorney's assessment, it is useful as a starting point. We make diagnoses from impressions gained from depositions as well: facility with the language, ability to explain complex or important issues, cooperativeness, and discernment should be assessed. From our impressions formed in these ways we develop working hypotheses about strengths and weaknesses of a witness, hypotheses that are modified on subsequent contacts with the person, depending on what we later discover.

In general, the typical practicum training, the experience, and the assessment literature of clinical psychologists probably constitute the best preparation for the diagnostic aspect of witness preparation. In contrast, the nonclinician frequently finds ideas in professional journals rather than in mundane observation, and in theory rather than in practical cause and effect. The experimental social psychologist learns to create situations containing important psychological and social requirements for research, rather than to discern the important social and psychological determinants of encountered situations. In the typical education and training of the nonclinician, there is no supervised practicum experience in development of diagnostic skills.

Intervention

Because witnesses are usually receptive to efforts to improve their testimony, the preferable intervention is often a simple, direct suggestion with a supporting rationale. Such inductions frequently bring about the required change in thinking, perspective, or behavior. However, the proper intervention must sometimes seek insight into self-attitudes that obstruct improvement in presentation of facts. In one such case, it appeared that although the witness believed he had acted properly given the information available, he also believed that he might have acted differently had he known everything that happened after the fact. In his meek manner he seemed to seek approbation and sympathy, when appropriately he should have been annoyed or angry at being the target of the suit. The witness was asked, "What things make you angry?" This question was the beginning of a brief but successful intervention that allowed effective mobilization of his intellectual and emotional resources as a witness.

The literature of social psychology, especially that concerning attitude formation and change (e.g., Zimbardo, Ebbesen, & Maslach, 1977), is useful to witness preparation. In witness preparation, the witness is the target and the consultant is the agent who induces change; the witness who then testifies at trial is the influencing agent in turn, and the jury or the judge is the audience. It is particularly useful to conceive of the situation in this way when planning intervention activities of witness preparation. Who should attempt the intervention? What is the best timing? To what degree should there be an emphasis on emotional content? How much change should be attempted in a single intervention? These and many other questions addressed in the attitude literature (e.g., Petty & Cacioppo, 1981) may be relevant at different points in witness preparation, with regard to both potential audiences and both potential influencing agents.

Consultants will develop their own expectations for witness change. How much one will attempt to achieve at any time will depend on considerations such as the intellectual ability and emotional status of the witness, the relationship between the witness and the consultant, and consultant style and preference. Defensiveness is usually not an obstacle, but we prefer incremental change to dramatic movement.

Evaluation

Evaluation is an assessment of the effectiveness of the intervention, that is, a diagnosis of performance after efforts by the witness to change. Most evaluation can be done during role-playing. Videotape provides feedback to the witness, detects problems in testimony that may be missed during the enactment, and verifies estimates of inadequacy or efficacy of the testimony. One can determine whether enough change has occurred, whether it has the desired effect, and can reevaluate its likely impact on jurors. Evaluation will usually focus initially on the specific changes that had been sought; those changes should then be assessed for their general impact on testimony.

Feedback to the witness is an integral part of evaluation. We try to assess change and provide feedback as a single process, believing that the immediacy of reinforcement for successful efforts to change is both informative and motivating. On reflection, new ideas may occur to us and are later used with the witness. Whatever the timing, feedback to the witness is often an intervention to induce additional change, either specific to the behaviors that were the target of the preceding effort or others, making evaluation and feedback part of the diagnosis–intervention–evaluation cycle.

ESCALATION OF PREPARATION

The actual testimony to be given by a witness evolves during trial preparation; owing to numerous factors, it is almost never foreseen by the attorneys or anyone else as an organized, integrated whole. The approach to witness preparation is a scenario rather than a blueprint. It is useful to begin with a discussion of the facts and to cover the areas of preparation described earlier in this chapter in a series of steps in a manner that increases performance demands by degrees tolerable to the witness. This procedure entails working initially with the witness's information without stressing presentational style. Important facts that will be part of the testimony are focused on in this stage. Before this stage is completed, one can slip into a second phase—role-playing segments of the testimony to be given under direct examination. These periods of role-play should be conducted with preliminary discussion and feedback for each segment, with videotape used as augmentation.

Once witnesses are reasonably comfortable with these periods of practice on direct testimony, they should be told that one of the next conferences will be devoted to practice for the cross-examination. In a simple statement the consultant should advise witnesses that the experience may be more intense than the preparation that has already occurred, but that it is helpful as a forerunner to the trial. The witness should not be further forewarned because an arduous experience during role-playing may toughen the usual witness. Someone who is fragile or overly sensitive may require gentler treatment.

Cross-examination, conducted as described in an earlier section, should be fairly intense, with the degree of stressfulness appropriate to the development of the witness. A witness who has been properly readied by the preceding steps will be able to appreciate the value of a grueling experience.

Efficiency during preparation sessions declines significantly after about a 2-hour period. Experience also shows that distributing the work sessions, with intervals of several days, is useful for promoting desired changes in behavior. During these intervals, witnesses think about what they have heard and seen and the work still to be done.

DO WITNESSES CHANGE?

We have been impressed with the degree to which witnesses are capable of modifying their behavior in order to present the evidence they must use in the best possible manner. This responsiveness may be owing in part to the unquestioned importance of the goals of the preparation and the obvious instrumental nature of the activity. The average person has seldom experienced the circumstances that can occur in witness preparation. It is meant to achieve the best presentation of the evidence and is focused on personal characteristics—the organization and presentation of ideas and personal styles of communication. Usually, when we are beseeched to change our actions or ideas it is because someone considers them distasteful or deficient for their purposes. However, in witness preparation, there is a shared goal which the witness eagerly accepts. This mutuality of purpose may account for some of the efficiency and effectiveness of witness preparation.

Chapter 6
Convincing the Jury: Evidence and Other Influences

The contest in the courtroom is for the minds and hearts of the jurors. They determine the true facts, based on the evidence presented, and fit those facts to the applicable law as given by the judge. In performing their role, jurors must make judgments of witnesses' credibility, weigh the relative importance of pieces of evidence, and achieve an understanding of the events that prompted the trial. In attempting to persuade jurors to view their side favorably, attorneys impose the most influential content, style, and structure at their disposal on the facts as they see them. The task of convincing the jury is tantamount to molding beliefs, feelings, and behavior, with the intent that convinced jurors will eventually persuade others and, finally, vote "correctly" on the verdict. No one on this planet would view the attorney's job as one of a mere presentation of the facts as though they spoke for themselves. Furthermore, the contest takes place in an adversary system in which anything that is within the rules is not only permitted but is expected of competent counsel.

Evidentiary circumstances and procedural law set limits on the behavioral consultant and the attorney. First, the consultant and attorney operate within the constraints of the evidence in the case: They must work with what they have. The consultant is further constrained by the theory of the case as developed by the attorney—the scenario of events that the attorney wishes the jurors to accept and one that is developed in response to the facts and in turn influences their organization and presentation. The plaintiff's theory in a libel case may be that the defendant knowingly published an untrue, defamatory article with the intent to damage the reputation of the subject as a means to deprive him of political influence. A physician-defendant being sued for a death following surgery may claim that the procedures used in the surgery followed the standard of care in all particulars, and that the death was a consequence of the inherent risks of general anesthesia, which are recognized but not well understood. In a criminal defense in a capital murder trial, the attorney's theory may entail diminished capacity in the form of extreme emotional distress. The consultant may at times participate in the formulation of the theory of the case, but usually does not because it has been worked out prior to consultation. The theory of the case depends on the available facts and on the applicable law, but there is latitude for a construction and a presentation of the facts that promote a particular interpretation of events.

Procedural constraints set by law either limit the manner in which facts may be presented or prohibit their presentation. Although such constraints vary in different jurisdictions, the following are examples: attorneys may not ask their own witnesses leading questions, but may do so when cross-examining witnesses for the other side; a defendant's prior record cannot be introduced unless his previous crimes raise issues of veracity and bear on his credibility as a witness; and, on redirect examination, only those issues covered in the cross-examination can be addressed. Such fetters attached to attorneys, and therefore to behavioral consultants, limit behavioral intervention in trials. Nonetheless, there is ample opportunity to modify social and psychological influences at work in the courtroom (Dillehay & Nietzel, 1986).

THE COMMUNICATION PARADIGM: APPLICABLE BUT LIMITED

For years, social psychologists have used the communication paradigm —who says what to whom in what channel—to study persuasion and attitude change (e.g., Hovland, 1954; McGuire, 1969). Thus, characteristics of communicators, such as attractiveness, expertness, and power, as well as features of the communication such as the internal ordering of arguments or the use of emotional appeals, have been examined for their effects on recipients of the communication. In turn, the characteristics of audiences have been studied for their influence on the success of persuasive appeals: Does intelligence, existing attitude, or prior experience affect the impact of a communication? Are certain personality factors associated with persuasibility? Zimbardo, Ebbesen, and Maslach (1977) present a highly readable summary of this literature; Saks and Hastie (1978) apply it to courtroom issues. Within the communication framework, the psychological processes involved in the effect of persuasion on attitudes and behavior have been described as attention, comprehension, yielding (accepting the conclusions of the communicator), retention (remembering the facts or conclusions), and action (behavior) (McGuire, 1969). Research both inside and outside the laboratory documents influential factors in each of the categories of the communication framework that affect these processes.

The persuasion model is, however, too narrow a research and theoretical base for examination of influences on jurors. Persuasion (using argument to engender the communicator's conclusions) is strictly applicable only to the closing arguments of a trial, in which the attorney reviews and summarizes the evidence and highlights desired conclusions. Closing arguments are termed such for good reason. Arguments are not permitted elsewhere in the coverage of evidence, although in some courts we have heard opening statements that resembled closing arguments but did not result in intervention of the judge or objection from the other side. However, the evidence given between the opening statements and closing arguments and which comprises the bulk of a trial, appears in fragmented and disorganized form, is laced with gaps and ambiguity, and comes from a variety of witnesses. The facts are almost always challenged immediately by the other side in cross-examination and, later, conflicting evidence is usually heard. This process is not persuasion in the sense in which it is conceived and researched. It is certainly social influence, however, and suggests literatures beyond the persuasion literature that may apply.

Education, identification, compliance, obedience, and conformity are social influence processes that operate to varying degrees in the life of a juror as juror. To recognize these processes and their various features is to be aware of different potential interventions to influence jurors. Information is the hallmark of education, and the necessities of a specific case may suggest the importance of specific information, as in a medical malpractice case in which an obscure anatomical structure may be a central matter. Identification is based on a positive affective relationship to another person—a witness, party, or attorney—which may be used to induce acceptance of a particular interpretation of the evidence. Identification as an affective process derives in turn from perceived similarity to the other person, admiration, or other motivational states. Jurors may be said to be compliant or obedient when they respond to the direct requests or commands of another person, often an authority figure, who wishes to achieve a particular behavioral effect. Conformity is adherence to social norms; its operation is most evident in deliberation, although adherence to community standards as a basis for individual juror decision-making is a concern in certain cases.

Other literatures are germane to conceptualizing juror attitudes and behavior as targets of influence. There is considerable research on social motivation underlying attitudes and behavior (e.g., Fishbein & Ajzen, 1975; Wicklund & Brehm, 1976) that also does not follow the communication paradigm, and voluminous theory and data on basic processes in social perception and attribution (e.g., Harvey & Weary, 1981; Heider, 1958), which are potentially relevant to the forensic consultant. Moreover, from the literature on social power, we are aware of varying bases of social influence—legitimate, coercive, reward, attraction, and expert (French & Raven, 1959)—that can be helpful in understanding juror reactions.

We believe that the theory and practice of courtroom consultation can be based on behavioral science theory and research. Theoretical, metatheoretical, and practical aspects of this knowledge base are treated in chapter 7. However, we wish to reaffirm that the consultant must combine a knowledge of the literature with a diagnosis of the case to formulate a course of action, advising and intervening with attorneys as clients. In itself, a knowledge of behavioral principles derived from research is no more sufficient as professional preparation for the forensic consultant than is a thorough knowledge of physics for the mechanical engineer on a construction project.

The present legal literature contains much information derived from the theory and research of the behavioral sciences on communication and persuasion. Whether the authors are behavioral scientists (e.g., Sannito, 1981; Vinson & Anthony, 1983) or attorneys (e.g., Begam, 1980; Colley, 1981; Lawson, 1969), the articles call attention to principles of behavior examined and to some degree supported in the psychological and sociological literatures. If our clients read their own literature, they would learn a moderate amount of behavioral theory and principles based on research, reasonably updated, with few reporting errors and numerous specific examples of application to cases. However, busy attorneys have little time to read much of this literature; it neither serves as the precedent case for a motion nor provides a legal basis for a pleading. If they were to read the translations of behavioral principles to the courtroom, they would probably still seek behavioral consultation for two reasons: authentication of what the translators were claiming, and assistance in behavioral aspects of specific cases.

TRIAL SEGMENTS AND
JUROR INFLUENCE

Both civil and criminal jury trials may be considered as containing six segments in which jurors participate. Each segment represents an opportunity to influence the jurors in some way. The first segment is voir dire, during which jurors form impressions of the case they will hear—of the attorneys, the judge, and the defendant if it is a criminal proceeding, or of the parties to the dispute, if it is a civil matter. Once the jury is seated and sworn, the second phase begins; the plaintiff or the prosecution makes an opening statement, after which the defense may do the same. If the defense so chooses, it may, in the typical jurisdiction, either defer the opening statement until the time during the evidence phase when it presents its case-in-chief or decline to make any opening statement at all; the latter seldom occurs. The third phase entails the presentation of the evidence, usually through live testimony; sometimes other means, such as video-tapes and visits to scenes of important incidents, are used. Following the presentation of the evidence, each side makes closing arguments, which comprise the fourth segment. In the fifth segment, the jury receives instructions from the judge on the law and its application to the case. The sixth phase is jury deliberation. Although procedural requirements derived from statutes and case law for each segment limit the kinds of influence that can occur, judges have wide latitude over what happens in their courtrooms.

In the following sections, we discuss the more important issues on which attorneys seek behavioral consultation concerning ways to influence jurors during the trial and some of the considerations we have made in dealing with those issues. The trial segments just described provide a framework for the remainder of the chapter.

How Much Will Jurors Know
Before They Hear Opening Statements:
Publicity and Voir Dire

Consultants are usually not participants in ordinary cases, but participate in cases that involve serious sentences such as life imprisonment, the death penalty, or in which large sums of money are in dispute. In trials with such extreme possible consequences, jurors may have pertinent information, correct or not, before coming to the courtroom, received from the media or personal contacts. Consultants cannot expect that jurors with information about the case will be excused by the judge during voir dire. Judges do not excuse a juror who will answer yes when the judge asks whether the juror can put aside what has been read or heard about the case, listen objectively to the evidence presented in court, and return a true verdict based on that evidence alone. Demand characteristics and social desirability are so strong that few jurors admit unresolvable bias. There may still be some prejudiced jurors even after peremptory strikes.

In addition, if voir dire has been extensive, jurors will form impressions of the facts of the case, however erroneous they may be. The content of voir dire questions helps jurors begin to frame the issues in the case, and questioning during juror deselection should be recognized for its de facto influence on jurors' opinions (Suggs & Sales, 1978).

In court, jurors also will have heard the criminal indictment or the civil pleadings read before the opening statements are made. The charge or pleading will be encoded as part of their own perspective, which we can expect to be a limited but embellished personal construction of the actual circumstances.

In these three ways, jurors may preform ideas about the facts and the defendant or plaintiff before "official" presentation of the evidence takes place. The blank or open mind of the juror is a myth.

Opening Statement

The opening statement is the first opportunity for both sides to provide an integrated view of the case. This statement to the jury is not supposed to be argumentative in style or content; rather it is restricted to what the evidence will show, as seen by each side of the case. False claims are costly, because they serve as grounds for a mistrial, although we have observed considerable differences in the tolerance of trial judges in regard to "what the evidence will show." The statements tend not to be lengthy, usually lasting no more than 20 to 30 minutes even in the most serious of trials. The prosecution or the plaintiff speaks first, and the defense follows. In preparing the opening statement, both attorneys must decide how much to say about the ensuing evidence, and the defense attorney must choose whether to make an opening statement immediately following the prosecution/plaintiff's opening or to wait until just before presenting the defense's case-in-chief.

Should the defense wait? Consider the juror's state of mind after the prosecution's opening statement. The juror knows that there are conflicting claims, but after the prosecution or plaintiff has outlined its case—assuming it has done so with proper emphasis—there is a clear and predominant perspective. Even the skeptical juror, who may try to imagine what the defense can show, is faced with a considerable task if left to do it alone. Juror confusion or uncertainty at this point is probably inimical to the defense; not only is the point of view of their adversary salient as a theory to the juror, but the adversary presents evidence first. The behavioral principle involved is that the theory and information presented by the side which goes first provides a perspective, a theory with its supporting facts, which determines in part how subsequent conflicting information will be processed. The plaintiff/prosecution builds its case over little opposition, without a competing perspective; the defense does not have that advantage. Because an advantage in early structuring exists in the absence of a competing account (see Jones & Brehm, 1970), the defense should not let its opponent's perspective persist unchallenged any longer than necessary, certainly not through accumulation of supporting evidence.

How many and which facts to be presented to the jurors should be brought out in the opening statement? What is said then tells not only the jurors but the other side what your theory and evidence will be. Legal procedures for pretrial discovery permit each side to know much of the substance of the opposition's case. But neither knows with certainty what will be emphasized or what theory will be developed to strengthen and support the adversary's claims and, therefore, what major refutations are required. Anyone who doubts the potential importance of this fact should watch the notetaking by the opposition that accompanies the opponent's opening statement. How much to disclose depends on what is requisite to the particular circumstances: the value of surprise, the role of the facts in creating the perspectives of jurors, the complexity of the case, etc.

Consultants and attorneys on some capital cases face a special issue: How much of the guilt of the defendant should be admitted during the opening statement? This consideration arises because capital trials are bifurcated, with a first phase during which the jurors return a verdict and a second phase in which they fix the penalty if the verdict permits the death penalty. In most jurisdictions, it is not possible to plead guilty to capital murder and then to have a jury deliberate the penalty. If evidence strongly indicates the guilt of the defendant and if there is no basis for a serious refutation during the first phase of the trial, what can be said by the defense during the opening statement? From the point of view of the defense the real issue in the trial phase is life or death. Thus, in such cases, we believe that the jury should be informed in the opening statement that its real task is to examine the facts surrounding the act, the state of mind of the defendant, and the defendant's worth as a person. The facts of the case will determine the best language to be used in accomplishing this. Such strategy constitutes a meritorious trial principle: Weaknesses or liabilities in your case that will be brought out by the other side are best presented first by you; this allows for your own construction of the issue, eliminating the surprise value for the other side, and fostering the impression of honest admission of true shortcomings. However, admission of anything that would not otherwise be heard by the jury would be a tactical blunder; careful judgment is indispensable.

The Evidence: Witnesses, Parties, and Attorneys as Influencing Agents

Every word or act of an attorney, a witness, or a party to the case within sound or sight of a juror has a potential influence on that juror's mind and behavior. As sources of influence, these individuals can be thought of as communicators, although clearly they affect others not only (if at all) by what they say. In addition to what is said, in itself complex, the style and substance of what else we perceive while words are spoken influences us: expressive behavior, tone of voice and other paralinguistic behavior, clothes, social interactions, etc. In general, the characteristics of actors that are influential outside the courtroom produce their effects inside the courtroom as well. Attorneys are usually well aware of the potential importance of such social influence effects.

Of the communicator variables that are important in court, credibility is probably paramount. Typically defined as expertness and trustworthiness (McGuire, 1969; Saks & Hastie, 1978), this factor has been shown repeatedly to influence attitudes and opinions. Furthermore, other communicator variables that shape juror responses may do so because they alter perceived credibility. Power of the communicator, such as impressions conveyed through speech style or content (O'Barr, 1982), communicator attractiveness, or general knowledgeability may produce their effects through increased apparent credibility. In the judgment of Michael Colley (1981), a former President of the Association of Trial Lawyers of America, increasing juror attributions of attorney credibility is one of the two main tasks of voir dire. Maximizing credibility is also one of the major tasks of the behavioral consultant in the courtroom.

The more important communicator variables that effect successful influence are summarized in Box 6.1. These factors are derived from basic re-

---

Box 6.1. Source Characteristics That Affect Persuasiveness

There is a distinction to be made between persuasion, in which communicators attempt to change attitudes and behavior through persuasive communication, and other categories of social influence. In the latter, we can think of changing attitudes and behavior through mechanisms that produce their effects by means other than successful argumentation. Social influence processes that do not entail persuasive communications and a communicator in the usual sense are admonishments by an authority figure (obedience), requests without obvious sanctions attached (compliance), and transmissions of group standards (conformity). All of these processes can operate in the courtroom. Usually, in regard to the source of information, those characteristics of a communicator which facilitate success in persuasion probably also contribute to success in other forms of social influence.

Based largely on laboratory research, the following characteristics of *communicators* have been found to affect the reactions of audiences through persuasive communications.

(continued)

Credibility: Expertise

The more the communicator is judged to be expert on the subject of the communication, the greater the influence of the communicator on the audience.

With increasing discrepancies between the position advocated in the communication and the views of the audience, experts produce increasing amounts of change, whereas those who have little expertise induce decreasing amounts of change.

The expertise of a communicator may interact with the initial degree of agreement between the communicator and the audience. When information is derived from a source that is presumed expert, it elicits less thinking about the message; therefore, an expert is better able to overcome the tendency of an initially opposed audience to conceive counterarguments to the message received from the expert. However, an expert who addresses an audience already in agreement causes less thinking in support of the existing point of view than does a communicator who is not expert. Presumably the more the generation of thought in support of a given position, the less the susceptibility of a person to subsequent counterargument.

Credibility: Trustworthiness

The more the communicator is perceived as trustworthy, the greater the influence of the communicator.

As the listener becomes more personally involved in the topic, the trustworthiness of the communicator becomes more important.

Vested Interests

One who is perceived as arguing against one's own vested interests is more persuasive than one who is perceived to have vested interests consistent with the conclusions.

(continued)

search. The applicability and utility of these variables depends not only on their general truth, but also on the specific factors predominant in a concrete situation, and are thus a matter for careful assessment by the consultant.

Some social influences that operate in other situations may at first appear inapplicable to the courtroom. Obedience or compliance (Kelman, 1960), for example, which is manifested as adherence to the demands of an authority or requests from others and which occurs largely because of the powerful position of the communicator, would not seem to be a potential aspect of courtroom influence. Attorneys and witnesses do not normally brandish power displays in a trial, and jurors who have relationships with attorneys and other principals that may entail such a factor are excused for cause. The *judge*, however, has both reward and coercive power, and there are ways in which they may be used to advantage. For example, the judge can be asked to admonish the jurors not to make up

Intent to Persuade

Forewarning an audience about intent to persuade reduces the success of the communication for recipients personally involved with the issue. Presumably, this occurs because the audience actively counterargues while listening to views they oppose.

Perceived intent to persuade does not affect the comprehension and retention of the message, although it does reduce acceptance.

Attractiveness

An attractive communicator is more effective. As with other factors, the audience's definition of attractiveness is a key element.

Similarity Between the Communicator and the Recipient

Much experimental research concludes that, other factors being equal, similarity between a source and an audience increases liking and persuasiveness.

However, other research indicates that similarity of the source is not uniformly advantageous for social influence, and may be a liability if the similarity is threatening, as when it implies that the misfortune of a defendant might also befall a recipient.

Note: In the courtroom, comprehension, acceptance, retention of the content or conclusions of testimony or argument, and action are probably the processes that must be targeted by attorneys and witnesses. Attention is less an issue, although it should not be routinely eliminated as a potentially significant concern. In long, drawn-out civil trials we have seen jurors sleep in the jury box during testimony; in other cases, jurors have been so somnolent that it mattered little that their eyes were open.

Some jurors may have difficulty recalling the sources of significant parts of the testimony in lengthy trials; during recall, jurors may even confuse some of the testimony with that of witnesses for the other side (Austin, 1982). Maximizing source distinctiveness, through visual or verbal cues, can be important in some cases; priming processes in closing arguments that facilitate recall through distinctive features of the source should be considered.

---

their minds before all evidence is in, a statement that some judges are wont to make in any case. The judge's admonishment encourages jurors to suspend judgment and reminds them that another and contrasting side to the case will be presented next by the defense. Basic research (Jones & Brehm, 1970) supports the assertion that mere awareness of the existence of another side to the issue has effects on opinions; keeping such awareness salient should be helpful. Attorneys themselves can make direct requests of jurors during voir dire and in closing arguments that have some of the characteristics of inducing compliance. Jurors may be asked to indicate that they will not be prejudiced against a defendant who does not testify and may be reminded again of the request during closing arguments. Requests for certain behaviors are discussed later as an aspect of juror characteristics.

Attraction to the attorney or witness, sympathy for the defendant, and other forms of positive affective states should be considered in light of the personal characteristics of the attorney and parties. Serious attention should be given to eliminating or minimizing attorney or witness behaviors that provoke such negative emotions as repulsion, antipathy, annoyance, and impatience. Because trial preparation is often hurried, one must eliminate problems rather than improve on advantages. There are strong arguments that affect precedes cognition (Zajonc, 1984), but whether positive feelings for an attorney or witness induce positive evaluations and acceptance of their conclusions, or whether the process works in reverse, the principle of cognitive-affective consistency offers convincing evidence of the importance of supportive affect.

Jurors' attributions about attorneys, judges, and witnesses deserve careful attention. Attributions (Kelley & Michela, 1980) are efforts to explain behavior or ascriptions of personality characteristics. In the normal course of social perception and cognition, attributions precede at times and follow at other times the judgments we make about others. For example, jurors may learn that an expert is receiving $100 per hour for his testimony. If this seems like a lot of money to a juror, a subsequent lengthy and contentious cross-examination of the usual sort in which the expert uses his right to explain his answers may be interpreted by jurors as a deliberate prolonging of the exchange to earn a larger fee! An incident of this kind is described by Austin (1982), whose juror interviews also underscore the point that as the proceedings draw out or become tedious (as courtroom actions do, contrary to the image conveyed by television and the movies), jurors shift their attention from the issues to the personalities of the contestants. Consequently, a consultant must consider which personal characteristics of the actors will wear well with jurors and which will not.

The principle that similarity between a source of influence and an audience yields attraction to that source, and therefore increases potential for influence, is a much replicated experimental result (Berscheid & Walster, 1978; Byrne, 1971). Some of our earliest observations in the courtroom, however, contradicted this principle. For example, black jurors were not necessarily best for black defendants, and women jurors did not automatically favor victims in rape cases. Indeed, these instances suggest that jurors may need to preserve their assumptions about their own susceptibility to the misfortunes of the defendants who, in some respects, are apparently like themselves. Rather than believe that "There but for the grace of God go I," which is basically an identification of the juror with the defendant, jurors may believe that the defendant is deserving of punishment because of some weakness in character or some ill-advised behavior. In this way, the defendant is perceived to be different from the similar juror, and the juror is thus able to preserve the idea of a just world (Lerner, 1977).

We have also seen this process operate in juror selection strategy in a simulation of a personal injury case in which a motorcyclist was suing for damages from a motorist after a collision between the two. Attorneys *and trial consultants* alike predicted that a woman who was married and middle-class in most respects but who was also a motorcyclist would favor the plaintiff. They thought that because both she and the plaintiff rode motorcycles the woman would be good for the plaintiff and bad for the defense. They were wrong. Subsequent interviews with the woman revealed that she believed that if plaintiff had not been careless the accident never would have happened. How can an attorney or behavioral consultant know when condemnation of an otherwise similar victim or defendant, rather than attraction and sympathy, will determine perception and judgment? One must look carefully at the facts of the case and at the characteristics of the witness, the defendant, or the plaintiff, and at the makeup of the juror as the target of social influence.

Should the defendant take the stand? In a civil proceeding it seems beyond question that the parties will testify, if they are physically and psychologically able. In a criminal case, defendants sometimes do not, but should they? Defense attorneys face this question in almost every trial. At times, the answer is easy: the defendant may be the only one who can supply a vital element of testimony, or may make an excellent witness on his or her own behalf; alternatively, it may be essential to keep the defendant off the stand because certain injurious information is available to the other side only if the defendant testifies. When the decision is less clear, the behavioral consultant may be asked for advice. Our view is that generally, it is better for the defendant to testify, although occasionally we make a contrary recommendation. Jurors want to hear the defendant's own statements, and try though they may not to, they believe the silent defendant has something to hide. This attribution is particularly marked in potential jurors who would qualify in capital cases, that is, those who say they would consider giving the death penalty (Fitzgerald & Ellsworth, 1984). Therefore, in considering behavioral factors of a defendant-witness, one must also consider the characteristics of the jurors and of the defendant. Available experimental research concerning the defendant who does not testify is of less guidance here than is a careful psychological analysis of the actual trial circumstances.[1]

The Evidence Itself

How much do the facts of the case affect jurors' decisions? Prominent trial attorneys like former President of the Association of Trial Lawyers of America Michael Colley (1981) aver that impressions and not content decide cases; juror interviews (e.g., Austin, 1982) can be cited to support this contention. How are those impressions conveyed by the content of the information given to jurors? By such factors as the amount of information and its figure-ground quality, the timing of presentation of facts, the language used, and the emotional content of the message.

The facts available to the attorney and the theory of the case determine what will be presented to jurors. The consultant must know both and should select a few major points, essential to the conclusions desired of the jurors, to be stressed. These few elements provide the framework on which all supporting information should hang. The case determines these facts; the law may affect their relevance. For example, if the jurors must believe the fire started from faulty wiring in the wall of the restaurant and not at an unattended stove, that it smoldered for several hours, and then intensely and quickly engulfed the dining room, a few major, essential facts should be the illuminated points of evidence. Three or four key elements deserve special focus; the rest of the evidence is built to support these few conclusions. The message received by the jurors must be well-punctuated and clear.

Social psychological research on attitudinal consequences of persuasion shows that punctuation that provides conclusions is usually more effective than is presentation of clear arguments that leave conclusions to be drawn by the audience. This is a principle not easily followed in the courtroom; attorneys ask the questions and witnesses answer them; inferences or conclusions are often left for the jurors. (The exception is the expert witness, who offers both his opinions and conclusions.) The way in which evidence is presented can enhance the point of the testimony, which is the conclusions the jurors should reach, by the timing and the emphasis of its content. In addition, according to some analyses (Petty & Cacioppo, 1981), there is an advantage to prompting an audience to draw its own conclusions, when it is both able and inclined to do so (see Box 6.2).

The most effective order for presentation of evidence is an aspect of the content of social influence that is of natural interest to trial counsel. We can distinguish gross order within the trial, that is, who goes first and who goes second, from internal order within a smaller segment, that is, the way in which testimony within the case-in-chief of either side is ordered. The climactic versus anticlimactic ordering within the testimony of a single witness is a still smaller unit. The breadth of the unit of focus is conceptually arbitrary as long as it is psychologically meaningful.

Social psychologists' discussions (Hovland, 1958; Lind, 1982; Saks & Hastie, 1978) of theory and research on primacy/recency seem to be cast at times in terms of the entire trial and at others to be aimed at the closing arguments alone. Research on this aspect of content in social influence has been done on impression formation (e.g., Luchins, 1957) and on persuasion as well (e.g., Miller & Campbell, 1959). The communication framework and the persuasion literature may come quickly to mind, but that focus is much too narrow for the circumstances, which command a social influence perspective. If we concentrate on persuasion, as distinct from other forms of social influence, it can be argued (Lawson, 1969) that the only segment of the trial that is directly relevant is the closing argument (discussed later). The advocate's effort is always to convince the jury; persuasion and other means are used to do it, and the consultant should not make use of only the persuasion literature.

Gross order effects in the presentation of evidence are determined by procedural law: the plaintiff/prosecution goes first in the opening, the case-in-chief, and sometimes in the closing arguments, although in some jurisdictions the defense goes first in the latter. When the prosecution is first in the closing, it is usually also last, with the defense appearing in between. However, choices are permitted in the ordering of facts and arguments within one's case as to sequence of witnesses, content of testimony for each witness, and issues within the closing statement. Which has the greater impact, ideas presented first (a primacy effect), or those that come last (a recency effect)?

Experimental research (see McGuire, 1969; Petty & Caciappo, 1981; Zimbardo et al., 1977) reveals that the answers are not simple; it depends in part on the timing of persuasion and the assessment of effects (Miller & Campbell, 1959). For example, a primacy effect is observed when each side follows the other closely in time and the effects are assessed after some time has passed. Recency occurs when there is a time interval between the two sides but none between the second presentation and the assessment of opinions. Impression formation literature (Luchins, 1957), shows that forewarnings about a second point of view to come reduces a primacy effect. In addition, Lind (1982) points out that research on decisions about general issues typically shows recency effects, whereas primacy effects are more likely to be found when personal characteristics are studied. Finally, experiments on mock juries (Thibaut & Walker, 1975) show strong recency effects in the presentation of simulated evidence; one interpretation of such results is that subjects wait to hear the second side before making up their minds. Our impressions are that jurors do not suspend judgment very long at trial, and that they engage in something akin to hypothesis testing with incoming information, perhaps even biasing that information toward their personal structuring of the case. Various research leads us to conclude that facts or arguments presented either first or last will have a distinct advantage over those presented in between.

The internal ordering of facts can be framed as climax and anticlimax, as building to a strongest element late in the presentation versus hitting with the strongest fact first. A decision in a particular case should rely on the facts and circumstances at hand. If presenting the strongest fact first leaves some jurors unattentive thereafter because they accede to your conclusions, they may miss the full effect of your other facts and be less able to defend their position later in deliberations. Under such circumstances, it would be better to keep jurors' attention and to build to a climax with the strongest element. When the strongest fact presented first is likely to increase jurors' attention to what follows, an anticlimax order is preferred. Begam (1980) illustrates this reasoning with a hypothetical personal injury case in which plaintiff was struck by a driver who was drunk, speeding, and ran a red light:

> I would suggest that the first thing you do is let the jury know that in this case your (attorney's plaintiff/client) was injured because the other driver failed to yield the right-of-way and the cars came together. In addition to that, the other driver was not looking. On top of that he was going too fast. On top of that he ran a red light. Beyond anything else he was drunk. (p. 37)

Hearing first that the driver was drunk, the jurors may not hear the rest of the story.

Attorneys will often know from either the discovery process preceding trial or the voir dire that the other side will introduce one or more facts about the consultant's case that are weaknesses. Attorneys usually believe that it is advantageous to bring out one's own weaknesses before one's adversary does, allowing oneself the opportunity to interpret the weaknesses and to project an appearance of balance and fairness in presentations (Begam, 1980). Social psychological research (McGuire, 1969; Petty & Cacioppo, 1981) indicates that two-sided presentations (communications that include not only arguments for one's own conclusions but also a recognition of the other side's points, which would include one's own weaknesses) are more effective in changing opinions than are one-sided communications when the audience is initially opposed to your conclusions or when the audience is especially intelligent. Two-sidedness is not only more effective in persuading people to the communicator's point of view, but also serves to make the audience resistant to subsequent opposing arguments and conclusions.

The behavioral consultant must attend carefully to the language style and content of attorneys and witnesses. Because language permits varied descriptions of the same event or object, significant variation in meaning can be conveyed by the choices made. Was it an "encounter," an "exchange," or an "argument?" Did the person "leave" or "flee from" the scene? Such variations have effects on perception and memory for experimental subjects (Loftus, 1979), and probably affect jurors as well. Furthermore, speech styles may be used to judge credibility or to reach conclusions about deservingness. Studies of actual courtroom language by O'Barr and his colleagues (O'Barr, 1982) indicate the weight of speech styles on judgments about the speakers. Careful witness preparation on such matters can strengthen considerably the message delivered in the courtroom. Some highlights from this research relevant to the courtroom are provided by Andrews (1983).

Box 6.2 summarizes some of the major findings from experimental research on message factors that affect attitude change through persuasion.

Box 6.2. Message Factors That Affect Persuasion

Fear Appeals

In persuasion, the use of fear may be more effective if the audience is persuaded that (a) a very severely negative state of affairs (b) is likely to befall them unless (c) they take steps that are explicitly described in the message.

One-sided versus Two-sided Messages

A one-sided message from a single source is a communication containing only the communicator's arguments and conclusions; a two-sided communication contains arguments from the other side that are refuted in turn by argument. One-sided arguments are more effective only with audiences who already agree with the conclusions or who know little about the topic. Otherwise two-sided communications are better.

Audiences who may generate more thoughts on the topic (more intelligent, informed, or highly motivated) after hearing a two-sided communication will be less susceptible to subsequent counterarguments.

Order of Presentation: Primacy/Recency

With both sides presenting their own arguments, is it better to speak first, or to have the last word? Strong recency effects are shown by experiments that attempt to mirror trial characteristics; other research suggests that recency effects depend on (a) the interval between the first and the second communication, and (b) the length of time that elapses between second arguments and assessment of attitudinal effects. With a delay between the arguments and measurement of the effects right after the second communication, it is better to speak second. If the arguments are presented one after the other, with a delay in assessment of the effects, it is better to speak first. For other combinations, neither side has the advantage.

Style: Powerful Speech

Speakers who qualify their statements with phrases such as "kind of," and "sort of," are less effective.

Distraction

Mild distraction during persuasion increases its effectiveness.

Drawing Conclusions

It is better to draw conclusions if the audience is unable (e.g., does not have the competence to deal with the message) or is unwilling to draw its own conclusions; if the audience is both willing and competent, it is advantageous to have the audience draw its own conclusions.

Jurors as an Audience
React to the Evidence

Between the time a jury is sworn and the time it begins to deliberate, it occupies a unique position as an audience: jurors will spend hours, days, or even weeks listening to opening statements, evidence, and closing arguments under the directive to talk to no one about what they have heard and seen. They are not allowed (in most jurisdictions) to seek clarification of the issues by asking questions of attorneys, witnesses, parties, or the judge during this period. They are to form their views in psychological isolation, neither influencing nor being influenced by others. Our sentiments usually are not formed in this way, and this peculiarity of opinion formation in jurors has not been studied as a phenomenon, and we do not know its real implications. However, a curious paradox exists: in the opinion formation stage, jurors are like experimental subjects who are exposed to an attempt at social influence and who are not permitted to explore their ideas with others before being asked what they feel. Have social psychologists always been studying social influence, including communication, persuasion, and attitude change, in circumstances that mimic the isolation of the predeliberation juror?

Are there juror characteristics that influence attention, comprehension, acceptance, and retention, processes that should be important during this opinion formation phase of the trial and affect deliberation behavior and voting? It is obvious from our discussion of jury deselection (chapter 3) that we believe the constitution of a jury is important. As much as possible, we try to fit the jury to the case by eliminating during voir dire jurors who are dispositionally opposed at the outset, such as those who are conviction-prone in a criminal proceeding. This tactic has limited success because dismissals for cause are at the discretion of the judge, and peremptory challenges in most jurisdictions are few, especially in civil cases. Even in criminal cases in which each side has more than 20 peremptory challenges, this number is attenuated; in such cases, judges tend to sustain fewer motions for cause dismissals, apparently believing that the relatively high number of peremptories will eliminate questionable jurors. After the necessarily incomplete efforts to eliminate potentially contrary jurors, the strategy becomes an effort to tailor presentation of the facts to the particular individuals in the jury box.

Research (Davis, Bray, & Holt, 1977) on the social and psychological characteristics of jurors or mock jurors and verdicts or group decisions is generally interpreted as revealing that juror states and traits do not influence verdicts.[2] However, with the exception of Kaplan (1982), this research does not address the potential benefits of appeals tailored to the characteristics of jurors. Attitudes serve several major functions in adjustment (Katz & Stotland, 1959; Kelman, 1958; Smith, Bruner, & White, 1956), and functional analysis of attitudes leads to the conclusion that motives underlying attitudes should be considered when attempts are made to change the attitudes. For example, jurors concerned largely with the social anchorage of attitudes will be responsive to appeals different from those that interest jurors whose relevant attitudes are formed because of their implications for central values. Content and style of evidence and argument should be directed consistently at the personal concerns of the jurors on the case.

Information about jurors is obtained in several ways in the usual trial. First, the juror questionnaire and voir dire reveal much information about each juror, and a profile can be developed. Second, in-court observation provides nonverbal clues about reactions to the attorneys, the witnesses, and the evidence. These observations depend on differential response to the contestants, focusing on attentiveness, interest, and signs of approval or disapproval. Jurors who have made up their minds will tend to show less interest in what the disfavored side is presenting, letting their gaze roam around the room or appearing preoccupied with their own thoughts. The opposite is true when the favored side is presenting or making a point. This kind of diagnosis is difficult and tenuous, but can be combined with other bits of information to permit defensible speculations. The social interaction among jurors when not in court is also helpful information: What groups form in the hallways? Who leaves and who arrives with whom? Are there social isolates? In long trials especially, we can expect that people of like dispositions will associate with one another, making it possible for the consultant to infer the leanings of more inscrutable jurors from associated, more transparent ones.

During the evidence and argument phase the attorney can talk more directly to a few of the jurors, especially those who are opposed or who are the potential opinion leaders. A sociogram can be useful in considering the possible effects of such a strategy. Care should be taken not to overlook the other jurors in the box.

A juror characteristic to be utilized during closing arguments is commitment previously obtained from a juror during voir dire to fairness and impartiality for the defendant/plaintiff. The commitment should be a behavioral commitment, a public statement if possible. Jurors should be reminded of their agreement. The substance of the agreement should be a commitment not to hold a particular feature of the defendant/plaintiff or the case against the party. The entire jury should be reminded, but particular sensitivity should be used with those jurors for whom consistency between their dispositions and behaviors is seemingly important.

Closing Arguments

The closing argument is the first full-scale opportunity for the advocate to integrate the evidence, address the issues, and put the best face on the advocate's side of the case for the jury. Evidence will have been introduced in bits and pieces, fragments organized to some degree by their nature and order. However, no integrative comment, no connective words or phrases, no explicit interpretation by the witnesses or attorneys or the judge is presented with the evidence. It is a montage, often assembled in very slow motion, and the glue for the pieces is supplied wholly by the juror.

Much of the structure for the evidence and the relative importance of the different pieces of evidence have been left to the juror during the evidence phase. Testimonial facts are not interpreted until the closing; therefore, their meaning may be unclear. Important facts may not be remembered; if they are, their significance may be missed. Jurors will have a theory of the case, however, and most of them will have reached conclusions, based on feelings and their own conception of what has happened. Because of an overload of information and confusion about factual importance, feelings and partially evaluated propositions hold sway at the end of the evidence phase.

Two major goals of the closing, then, should be to simplify the evidence and to highlight differential importance. The attorney should pick the few essential points and mold the evidence around them, simplifying the issues for jurors and helping them evaluate the evidence. One must address one's own weaknesses and the opposition's strengths, counterarguing them as fully as possible because jurors often are actively thinking about an adversary's points while an advocate raises his or her own. The strong arguments by Thibaut and Walker (1975), based on their laboratory experiments for recency effects, suggest that a climax internal ordering is strongest; in any given case, a judgment should be based on the technical nature of the evidence and the apparent motivation of the jurors.

In closing arguments, one should tailor the appeals used to the salient motives of the jurors and pay particular attention to the likely concerns of jurors who may be supportive in the deliberations. Just as the evidence can be presented with an eye toward the sensitivities of the jury, so can the closing be handled, at least in part, by covering the available arguments well and giving special attention to those that may strike a responsive cord with a particular jury. If the reputation of some witnesses and the inconsistency of the facts are both to be addressed, a decision as to which is more important to the specific jury under the circumstances may suggest emphases in the arguments.

Jurors who are likely to be spokespersons for the consultant's side in the deliberations should receive special attention. The attorney should attempt to reach each of the jurors through eye contact, body language, and individual attention during the closing. Extra emphasis, with particular points in the presentation, can be directed to opinion leaders and socially influential members of the jury.

Instructions to the Jury

The trial judge instructs the jurors on the law they must apply to the facts in the case to reach a verdict or set a penalty. However, this instruction comes after the jury has heard the evidence and the closing arguments, all of which they must use in making their decision. Without knowing the law as they make up their minds about the facts, it is hard for jurors to know just where to focus their attention in the panorama of points made by attorneys and witnesses; the emphases supplied in the questions of attorneys can be lost or confusing if the reasons for them are not apparent. Jurors resemble carpenters who, not having seen the plans for a house, are asked to evaluate a load of wood from the lumber yard as sufficient material to construct it. Occasionally, to facilitate jurors' evaluation of the facts, we have recommended that the judge be requested to give part of the instructions to the jury before the evidence is heard. In all fairness, the judge knows few facts of the case at the outset and may find it difficult to determine exactly what instructions are appropriate. Elwork, Sales, and Alfini (1977) have suggested the potential of this approach, based on their research on comprehension of judges' instructions (see also Kassin & Wrightsman, 1979, and Prettyman, 1960, who, as a judge, suggested the idea long ago). The value of pre-instructed jurors can be seen by considering that in almost all trials, jurors are asked to make distinctions contained in law spelled out after the evidence phase and final arguments (e.g., murder punishable by death vs. manslaughter), and to relate such distinctions to the facts of the trial. (Was the killing premeditated or was it committed in the heat of passion?) The preinstructed juror should be better prepared for necessary decisions if rules they must later follow are made clear before the evidence is heard. It is of some value to the defense to have the jurors think about distinctions in the law that suggest or allow alternative interpretations of the facts.

The Jurors Deliberate

Is the verdict already determined by the cast of mind of the jurors when they enter the juryroom? Will the extant views of the majority of individual jurors, arrived at in isolation during the trial, predetermine the jury verdict? Research (Kalven & Zeisel, 1966) based on interviews with actual jurors indicates an affirmative answer. Their study, with unanimous decision rules and 12-person juries, revealed that the verdict in ~90% of the cases was presaged by the initial ballot: a majority for guilt eventually yielded a guilty verdict; a minority for guilt predicted acquittals. Experimental research (Davis, Bray, & Holt, 1977) reveals that in laboratory groups a two-thirds majority on predeliberation opinions typically points to the ultimate group outcome.[3]

Is there no real-life Henry Fonda who, as in "Twelve Angry Men," persuades his 11 companions that they are wrong? Not often, apparently, but the possibility exists; consultants must remember an important consideration regarding the discussions of juries.

In actual juries, the first ballot does not necessarily precede discussion; the jury determines the sequence. When balloting occurs before formal discussion, jurors can and do express or exchange views prior to discussion, perhaps eagerly—after having been gagged for the duration of the trial. Jurors have reported that there are exchanges of views or exclamations made before any formal deliberation begins. We hear of comments such as, "We'll all be safer with him off the streets," or "I'll never vote guilty on this one." How much comment and discussion occurs before the first ballot and how much it influences voting and verdicts has not been determined.

Jurors are not created equal in deliberation (or, perhaps, in anything else). Gender, socioeconomic status, occupation, and personality determine participation rates and social influence in decision-making. Research on actual juries (Dillehay & Nietzel, 1985; Kerr, 1981; Werner, Strube, Cole, & Kagehiro, 1982) shows that men are chosen most often as forepersons, as are experienced jurors and those who have previously been forepersons (Dillehay & Nietzel, 1985). Do people in such positions exert more than average influence? Experimental research shows that they do (see Hastie, Penrod, & Pennington, 1983; Nemeth, 1980).

Evidence and arguments can be partially tailored to juror characteristics; to the extent that tailoring is successful, one can expect to have advocates in the jury room. As first priority, each individual juror should be convinced of the merits of the advocate's position, before all jurors share their views. Alternatively, an advocate should attempt to create willing spokespersons among the jurors.

NOTES

[1]In capital murder cases, it is vital that the defendant either testify or reach out to the jury in some other communication fashion, either during voir dire, the opening statement, or the closing arguments to counteract tendencies of a jury to view silent defendants as less than human. The perceived human qualities of the defendant are vital during the penalty phase when the jurors decide on life or death.

[2]Research reviewed by Dane and Wrightsman (1982) also indicates that defendant and victim characteristics are only weakly related to group decisions of mock jurors or verdicts of actual jurors. They note important exceptions.

[3]These and other more complex prediction models for alternative degrees of guilty verdicts are described by Hastie, Penrod, and Pennington (1983).

Chapter 7
Evaluation and Professional Issues

Like many other human endeavors, trial consultation is an art that relies on a blend of science, experience, and personal characteristics of the consultant. Psychology and other behavioral disciplines are the source of principles which describe behavior and its determinants, providing a scientific knowledge base for the consultant. Although we have discussed several of these principles in preceding chapters, they are not in a form that can be simply and directly applied in the complex social circumstances of the consultant, distant as they are from the settings in which the behavioral generalizations were themselves developed. Through training and experience, the consultant must develop the perspicacity essential to selection and selective application of those generalizations. In turn, good consultation provides opportunity for learning the utility of principles of behavior, the important variations in settings, and methods of assessing one's efforts to produce intended behavioral effects in jurors and others. Ethical considerations which arise also must be kept in focus. In this chapter, we discuss these several matters.

EPISTEMOLOGY AND THE BEHAVIORAL CONSULTANT

Our accounts of our own consultations reveal our perspective on epistemology for the behavioral consultant. This volume delineates a reliance on three sources of knowledge for consultation: *basic science* in social psychology, psychology, and sociology; *applied science*, primarily in the same disciplines but also including the work of anthropologists; and *"clinical" experience* with participants in legal matters and actual cases. Each of these sources encompasses assumptions about ways to acquire valid knowledge for forensic psychological practice. In addition, we use knowledge from and about law, both its procedural and its substantive aspects, although this knowledge differs qualitatively from the rest since law is prescriptive rather than descriptive. Law exists because systems of authority have created it; its validity is achieved by interpretive internal rule. In contrast, the truth of behavioral propositions depends on correspondence with the natural phenomena to which they are applied.

Basic Science as a Knowledge Base

Overall, the behavioral sciences seek to develop principles of behavior, with overlapping specialization in terms of individual, social, organizational, institutional, or cultural foci. Even those (Sampson, 1983) who argue that modal nomothetic science is misguided seem to assert that a proper understanding of human actions can be attained by examination of behavioral uniformities. As psychologist consultants, we are no exception. In this book, we make numerous references to research on such topics as detection of deception, attitude formation and change, attribution, and social power that are taken from the core of psychology, especially from social psychology. Such research is often termed basic to differentiate it from applied research. We prefer to call it disciplinary research (Ford, 1977) to indicate that it is conducted with respect to advancing general knowledge within a discipline. The impetus for the work derives from the ideas of the field in which it is done, and its most prominent audience consists of colleagues in the discipline of the investigator. The value connotations of the appellation "basic" make it a less desirable descriptor. Our reliance on these literatures bespeaks a belief in disciplinary research as a path to knowledge that is useful in understanding and changing behavior in legal settings.

Several criteria must be satisfied by disciplinary research before one can consider its applicability to the law. These criteria are the tests of good science (Cook & Campbell, 1979): statistical conclusion validity, construct validity, internal validity, and external validity. Although psychologists and other scientists are trained to read research reports critically, they rely heavily on stringent and thorough editorial review to forestall publication of inadequate research, work that does not meet at least the first three criteria listed above. The fourth criterion—external validity—is often another matter.

External validity is a question of generalizability to persons, situations, and times other than those investigated in the research. It presupposes internal validity and requires that there be no interaction between the variables manipulated or measured in the research and variations in persons, places, and times. External validity demands that the explanations for the effects hold regardless of such variations. Frequently, however, boundary conditions for effects are not well explored. However, as conceptual replications and related variations are published and a research literature is integrated, we can be more confident of the surviving principles of behavior.

The persons, places, and times encountered by consultants in trial preparation and conduct are typically different from those used in research. How do we know that the principles apply to the settings we face? The answer must be that an assessment of these settings reveals no apparent reasons to suspect that the determinants of behavior are different from those in the circumstances of research. This judgment demands perceptual acumen, careful reasoning, and a broad knowledge of the determinants of behavior. Thus, for example, a consultant must be able to judge whether similarity in the situation between jurors and a plaintiff will induce attraction and sympathy or aversion and rejection. Research shows both results.

To address the matter of applicability to legal settings, researchers have attempted to create structural verisimilitude (Diamond, 1979) in their research. That is, psychologists and others have tried to make the language and actions in research sound and appear like those of the courtroom. Instead of investigating the effects of order or arguments on attitude change, for example, they have studied the effects of "prosecution and defense" arguments on jurors' judgments of "guilt" of "defendants." None of the research is ecologically authentic, since the experiments are contrived. The results of this experimental, laboratory research are treated as though they were based on observations of actual jurors and represent generalizations about jurors that bypass serious questions about external validity. The difference between generalizations about behavior based on research on actual trials and research based on mock-ups in the laboratory is ignored or minimized.

Serious problems result from this practice, both in the research that is done and in its application (Dillehay & Nietzel, 1980a, 1980b). Because of the language used to describe the experiments, researchers and others conclude that something is learned about jurors, courts, judges, and trials, whereas the most that can be gained from such research is an understanding of psychological and social processes. The latter objective may be compromised in the research itself because the requisite conceptualization and methods for the investigation of perception, cognition, attitudes, interpersonal processes, group decision-making, etc. are overlooked in favor of legal terms (defendant, judge, etc.) and superficial similarities to trial proceedings (reading a synopsis of a case, watching a videotape of a dramatized trial, etc.). We discuss these problems and their solutions at length elsewhere (Dillehay & Nietzel, 1980a, 1980b). Mock trial or mock jury research can be valuable as a means of understanding psychological processes if proper theory and methods are used in the experiment. Often, they are not (see Ebbesen & Konecni, 1975 for a discussion of a related issue).

Policy-Action Research as a Source of Knowledge

We designate investigations of actual jurors, courts, defendants, victims, and trials as policy-action research rather than applied research. Such investigations will always be nonexperimental, making use of such methods as interviews or questionnaires involving participants in the legal arena and observations of their behavior, or archival analyses of information created in the operation of the legal system. These investigations shed less light on alternative, specific psychological and social processes that produce effects in the legal system; as a result we will acquire knowledge about attitudes, perceptions, and group decision-making that is more ambiguous than that derived from experiments. However, what we discover in sound policy-action research has direct relevance for outcomes in the system. Done well, this is research "at the scene."

The Contribution of Experience

Attention to important behavioral factors in a case, analysis of their implications, formulation of consultation strategy and tactics, execution of the plans, and assessment of their effects are skills that depend on practice and benefit from feedback. One learns very quickly that guesses about wide variations in the character and behavior of judges are correct, and that what is done in one courtroom is not necessarily done in another. Experience also teaches us that some considerations may be overriding, taking precedence over others that should be assessed. A venue change is one such consideration. We have found that implicit community pressure may be so great that even the most independent, self-assured, seemingly rational jury can be swayed toward a popular decision, accepting arguments and evidence that would not normally affect them. Such experience can best be acquired through supervised activities or through collaboration with another veteran professional. We found it highly informative to do our early work as a pair, acquiring not only a second perspective but much more observational coverage—two heads, four eyes, and four ears are better than half as many in and around the court. There is also much to be said for doing research on trial issues, perhaps with attorney collaboration, in the courtroom rather than in the laboratory; it provides valuable experience for the consultant.

ASSESSING THE EFFECTS OF CONSULTATION

It is very difficult to determine successful behavioral consultation. The problems are both definitional and practical. What are the conceptual criteria by which to gauge whether the consultant has performed well?

Shall we define success in terms of process or effects? If process is the focus by which success is determined, what are the actions and interactions to be considered? If we conceptualize success in terms of outcomes, how large a unit should be used—a witness's testimony? The verdict or changes in attorney behavior? Operations to be selected for the definition adopted must correspond faithfully to the concept selected and must be accessible and reliable.

Is it reasonable to believe that successful consultation can be measured at all, given the complexities of consulting and the inherent ambiguities in most indices? Moreover, is it likely that there will be opportunity for evaluation in the fast, fluid, task-centered environment of trial work, where the farthest thing from the trial lawyer's mind is an adequate evaluation of behavioral intervention? For the attorney, the ultimate measure of success is the verdict or settlement, weighed by some subjective calculus of emotion and reason that defines what was indeed possible given the facts in the case. Getting the best result possible is not an unreasonable standard for an attorney, although conceptually and practically it may be difficult to determine what that result is.[1] The behavioral consultant should not use the trial outcome as a reasonable determination of performance of work, although reputations are based in part on such outcomes. Invariably, in the course of working with a new attorney, we are asked how effective we have been in previous work, in which case the definition of effectiveness is determined by the nature of the case (e.g., success often may be a result less than the death penalty in capital cases, or a finding of no negligence in a civil case). The issue of successful work is quite real and important, however, no matter what the difficulty in its determination. Because the targets of change are the attorney and witnesses whose behaviors the consultant attempts to modify in some way (a new sequence of testimony, an alternative mode of presentation, or a new form of questioning), these behaviors serve as a point of departure for assessing effects.

The social structure of the consultation circumstances varies by case. Usually, the behavioral consultant's client is the attorney, not the party to the dispute, who is in all cases the attorney's client. The work of the behavioral consultant is done for and provided to counsel. However, some interaction with the attorney's client (the plaintiff or defendant) will always occur, and in civil cases in which witness preparation with the litigant is extensive, much contact necessarily occurs. Despite such interaction, case management decisions are always made by the attorney.

This basic social structure of psycholegal consultation represents only the most rudimentary of relationships. The situation in most trials will be more complex. Often, there is more than one attorney, paralegals frequently are participants, several parties may be your attorney's clients, and a spouse or other relative of the litigant may participate substantially. Some or all of these individuals may be targets of behavioral intervention in a given case.

The first level of effects of interventions with these targets is to be found in the behaviors of the targets themselves, which is the most logical place to look for evidence of successful consultation. Do the attorneys modify their questioning in keeping with your efforts? Are witnesses better able to respond to questions during cross-examination? Do the attorneys include evidence of the kind you suggest for the jury at hand? These effects are highly visible, often easily determined, and form the basis of subsequent interventions during preparation for trial. With witnesses, the consultant can frequently use videotape to compare before and after samples of behavior. Linking these local effects with trial outcome is as difficult as it is to tie efforts of attorneys to jurors' decisions. Reasonable investigative steps can often be taken, however, to determine whether the consultant was correct in anticipating certain effects in the jurors from events that the consultant tried to create at trial.

Jurors are probably the most important ultimate source of evaluation information. By various methods, we and other trial consultants often get information from the jurors about their perceptions of the facts, the participants, and the deliberation process. Only jurors can supply a view of the trial from the perspective of fact-finders, and what they reveal can be surprising and illuminating. Their comments are often especially appropriate to assessment of the effects of behavioral consultation; almost everything the trial consultant does is designed to affect jurors' perceptions, attitudes, deliberation behaviors, and voting. One juror's view of what occurred may not agree with another juror's perceptions and recollections; therefore, consultants are fortunate to have up to 12 separate sources of information to use in piecing together trial impact.

Several categories of information are available from jurors who consent to be interviewed, categories that vary in their applicability to important questions. The major categories of information may be designated as (a) the juror as observer, (b) the juror as naive psychologist, and (c) the juror as barometer.

The juror can serve as *an observer of trial events* that are not accessible to the consultant or, in some instances, to the attorney, such as behavior during deliberations, which can be directly observed only by jurors. Interactions among jurors during breaks and before and after court time and courtroom events that occur when the consultant is not present are also observed only by jurors. The consultant may be interested in conversations among jurors, the time of first ballot, the breakdown of votes, the pieces of evidence which received most attention during deliberations, arguments used by jurors in efforts to persuade their fellows, etc. Such information is a recounting of events, a description that is as similar to the objective as possible: raw facts, uninterpreted by the observer.

The juror can also serve as *a naive psychologist*, providing a layperson's perspective on causal sequences of events and the determinants of relevant behaviors. Significant portions of social psychology deal with naive psychology, examining the layperson's interpretation of behavior (Heider, 1958; Kelley & Michela, 1980). The test of veridicality in juror's perceptions can be consensus; disagreements can be diagnostic as well.

As a third category of information, juror self-report is a source of the impact of trial events which serves as *a barometer*, revealing the success of important consultant efforts. Perceptions, cognitions, feelings, dispositions, and evaluations can be assessed with jurors just as with others, with proper safeguards to protect against demand characteristics and social desirability effects. As in other contexts, one can also ask jurors to tell why they acted as they did, although it is doubtful whether individuals can identify accurately the actual causes of their own behavior (Nisbett & Wilson, 1977). By use of proper interviewing technique, however, one can obtain useful information about the results of behavioral interventions from juror self-report.

Before the consultant interviews jurors after trial, the legal status of follow-up interviews with jurors in the particular jurisdiction should be determined. Some jurisdictions, such as Oregon, statutorily or by rules of court, prohibit juror interviews by the trial attorneys or their representatives at the conclusion of a case. Some local jurisdictions have a comparable court order, as in Lexington, Kentucky, where five of the six judges in the Circuit Court have signed an order prohibiting juror interviews by parties. Interviewing the jurors of a trial in which you were involved may lead to contempt actions or other criminal prosecution.

Legislators and courts have been clear in their concerns to protect jurors. One reason for such protection is that the deliberation process could be affected if jurors believed that the privacy of the jury room was seriously threatened (*Harvard Law Review*, 1983; Sharp, 1983; *United States v. Driscoll,*[2] 1967). Knowing that they may be questioned about their verdict, jurors may be reluctant to reach decisions that are unpopular although warranted by the facts. Judges are also concerned that potential jurors, fearing publicity, may be reluctant to serve, making it difficult to impanel fair and impartial jurors who represent a cross-section of the community. Yet another reason cited for controlling post-verdict contact with jurors is protection of jurors from the prying interests of counsel and others who wish to learn more about the deliberation process that occurred, whether to present an account of it to a wider audience, whether their speculations about important influences on the jurors are correct, or whether there are indications of juror misconduct that may be a basis for retrial. The individual right to privacy is cited (see Sharp, 1983) as one basis for insulating jurors from posttrial interviews, with the view that this right is as fundamental as those that are spelled out in the Constitution. Although the nature and extent of the right to privacy are not clear, neither are the matters of how and by whom this right can be asserted.

Statutory and case law on posttrial interviews with jurors has arisen concerning: (a) the tension between first amendment rights of the press to obtain and publish information on the one hand, and juror harassment, annoyance, and privacy on the other; (b) interests of the parties in determining whether a fair trial, free of juror misconduct, has occurred; (c) interests of the parties in learning about juror reaction to evidence and individuals in the trial in anticipation of further litigation, either in a retrial or with other similar cases; and (d) scientific interest in the nature of the deliberative process.

Litigation on the issue of first amendment freedoms of the press is generally interpreted as providing a broad latitude for gathering information and discouraging judicial restrictions (American Bar Association Journal, 1983; Sharp, 1983).

Statutory (Rule 606(b), Federal Rules of Evidence) and case law (e.g., United States v. Cauble,[3] 1982) on the point of determining juror misconduct specify the circumstances under which jurors may be questioned, under the supervision of the court, and the matters on which they may not be queried. Thus, Rule 606(b) provides:

> A juror may not testify as to any matter or statement occurring during the course of the jury's deliberations or to the effect of anything upon his or any other juror's mind or emotions as influencing him to assent to or dissent from the verdict or indictment or concerning his mental processes in connection therewith, except that a juror may testify on the question whether extraneous prejudicial information was improperly brought to the jury's attention or whether any outside influence was improperly brought to bear upon any juror.

One can easily see the potential for abuse by parties who desire a jury issue in order to upset a verdict and gain a new trial.

With a retrial already pending, owing to a hung jury or to some other cause of mistrial, attorneys may wish to interview jurors to learn about the impact of evidence on juror decisions specific to the issues in the case, and it is not uncommon for behavioral scientists or other investigators to be retained to gather relevant information. In such instances, all three kinds of information discussed above will be relevant to the inquiry.

Although not new (see chapter 1, and Loh, 1984), postverdict research with jurors has intensified dramatically in the last 15 years for several probable reasons: the involvement of behavioral scientists in jury selection leads naturally to an examination of their theories about juror behavior; social scientists during the 1970s responded to exhortations, initially from student activists, to become involved with social and political issues, and concern with the jury trial became relevant; social science in civil litigation has become a growth industry, with millions of dollars at stake and resources sufficient to leave no stone unturned, including jury analysis, in the conduct of trials and preparation for future cases. Undoubtedly, postverdict research on jury behavior has not yet had its full impact on legal response to protect the integrity of the jury, because the factors requisite to an effective system, such as the free exchange of ideas in the deliberation process and the protection of the privacy of individual jurors, have not been trammeled. Neither has society's need for final resolution of disputes been thwarted by social research. Instead, in the legal literature, one encounters concern with abuses by litigants seeking jury misconduct issues for retrial and with free press/fair trial tensions. However, an historical object lesson regarding the legal system's response to social science research that may be a harbinger for postverdict jury investigations can also be found.

In the mid-1950s, members of the research team of the Chicago Jury Project, with judicial approval, recorded jury deliberations in an effort to study jury dynamics. The jurors did not know they were being recorded. This study was only one of a number of investigations that used interviews, questionnaires, and experimental methods to examine diverse behavioral issues in the law (Broeder, 1958; Kalven & Zeisel, 1966; Strodtbeck, 1962). Nonetheless, public and official reaction to these recordings led promptly to an addition to the U.S. Code: Article 1506 provides for a fine of up to $1,000 and imprisonment up to 1 year for anyone who records, listens to, or observes the proceedings of grand or petit juries while they are deliberating or voting. As Sharp (1983) observes, the "rationale for maintaining absolute secrecy during jury deliberations applies with equal force when dealing with postverdict interrogation of jurors" (p. 8).

What is the social scientist or consultant who has legitimate interests in the myriad influences on jury behavior to do?

It is fortunate that the social scientist's need to understand jury behavior does not require the sacrifice of anonymity of the sources of information. In addition, in contrast to the interests of the press, the search for social science principles or behavioral intelligence for specific cases does not entail publication of information that is designed for mass appeal. Courts are concerned that inquiry for social science or specific case intelligence should not take on the adversarial and at times almost accusatory character of investigation by the parties in search of a retrial issue. The courts should recognize the importance of social science inquiries and distinguish between them and other inquiries. Postverdict access to jurors, with proper safeguards, is essential to the evaluation of the consultant's efforts. Our concern with the vitality of the jury system and the sensitivities of individual jurors, translated into care in the exercise of the craft, should preserve essential distinctions among the behavioral scientist/consultant, the press, and the parties investigating juror misconduct.

Another kind of evaluation is possible when consultants work in pairs on the litigation team. With high levels of trust, keen cooperation, mutual respect, and group rather than individual goals and reward structures, there are distinct advantages to working in tandem. Perception checking is then possible, as is comparison of adequacy of analysis and formulations of interventions. A partner can also help to clarify the complex issues that are typically encountered. Working in pairs not only provides ability to determine formative and summative success, but also affords the opportunity to manage the vagaries of scheduling with multiple parties in a system that does not yet take into account the demands on the time of behavioral consultants as well as it does those of judges and attorneys.

The assessment of behavioral interventions as a generic category invites reference to the literature on evaluation as a research process and its relationship to the use of interventions. The distinctions between formative and summative evaluation, and among context, input, process, and product as evaluation concepts (Joint Committee on Standards for Educational Evaluation, 1981) have relevance for psycholegal consultation. A formative evaluation focuses on the activities of consultants themselves to determine whether they are carrying out activities necessary to produce desired effects. A summative evaluation is a determination of the outcomes of those activities and the objectives of the consultation plan, whether it focuses on effects on the targets of change or on the results of their behaviors on the jurors' verdict. In the model of the Joint Committee, context refers to the circumstances existing at the point of initial involvement of the consultant —the behaviors of the attorney-client, the parties, the witnesses, as well as the existing plans for handling evidence. Input is the intervention plan that is developed in an effort to create the desired results. An evaluation of process effects is tantamount to a determination of whether the steps in the intervention have been successfully taken. For example, has the new order of presentation of evidence been thoroughly discussed? Have the practice sessions with the expert witness been conducted? Finally, product evaluation examines the outcomes; it is equivalent to summative evaluation. Although these formal evaluation models can be useful to the consultant as models for conceptualizing an evaluation of their work, just as are program evaluations in other domains, the most beneficial effect of the evaluation may be seen in improvements in the work itself.

ETHICAL ISSUES

In 1975, the American Psychological Association's Board of Social and Ethical Responsibility for Psychology appointed a Task Force on the Role of Psychology in the Criminal Justice System to investigate involvements of psychologists in the criminal justice system and the ethical issues arising from these involvements. Under the chairmanship of John Monahan, the Task Force formulated 12 recommendations on the major ethical issues that psychologists face in the area. These recommendations, together with background papers on psychologists working in police agencies, court settings, corrections systems, and the juvenile justice system were published as *Who Is the Client* (Monahan, 1980). Table 7.1 lists the 12 recommendations of the Task Force; many of them are relevant to the activities of the trial consultant and/or expert witness.

Ellsworth Fersch's (1980) background paper for the Task Force discusses more fully the special ethical dilemmas the psychologist faces in the courtroom. Among the thornier problems created by psychologists' participation in litigation are the following, according to Fersch.

1. Although psychologists are often used to challenge the assumptions and/or procedures relied on by the court system, at other times their involvement in the system lends tacit endorsement to current procedures that may be inimical to the best interests of an individual or society. Testifying about the inadequacy of certain voir dire methods illustrates the first principle, attempting to predict future dangerous behavior of a convicted defendant exemplifies the second. Psychologists in court risk the possibility that their testimony will be misused by others, primarily because of the adversarial nature of the system. The preamble to the *Ethical Standards of Psychologists* (1981) commits psychologists to protect against the misuse of their skills by others. In addition, Principle 4 states:

> Psychologists present the science of psychology and offer their services, products, and publications fairly and accurately, avoiding misrepresentation through sensationalism, exaggeration or superficiality.

However, one of the hallmarks of skillful cross-examination is to force certain distortions and exaggerations on the witness.

2. Assessing an individual's psychological condition as a basis for giving expert testimony about that individual's sanity, competence, or mental state entangles psychologists in several ethical snares, particularly when the person is assessed by court order. Such activity will probably conflict with Principle 3c:

> In their professional roles, psychologists avoid any action that will violate or diminish the legal and civil rights of clients or of others who may be affected by their actions.

Table 7.1. Recommended Ethical Principles for Psychologists
Working in the Criminal Justice System

Recommendation 1: Psychologists in criminal justice settings, as elsewhere, should inform all parties to a given service of the level of confidentiality that applies and should specify any circumstances that would constitute an exception to confidentiality. This should be done in advance of the service, preferably in writing.

Recommendation 2: The ideal level of confidentiality of therapeutic services in criminal justice settings should be the same as the level of confidentiality that exists in voluntary noninstitutional settings.

Recommendation 3: Other than for legitimate research purposes, psychological assessments of offenders should be performed only when the psychologist has a reasonable expectation that such assessments will serve a useful therapeutic or dispositional function.

Recommendation 4: Psychologists who work in the criminal justice system, as elsewhere, have an ethical obligation to educate themselves in the concepts and operations of the system in which they work.

Recommendation 5: Since it is not within the professional competence of psychologists to offer conclusions on matters of law, psychologists should resist pressure to offer such conclusions.

Recommendation 6: Psychologists should be clear about what they are trying to accomplish in the criminal justice system and the state of the empirical evidence in support of their ability to accomplish it.

Recommendation 7: There is an ethical obligation on psychologists who perform services in the criminal justice system, as elsewhere, to encourage and cooperate in the evaluation of those services.

Recommendation 8: Psychological research in prisons should conform to the ethical standards proposed by the National Commission for the Protection of Human Subjects.

Recommendation 9: Psychologists should be exceedingly cautious in offering predictions of criminal behavior for use in imprisoning or releasing individual offenders. A psychologist who decides that it is appropriate in a given case to provide a prediction of criminal behavior, should clearly specify (a) the acts being predicted, (b) the estimated probability that these acts will occur during a given time, and (c) the factors on which the predictive judgment is based.

Recommendation 10: Psychologists should be strongly encouraged to offer treatment services to offenders who request them.

Recommendation 11: The American Psychological Association should strongly encourage graduate and continuing education in the applied ethics of psychological intervention and research.

Recommendation 12: The American Psychological Association should take steps to increase awareness among psychologists and those with whom they work of mechanisms to investigate and act upon complaints of violations of its Ethical Standards. Formal advisory opinions should be available to psychologists who request an interpretation of the Ethical Standards in specific fact situations.

Note. From *Who is the Client?* (pp. 5–16) by J. Monahan (Ed.), 1980, Washington, D.C.: American Psychological Association. Copyright 1980 by the American Psychological Association. Used with permission of the publisher.

In the case of predicting dangerous behavior or assessing psychological status in the past, Principle 8c should inspire considerable caution in the testimony of psychologists.

> In reporting assessment results, psychologists indicate any reservations that exist regarding validity or reliability because of the circumstances of the assessment or the inappropriateness of the norms for the person tested. Psychologists strive to ensure that the results of assessments and their interpretations are not misused by others.

3. The issue of confidentiality as enunciated in Principle 5 of the *Ethical Standards* causes several problems for the psychologist, who often interviews a criminal defendant or party to a civil suit under conditions that are at least partially coercive. Principle 5 requires psychologists to avoid undue invasions of privacy and to inform clients about the limits of confidentiality, both of which may interfere with thorough, accurate evaluations. Another possible conflict occurs with Principle 8a, which states that

> In using assessment techniques, psychologists respect the right of clients to have full explanations of the nature and purpose of the techniques in language the clients can understand, unless an explicit exception to this right has been agreed upon in advance.

Fersch (1980) suggests that resolving any of these dilemmas will depend on psychologists keeping three important precepts clearly in mind:

> (1) They must be clear what role they are performing, (2) they must be aware of the limitations of that role and the conflicts it raises, and (3) they must inform all those with whom they deal of those limitations and conflicts.

In this book, we have emphasized roles that are primarily of a consulting nature, in which an individual client seeks the advice and expertise of a psychologist for the purpose of strengthening the client's position in the adversary system. The major exception to these roles occurs when the psychologist, testifying as an expert, offers testimony that may be detrimental to the person interviewed. This problem is compounded when the data for the testimony are obtained under conditions that are not fully voluntary.

In the typical consulting relationship, the client chooses to purchase the services of the consultant following a decision that those services may be beneficial to the client's case. Coercion is minimized in this type of transaction. In fact, applied to the use of forensic consultants, the principle of *caveat emptor* covers a multitude of sins.

However, not all sins are expiated by the buyer's responsibility. Psychological consultants must attend to Fersch's second and third precepts of remaining sensitive to the limits and conflicts of their roles even when those services are voluntarily contracted for and then informing clients of these problems. Several ethical principles can help to direct the consultant's behavior in this regard. For example, Principle 1a states in part, "In publishing reports of their work, (psychologists) never suppress disconfirming data, and they acknowledge the existence of alternative hypotheses and explanations of their findings," and Principle 1b continues,

> Psychologists clarify in advance with all appropriate persons and agencies the expectations for sharing and utilizing research data; they avoid relationships that may limit their objectivity or create a conflict of interest. Interference with the milieu in which data are collected is kept to a minimum.

Finally, in regard to the ways in which consultants describe the effectiveness of their work, Principle 4 states:

> Psychologists represent accurately and objectively their professional qualifications, affiliations, and functions, as well as those of the institutions or organizations with which they or the statements may be associated. In public statements providing psychological information or professional opinions or providing information about the availability of psychological products, publications, and services, psychologists base their statements on scientifically acceptable psychological findings and techniques with full recognition of the limits and uncertainties of such evidence.

It is essential that psychologists inform the attorneys and parties with whom they consult of the above limitations in their work. Although necessary, such candor is often difficult for several reasons. First, attorneys may not want to take the time to discuss such matters when faced with the time demands inherent in the life of the trial lawyer. There may also be pressure to inflate claims of consulting successes in the interests of boosting a litigant's sagging morale. At other times, real controversy exists about the effects of certain consulting activities; for example, we believe that several "ethical" summations of jury selection methods can be made, ranging from the very pessimistic to the guardedly optimistic.

The consultant is obligated to assess the willingness of attorney colleagues to respect the ethical requirements of psychologists. In most cases, an initial, forthright discussion of the ethical dilemmas posed by a certain activity should be sufficient to ensure that a satisfactory working relationship can be negotiated. When consultants are unable to work out an ethically satisfying relationship with an attorney, they will probably find it necessary to terminate work on the case or to avoid working with the attorney on future cases.

Although we can prescribe very few hard-and-fast rules for the forensic consultant, the following guidelines have served us well:

1. The consultant should not accept cases on a contingency fee basis, but should charge a fair rate based on the time spent on the case. Although it is obvious that an expert witness should not testify on a contingency

arrangement, it may not be as clear that a consultant who never appears before a jury should also avoid payment contingent on the outcome. Contingency fees run the risk of encouraging "win-at-all-costs" behavior that will inevitably place the psychologist in an ethically compromising position. Psychologists should also remember that a portion of Principle 6d of the Ethical Standards states, "(Psychologists) contribute a portion of their services to work for which they receive little or no financial return."

2. The psychologist should not testify as an expert on substantive matters before the jury in a case in which the psychologist also functions as a litigation consultant to one of the sides. Such testimony at best gives the *appearance* of conflict of interest. At worst, it is difficult to believe that the psychologist can deliver impartial testimony under such conditions, and an attempt to do so will probably be harmful to the profession and to the case.

3. The psychologist must be very careful in witness preparation work to do nothing that encourages or suggests changes in the "facts" to which a witness will testify. As discussed in chapter 5, we believe that interventions aimed at the way in which the witness presents these facts are legitimate activities. However, the line between improving the facts and improving the witnesses' presentation of them is a periously thin one: The consultant must guard against crossing or being pulled across the line. Because of this problem, we have decided not to engage in witness preparation of criminal defendants other than by commenting on the possible consequences of their physical appearance or general demeanor in the courtroom, believing that criminal defendants find themselves in a situation in which perjured testimony is a constant temptation. Even the most cautious consultant can become a part of this temptation; therefore, it is in both the defendant's and the consultant's best interests not to engage in witness preparation together.

4. The trial consultant must contend with multiple pressures to exaggerate (a) claims of competence and (b) estimates of impact. Attorneys may want some assurances that they are "better off" working with one consultant rather than another or rather than following their own instincts. The parties involved may seek a guarantee that they will win the case with the consultant's assistance. If the consultant testifies at a change of venue hearing or in support of some pretrial motion, the judge may press for more certainty in the consultant's testimony than the data warrant.

More than any other issue, we have found these temptations to oversell one's activities to pose the most difficult ethical dilemmas for the consultant. They are particularly troublesome during one's initial work with attorneys. Consultants must remain constantly aware of the way in which they represent themselves and their work. They may feel enthusiastic about what they do but should not let that enthusiasm either become or be perceived as promises of desired outcomes. The consultant is responsible for clarifying that although specific interventions aimed at specific goals will be provided, achievement of those goals cannot be guaranteed. If the consultant is requested to perform a task that she or he has performed several times before in cases somewhat similar to the instant one, the consultant can inform the client of the past "track record" associated with that function, for example, what percentage of trials have been relocated following use of the public opinion polling techniques described in chapter 3. However, even this information requires careful delivery; trial consultants do not currently know precisely which factors account for successful rather than unsuccessful outcomes. Therefore, in making statements about past results they must be careful not to connote a level of understanding or certainty that is in fact not present.

5. The question of whether the consultant can work for a criminal defendant while believing that the defendant is guilty must be resolved. We have worked for culpable defendants; thus, we cannot say that we never know whether the client is guilty. However, we trust the assumption of our legal system that the truth emerges from an adversary process. The trial consultant is but one resource that advocates can use in trying a case, and we do not believe that the availability of that resource should be restricted to clients whom we judge to be more deserving on certain a priori grounds. We feel no compulsion to accept every case but see no need to justify our acceptance of most cases.

We recognize that other consultants decide this matter differently and that their positions are ethically defensible. Some consultants choose not to work on certain types of cases (e.g., rape, child molestation) because they find the nature of the crime so offensive that they cannot in good conscience work for the interests of such a defendant. Others try to evaluate the merits of each individual case before deciding to intervene, assessing the strength of the evidence against the defendant or the probability that extraevidentiary influences may bias the proceedings against the defendant. Consultants who approach such cases may prefer to work for defendants who they think are more likely not to be guilty or who are less likely to receive a fair trial.

Trial consultants may often find themselves being asked either by colleagues or by the public to justify their working for criminal defendants who are charged with heinous offenses. The consultant must be able to respond thoughtfully to such inquiries because both the integrity of trial consultation and of psychology as a profession are being assessed. We do not believe that any one answer best certifies the integrity of either. However, consultants are obligated to understand the negative reactions prompted by their work (particularly in notorious criminal trials) and must be prepared to discuss the principles and values that legitimize the roles they perform.

NOTES

[1]Systematic research (Williams, 1983) examining the results of bargaining for settlements between experienced attorneys indicates that there is considerable variation in the dollar amounts that result. Is it reasonable to use the average of these settlements as a standard given the fact pattern in the case or would a better standard be something similar to the best settlements?

[2]276 F. Supp. 333 (1967).

[3]532 F. Supp. 804 (1982).

Appendix A:
Special Juror Questionnaire

1. Name _____
2. Age _____
3. Address _____
4. Place of birth _____
5. Other residences in past 10 years _____
6. What schools have you attended:
   a. Grade School _____
   b. High School _____
   c. College _____
   d. Vocational/Trade School _____
   e. Professional/Graduate School _____
7. Have you served in the military _____
   Branch _____   Rank _____
8. Present occupation _____
9. Present employer _____
10. Please describe your job duties: _____
   _____
11. Occupations before present employment _____
   _____
12. Marital status: Married   _____ Number of years _____
                             Separated   _____
                             Widowed   _____
                             Divorced   _____
13. If married, spouse's name _____
14. Spouse's education _____
15. Spouse's occupation _____

16. Please list other members of your immediate family:

Name	Relationship	Age	Occupation

17. Have you or has any member of your family been a victim of a crime? If so, please explain. _____

18. Are you or is any member of your family related to or a close friend of any law enforcement or prison official? If so, please describe. _____

19. Have you or has any member of your family ever worked for a law enforcement, judicial, or correctional agency? If so, please explain. ____

20. Have you ever been a witness in a criminal case? If so, please describe. _____

    In a civil case? If so, please explain. _____

21. Have you or has a member of your family ever been convicted of a crime other than a minor traffic offense? _____

22. Do you own your own home? _____ ,   Rent? _____
    Live with someone else?   _____ ,   Other _____

23. Are all the people in your neighborhood white? _____
    Black? _____   Both black and white? _____

24. Have you or has any member of your family ever been a party in a lawsuit? If so, please explain. _____

25. What church do you attend? _____

26. How often do you attend church? _____

27. (a) Have you ever served on a grand jury? _____ If so, what and when? _____

    (b) Have you ever served on a jury in a criminal case? _____ If so, what and when? _____

    (c) Have you ever served on a jury in a civil case? _____ If so, what and when? _____

28. Were any comments made to you by a member or officer of the court afterwards concerning the verdict in either the criminal or civil trial? _____ Who? _____

29. What clubs or organizations do you belong to, and what positions have you held, if any? _____

30. What do you like to do most in your spare time? _____

31. What newspapers and magazines do you read? _____

32. What type of T.V. programs do you watch most? _____

References

Adorno, T. W., Frenkel-Brunswik, E., Levinson, D. J., & Sanford, R. N. (1950). *The authoritarian personality*. New York: Harper & Row.

American Bar Association Journal. (1983). *69*, 968–969.

American Bar Association. (1978). *Standards relating to fair trial and free press* (2nd ed.). Washington, DC: American Bar Association.

Andrews, L. B. (1983). Trial by language. *Student Lawyer, 12*, 10–17.

Arnold, S., & Gold, A. (1978–1979). The use of a public opinion poll on a change of venue application. *Criminal Law Quarterly, 21*, 445–464.

Austin, A. D. (1982). Jury perceptions on advocacy: A case study. *Litigation, 8*, 15–17, 68.

Bailey, F. L., & Rothblatt, H. B. (1971). *Successful techniques for criminal trials*. Rochester, NY: The Lawyers Co-operative.

Bartol, C. R. (1983). *Psychology and American law*. Belmont, CA: Wadsworth.

Bazelon, D. (1974). Psychiatrists and the adversary process. *Scientific American, 230*, 18–23.

Begam, R. G. (1980). Opening statement: Some psychological considerations. *Trial, 16*, 33–37.

Belli, M. (1954). *Modern Trials* (Vol. I). Indianapolis: Bobbs-Merrill.

Bennett, C. E. (1977). Psychological methods of jury selection in the typical criminal case. *Criminal Defense 4*, 25–32.

Bergman, P. (1979). *Trial advocacy*. St. Paul, MN: West.

Berk, R. A. (1976). Social science and jury selection: A case study of a civil suit. In G. Bermant, C. Nemeth, & N. Vidmar (Eds.), *Psychology and the Law*. Lexington, MA: Heath.

Berk, R. A., Hennessy, M., & Swan, J. (1977). The vagaries and vulgarities of ''scientific'' jury selection: A methodological evaluation. *Evaluation Quarterly, 1*, 143–158.

Berman, J., & Sales, B. D. (1977). A critical evaluation of the systematic approach to jury selection. *Criminal Justice and Behavior 4*, 215–240.

Berscheid, E., & Walster, E. H. (1978). *Interpersonal attraction* (2nd ed.). Reading, MA: Addison-Wesley.

Bersoff, D. N. (1981). Testing and the law. *American Psychologist, 36*, 1047–1059.

Blau, T. H. (1984). *The psychologist as expert witness*. New York: Wiley.

Blauner, R. (Ed.) (1972). *Racial oppression in America*. New York: Harper.

Boehm, V. (1968). Mr. Prejudice, Miss Sympathy, and the authoritarian personality: An application of psychological measuring techniques to the problem of jury bias. *Wisconsin Law Review, 1968*, 734–750.

Boice, R. (1983). Observational skills. *Psychological Bulletin, 93*, 3–29.

Bonnie, R. J., & Slobogin, C. (1980). The role of mental health professionals in the criminal process: The case for informed speculation. *Virginia Law Review, 66*, 427–452.

Bonora, B., & Krauss, E. (Eds.) (1984). *Jurywork: Systematic techniques* (2nd ed.) New York: Clark Boardman.

Brodsky, S. L. (1977). The mental health professional on the witness stand: A survival guide. In B. D. Sales (Ed.), *Psychology in the legal process*. New York: Spectrum.

Brodsky, S. L., & Robey, A. (1972). On becoming an expert witness: Issues of orientation and effectiveness, *Professional Psychology, 3*, 173–176.

Broeder, D. W. (1958). The University of Chicago jury project. *Nebraska Law Review, 38*, 744–760.

Broeder, D. W. (1965). Voir dire examination: An empirical study. *Southern California Law Review, 38*, 503–528.

Bronson, E. J. (1970). On the conviction proneness and representativeness of the death-qualified jury: An empirical study of Colorado veniremen. *University of Colorado Law Review, 42*, 1–32.

Brown, M. (1926). *Legal psychology*. Indianapolis: Bobbs-Merrill.

Bryan, W. J. (1971). *The chosen ones*. New York: Vantage Press.

Buckhout, R. (1978). *U.S. v. Swinton*: A case history of jury selection. *Social Action and the Law, 4*, 27–29.

Burger, W. E. (1975). Dissenting opinion in *O'Connor v. Donaldson. U.S. Law Week, 42*, 4929–4936.

Burgess, J. A. (1967). The efficacy of a change of venue in protecting a defendant's right to an impartial jury. *Notre Dame Lawyer, 42*, 925–942.

Burtt, H. (1931). *Legal psychology*. Englewood Cliffs, NJ: Prentice-Hall.

Bush, N. (1976). The case for expansive voir dire. *Law and Psychology Review, 2*, 9–26.

Byrne, D. (1971). *The attraction paradigm*. New York: Academic Press.

Cahn, E. (1983). Winning big cases with trial simulations. *American Bar Association Journal, 69*, 1073–1077.

Cannito, J. A., & Becker, K. L. (1979). The case for limited use of polls in jury selection process. *Rutgers Journal of Computers, Technology and the Law, 7*, 111–134.

Christie, R. (1976). Probability vs. precedence: The social psychology of jury selection. In G. Bermant, C. Nemeth, & N. Vidmar (Eds.), *Psychology and the law*. Lexington, MA: Heath.

Christie, R., & Geis, F. L. (Eds.). (1970). *Studies in Machiavellianism*. New York: Academic Press.

Clarke, B. M. (1980). Voir dire and jury selection. In I. Hall & M. Eisenstein (Eds.). *Criminal defense techniques* Vol. 1A. New York: Matthew Bender.

Colley, M. F. (1981). Friendly persuasion: Gaining attention, comprehension, and acceptance in court. *Trial, 17*, 42–46.

Cook, T. D., & Campbell, D. T. (1979). *Quasi-experimentation: Design and analysis issues for field settings*. Chicago: Rand-McNally.

Constantini, E., & King, J. (1980). The partial juror: Correlates and causes of prejudgment. *Law and Society, 15*, 9–40.

Cowan, C. L., Thompson, W. C., & Ellsworth, P. C. (1984). The effects of death qualification on jurors' predisposition to convict and on the quality of deliberation. *Law and Human Behavior, 8*, 53–80.

Dancoff, J. (1982). Hidden persuaders of the courtroom. *Barrister, 8–9*, 16–17, 52–54.

Dane, F. C., & Wrightsman, L. S. (1982). Effects of defendants' and victims' characteristics upon jurors' verdicts. In R. M. Bray, & N. L. Kerr (Eds.), *The psychology of the courtroom*. New York: Academic Press.

Darrow, C. (May, 1936). Attorney for the defense. *Esquire*, pp. 36–37, 211–213.

Davis, J., Bray, R., & Holt, R. (1977). The empirical study of decision processes in juries: A critical review. In J. Tapp, & F. Levine (Eds.), *Law, justice and the individual in society*. New York: Holt, Rinehart & Winston.

Deleon, P. H., & Borreliz, M. (1978). Malpractice: Professional liability and the law. *Professional Psychology, 9*, 467–477.

DePaulo, B. M., & Rosenthal, R. (1979). Telling lies. *Journal of Personality and Social Psychology, 37*, 1713–1722.

DePaulo, B. M., Zuckerman, M., & Rosenthal, R. (1980). Detecting deception: Modality effects. In L. Wheeler (Ed.). *Review of personality and social psychology* (pp. 125–162). Beverly Hills, CA: Sage.

Diamond, S. S. (1979). Does the microscope lens distort? *Law and Human Behavior, 3*, 1–4.

Dillehay, R. C. (1971). Authoritarianism and the authoritarian personality. In B. B. Wolman (Ed.). *International encyclopedia of psychiatry, psychology, psychoanalysis, and neurology.* New York: Aesculapius.

Dillehay, R. C. (1973). On the irrelevance of the classical negative evidence concerning the effect of attitudes on behavior. *American Psychologist, 28*, 887–891.

Dillehay, R. C., & Neises, M. L. (1984, October). *Social psychological ingredients in the assessment of prospective jurors.* Paper presented at the meeting of the Society of Southeastern Social Psychologists, Atlanta, GA.

Dillehay, R. C., & Nietzel, M. T. (1980a). Constructing a science of jury behavior. In L. Wheeler (Ed.), *Review of personality and social psychology* (pp. 246–264). Beverly Hills, CA: Sage.

Dillehay, R. C., & Nietzel, M. T. (1980b). Conceptualizing mock jury/juror research: Critique and illustrations. In K. S. Larsen (Ed.), *Social psychology: Crisis or failure.* Monmouth, OR: Institute for Theoretical History.

Dillehay, R. C., & Nietzel, M. T. (1985). Juror experience and jury verdicts. *Law and Human Behavior, 9*, 179–191.

Dillehay, R. C., & Nietzel, M. T. (1986). Psychological consultation in trial preparation and conduct. In M. F. Kaplan (Ed.), *The impact of social psychology on procedural justice.* Springfield, IL: Charles C Thomas.

Dittman, A. T. (1972). *Interpersonal messages of emotion.* New York: Springer.

Dixon, T. E., & Blondis, R. H. (1976). Cross-examination of psychiatric witnesses in civil commitment proceedings. *Mental Disability Law Reporter, 1*, 164–171.

Ebbesen, E. B., & Konecni, V. J. (1975). Decision making and information integration in the courts: The setting of bail. *Journal of Personality and Social Psychology, 32*, 805–821.

Edinger, J. A., & Patterson, M. L. (1983). Nonverbal involvement and social control. *Psychological Bulletin, 93*, 30–56.

Ekman, P., & Friesen, W. V. (1969). Nonverbal leakage and clues to deception. *Psychiatry, 32*, 88–106.

Ekman, P., & Friesen, W. V. (1974). Detecting deception from the body or face. *Journal of Personality and Social Psychology, 29*, 288–298.

Ekman, P., Friesen, W. V., & Scherer, K. R. (1976). Body movement and voice pitch in deceptive interaction. *Semiotica, 16*, 23–27.

Ellison, K. W., & Buckhout, R. (1981). *Psychology and criminal justice.* New York: Harper & Row.

Ellsworth, P. C., Bukaty, R. M., Cowan, C. L., & Thompson, W. C. (1984). The death-qualified jury and the defense of insanity. *Law and Human Behavior, 8*, 81–94.

Elwork, A., Sales, B. D., & Alfini, J. J. (1977). Juridic decisions: In ignorance of the law or in the light of it? *Law and Human Behavior, 1*, 163–189.

Emerson, C. D. (1968). Personality tests for prospective jurors. *Kentucky Law Journal, 56*, 832–854.

Ennis, B. J., & Litwack, T. R. (1974). Psychiatry and the presumption of expertise: Flipping coins in the courtroom. *California Law Review, 62*, 693–752.

Etzioni, A. (1974). Creating an imbalance. *Trial, 10*, 28, 30.

Farmer, M. W. (1976). Jury composition challenges. *Law and Psychology Review, 2*, 45–74.

Fersch, E. A. (1980). Ethical issues for psychologists in court settings. In J. Monahan (Ed.)

Who is the client? (pp. 43–62). Washington, DC: American Psychological Association.

Feyerabend, P. K. (1970). Against method: Outline of an anarchistic theory of knowledge. In M. Racher & S. Winokur (Eds.), *Minnesota studies in the philosophy of science* (pp. 17–26, 91, 92). Minneapolis: University of Minnesota Press.

Finkelstein, M. (1966). The application of statistical decision theory to the jury discrimination cases. *Harvard Law Review, 80*, 338–376.

Fiora-Gormally, N. (1978). Battered wives who kill: Double standard out of court, single standard in. *Law and Human Behavior, 2*, 133–166.

Fishbein, M., & Ajzen, I. (1972). Attitudes and opinions. *Annual Review of Psychology, 23*, 487–544.

Fishbein, M., & Ajzen, I. (1975). *Belief, attitude, intention, and behavior*. Reading, MA: Addison-Wesley.

Fitzgerald, R., & Ellsworth, P. C. (1984). Due process vs. crime control: Death qualification and jury attitudes. *Law and Human Behavior, 8*, 31–52.

Ford, T. R. (1977). The production of social knowledge for public use. *Social Forces, 56*, 504–518.

Fortune, W. H. (1980–1981). Voir dire in Kentucky: An empirical study of voir dire in Kentucky Circuit Courts. *Kentucky Law Journal, 69*, 273–326.

French, J. R. P., & Raven, B. (1959). The bases of social power. In D. Cartwright (Ed.), *Studies in social power*. Ann Arbor, MI: Institute for Social Research.

Freud, S. (1905). Jokes and their relation to the unconscious. In J. Strachey (Ed.). *The standard edition of the complete psychological works of Sigmund Freud* (Vol. 8). London: Hogarth Press, 1953–1964.

Fromm, E. (1941). *Escape from freedom*. New York: Rinehart.

Fugita, S. S., Hagrebe, M. C., & Wexley, M. C. (1980). Perceptions of deception: Perceived expertise in detecting deception, successfulness of deception and non-verbal cues. *Personality and Social Psychology Bulletin, 6*, 637–643.

Gaines, I. D. (1956). The psychologist as an expert witness in a personal injury case. *Marquette Law Review, 39*, 239–244.

Garfield, S. L. (1978). Research problems in clinical diagnosis. *Journal of Consulting and Clinical Psychology, 46*, 596–607.

Gass, R. (1979). The psychologist as expert witness: Science in the courtroom. *Maryland Law Review, 38*, 539–631.

Geen, R. G., & Gange, J. J. (1977). Drive theory of social facilitation: Twelve years of theory and research. *Psychological Bulletin, 84*, 1267–1288.

Geis, F. L., & Moon, T. H. (1981). Machiavellianism and deception. *Journal of Personality and Social Psychology, 41*, 766–775.

Gerbasi, K. C., Zuckerman, M., & Reis, H. T. (1977). Justice needs a new blindfold: A review of mock jury research. *Psychological Bulletin, 84*, 323–345.

Ginger, A. F. (1977). *Jury selection in criminal trials*. Tiburon, CA: Law Press.

Goldberg, F. (1970). Toward expansion of *Witherspoon*: Capital scruples, jury bias, and use of psychological data to raise presumptions in the law. *Harvard Civil Rights–Civil Liberties Law Review, 5*, 53–69.

Golding, S. L., Roesch, R., & Schreiber, J. (1984). Assessment and conceptualization of competency to stand trial: Preliminary data on the interdisciplinary fitness interview. *Law and Human Behavior, 8*, 321–334.

Greenberg, M. S., & Ruback, R. B. (1982). *Social psychology of the criminal justice system*. Monterey, CA: Brooks/Cole.

Grisso, T. (1981). *Juveniles' waiver of rights: Legal and psychological competence*. New York: Plenum Press.

Hafemeister, T., & Sales, B. D. (1984). Inter-disciplinary evaluations for guardianship and conservatorship. *Law and Human Behavior, 8*, 335–354.

Haller, T. (1982). Using public opinion surveys. *Litigation, 8*, 17–19.

Haney, C. (1980). Psychology and legal change: On the limits of factual jurisprudence. *Law and Human Behavior, 4,* 147–199.

Haney, C. (1984a). On the selection of capital juries: The biasing effects of the death-qualification process. *Law and Human Behavior, 8,* 121–132.

Haney, C. (1984b). Examining death qualification: Further analysis of the process effect. *Law and Human Behavior, 8,* 133–152.

Hans, V. P., & Vidmar, H. (1982). Jury selection. In N. L. Kerr & R. M. Bray (Eds.). *The psychology of the courtroom.* New York: Academic Press.

Harper, R. G., Wiens, A. N., & Matarazzo, J. D. (1978). *Nonverbal communication: The state of the art.* New York: Wiley.

Harrison, A. A., Havalek, M., Raney, D. F., & Fritz, J. G. (1978). Cues to deception in an interview situation. *Social Psychology Quarterly, 41 (2),* 156–161.

Harvard Law Review. (1983). *96,* 886–906.

Harvey, J. H., & Weary, G. (1981). *Perspectives on attributional processes.* Dubuque, IA: William C. Brown.

Hastie, R., Penrod, S. D., & Pennington, N. (1983). *Inside the jury.* Cambridge, MA: Harvard University Press.

Heider, F. (1958). *The psychology of interpersonal relations.* New York: Wiley.

Hepburn, J. R. (1980). The objective reality of evidence and the utility of systematic jury selection. *Law and Human Behavior, 4,* 89–102.

Himelein, M. J., Nietzel, M. T., & Dillehay, R. C. (1984). *Effects of prior juror experience on jury sentencing.* Unpublished manuscript.

Hocking, J. E., & Leathers, D. G. (1980). Nonverbal indicators of deception: A new theoretical perspective. *Communication Monographs, 47,* 119–131.

Horowitz, I. A. (1980). Juror selection: A comparison of two methods in several criminal cases. *Journal of Applied Social Psychology, 10,* 86–99.

Horowitz, I. A., & Willging, T. E. (1984). *The psychology of law: Integrations and applications.* Boston: Little, Brown.

Hovland, C. I. (1954). Effects of the mass media of communication. In G. Lindzey (Ed.), *Handbook of social psychology* (pp. 1062–1103). Cambridge, MA: Addison-Wesley.

Hovland, C. I. (1958). The role of primacy and recency in persuasive communication. In E. E. Maccoby, T. M. Newcomb, & E. L. Hartley (Eds.). *Readings in social psychology* (3rd ed.). New York: Holt, Rinehart, and Winston.

Hutchins, R. M., & Slesinger, D. (1929). Legal psychology. *Psychology Review, 36,* 13–26.

Joint Committee on Standards for Educational Evaluation. (1981). *Standards for evaluations of educational programs, projects, and materials.* New York: McGraw-Hill.

Jones, R. A., & Brehm, J. W. (1970). Persuasiveness of one-and-two sided communications as a function of awareness there are two sides. *Journal of Experimental Social Psychology, 6,* 47–56,

Jurow, G. L. (1971). New data on the effect of a "death-qualified" jury on the guilt-determination process. *Harvard Law Review, 84,* 567–611.

Kairys, D. (1972). Juror selection: The law, a mathematical method of analysis and a case study. *American Criminal Law Review, 10,* 771–789.

Kairys, D. (1975). *The jury system: New methods for reducing prejudice.* Philadelphia: National Jury Project and the National Lawyers Guild.

Kalven, H., & Zeisel, H. (1966). *The American jury.* Boston: Little, Brown.

Kaplan, M. F. (1982). Cognitive processes in the individual juror. In N. L. Kerr and R. M. Bray (Eds.), *The psychology of the courtroom.* New York: Academic Press.

Kaplan, M. F. (Ed.) (1986). *The impact of social psychology on procedural justice.* Springfield, IL: Charles C Thomas.

Kassin, S. M., & Wrightsman, L. S. (1979). On the requirements of proof: The timing of judicial instruction and mock juror verdicts. *Journal of Personality and Social Psychology, 37,* 1877–1887.

Kassin, S. M., & Wrightsman, L. S. (Eds.) (1985). *The psychology of evidence and trial procedure.* Beverly Hills, CA: Sage.

Katz, D., & Stotland, E. (1959). A preliminary statement to a theory of attitude structure and change. In S. Koch (Ed.), *Psychology: Study of a science* (pp. 423–475). New York: McGraw-Hill.

Kelley, H. H., & Michela, J. L. (1980). Attribution theory and research. *Annual Review of Psychology, 31,* 457–501.

Kelley, H. H., & Schenitski, D. D. (1972). Bargaining. In C. C. McClintock (Ed.) *Experimental social psychology* (pp. 298–337). New York: Holt, Rinehart, & Winston.

Kelman, H. C. (1961). Processes of opinion change. *Public Opinion Quarterly, 25,* 57–78.

Kerr, N. L. (1981). Effects of prior juror experience on juror behavior. *Basic and Applied Social Psychology, 2,* 175–193.

Kerr, N. L., & Bray, R. M. (Eds.). (1982). *The psychology of the courtroom.* New York: Academic Press.

Kerr, N. L., Harmon, D. L., & Graves, J. K. (1982). Independence of multiple verdicts by jurors and juries. *Journal of Applied Social Psychology, 12,* 12–29.

Kohlberg, L. (1969). Stage and sequence: The cognitive-developmental approach to socialization. In D. A. Goslin (Ed.) *Handbook of socialization theory and research.* Chicago: Rand McNally.

Kuhn, T. S. (1962). *The structure of scientific revolutions* (2nd ed.). Chicago: The University of Chicago Press.

Lassen, G. (1964). The psychologist as an expert witness in assessing mental disease or defect. *American Bar Association Journal, 50,* 239–242.

Lawson, R. G. (1969). The law of primacy in the criminal courtroom. *The Journal of Social Psychology, 77,* 121–131.

Lee, H. (1962). *To kill a mockingbird.* New York: Popular Library.

Lerner, M.J. (1977). The justice motive: Some hypotheses as to its origins and forms. *Journal of Personality, 45,* 1–52.

Levine, A. G., & Schweber-Koren, C. (1976). Jury selection in Erie County: Changing a sexist system. *Law and Society Review, 11,* 43–55.

Levine, M. (1974). Scientific method and the adversary model: Some preliminary thoughts. *American Psychologist, 29,* 661–677.

Levitt, E. E. (1969). The psychologist: A neglected legal source. *Indiana Law Journal, 45,* 82–89.

Lind, E. A. (1982). The psychology of courtroom procedure. In N. L. Kerr & R. M. Bray (Eds.). *The psychology of the courtroom* (pp. 13–38). New York: Academic Press.

Lipsitt, P. D., & Sales, B. D. (Eds.). (1980). *New directions in psycholegal research.* New York: Van Nostrand Reinhold.

Lipsitt, P. D., Lelos, D., & McGarry, A. L. (1971). Competency for trial: A screening instrument. *American Journal of Psychiatry, 128,* 105–109.

Littlepage, G. E., & Pineault, M. A. (1979). Detection of deceptive factual statements from the body and the face. *Personality and Social Psychology Bulletin, 5,* 325–328.

Litwack, T. R., Gerber, G. L., & Fenster, C. A. (1979–1980). The proper role of psychology in child custody disputes. *Journal of Family Law, 18,* 269–300.

Loftus, E. F. (1979). *Eyewitness testimony.* Cambridge, MA: Harvard University Press.

Loftus, E. F. (1980). Psychological aspects of courtroom testimony. In F. Wright, C. Bahn, & R. Reiber (Eds.). *Forensic psychology and psychiatry.* New York: New York Academy of Sciences.

Loftus, E. F. (1983). Silence is not golden. *American Psychologist, 38,* 564–572.

Loh, W. D. (1984). *Social research in the judicial process: Cases, readings, and text.* New York: Russell Sage Foundation.

Louisell, D. W. (1955). The psychologist in today's legal world. *Minnesota Law Review, 39,* 235–272.

Lower, J. S. (1978). Psychologist as expert witness. *Law and Psychology Review, 4*, 127–139.

Lowery, C. R. (1984). The wisdom of Solomon: Criteria for child custody from the legal and clinical points of view. *Law and Human Behavior, 8*, 371–380.

Luchins, A. S. (1957). Primacy–recency in impression formation. In C. I. Hovland (Ed.). *The order of presentation in persuasion*. New Haven: Yale University Press.

Marshall, J. (1966). *Law and psychology in conflict*. New York: Bobbs-Merrill.

Mauet, T. A. (1980). *Fundamentals of trial techniques*. Boston: Little, Brown.

McCarty, D. G. (1929). *Psychology for the lawyer*. New York: Prentice-Hall.

McClintock, C. G., & Hunt, R. G. (1975). Nonverbal indicators of affect and deception in an interview setting. *Journal of Applied Social Psychology, 5*, 54–67.

McCloskey, M., & Egeth, H. E. (1983). Eyewitness identification: What can a psychologist tell a jury? *American Psychologist, 38*, 550–563.

McConahay, J. B., Mullin, C. J., & Frederick, J. (1977). The use of social science in trials with political overtones: The trial of Joan Little. *Law and Contemporary Problems, 4*, 205–229.

McElroy, T. (1976). Public surveys: The latest exception to the hearsay rule. *Baylor Law Review, 28*, 59–76.

McGarry, A. L., et al. (1973). *Competency to stand trial and mental illness*. Washington, DC: U.S. Government Printing Office, Publication HSM 73-9105.

McGuire, W. J. (1969). The nature of attitudes and attitude change. In G. Lindzey & E. Aronson (Eds.), *The handbook of social psychology* (2nd ed., Vol. 3). Reading, MA: Addison-Wesley.

McReynolds, P. (1975). Historical antecedents of personality assessment. In P. McReynolds (Ed.). *Advances in psychological assessment* (pp. 477–532). San Francisco: Jossey-Bass.

Mehrabian, A. (1971). Nonverbal betrayal of feelings. *Journal of Experimental Research in Personality, 5*, 64–73.

Miller, G. R., & Burgoon, J. K. (1982). Factors affecting assessments of witness credibility. In N. L. Kerr & R. M. Bray (Eds.) *The psychology of the courtroom*. New York: Academic Press.

Miller, N., and Campbell, D. (1959). Recency and primacy in persuasion as a function of the timing of speeches and measurements. *Journal of Abnormal and Social Psychology, 59*, 1–9.

Mills, C. J., & Bohannon, W. E. (1980). Juror characteristics: To what extent are they related to jury verdicts. *Judicature, 64*, 23–31.

Monahan, J. (Ed.). (1980). *Who is the client?* Washington, DC: American Psychological Association.

Monahan, J. (1981). *Predicting violent behavior: An assessment of clinical techniques*. Beverly Hills, CA: Sage.

Monahan, J., & Walker, L. (1985). *Social sciences in law: Cases and materials*. Mineola, NY: Foundation Press.

Moore, M., & Wood, J. (1980). The use of handwriting analysis in jury selection. *Case and Comment, 85*, 38–41.

Morse, S. J. (1978a). Crazy behavior, morals, and science: An analysis of mental health law. *Southern California Law Review, 51*, 527–654.

Morse, S. J. (1978b). Law and mental health professionals: The limits of expertise. *Professional Psychology, 9*, 389–399.

Munsterberg, H. (1908). *On the witness stand: Essays on psychology and crime*. New York: Clark Boardman.

Mulvey, E. P., & Lidz, C. W. (1985). Back to basics: A critical analysis of dangerousness research in a new legal environment. *Law and Human Behavior, 9*, 209–219.

Nash, M. N. (1974). Parameters and distinctiveness of psychological testimony. *Professional Psychology, 5*, 239–243.

Nemeth, C. (1980). Social psychology in the courtroom. In L. Berkowitz (Ed.), *A survey of social psychology*. New York: Holt, Rinehart, and Winston.

Nietzel, M. T., & Dillehay, R. C. (1982). The effects of variations in voir dire procedures in capital murder trials. *Law and Human Behavior, 6*, 1–13.

Nietzel, M. T., & Dillehay, R. C. (1983). Psychologists as consultants for changes of venue. *Law and Human Behavior, 7,* 309–335.

Nietzel, M. T., Dillehay, R. C., & Himelein, M. J. (1984). *Effects of voir dire variations: A replication.* Unpublished manuscript.

Nietzel, M. T., Dillehay, R. C., & Rogers, G. (1976). *Method innovation in jury research: Alternative juries and archival data.* Paper presented at the meeting of the American Psychological Association, Washington, DC.

Nisbett, R. E., & Wilson, T. D. (1977). Telling more than we can know: Verbal reports on mental processes. *Psychological Review, 84,* 231–259.

Note. (1980). Juror bias: A practical screening device and the case for permitting its use. *Minnesota Law Review, 64,* 987–1020.

O'Barr, W. M. (1982). *Linguistic evidence: Language, power and strategy in the courtroom.* New York: Academic Press.

Okpaku, S. (1976). Psychology: Impediment or aid in child custody cases. *Rutgers Law Review, 29,* 1117–1153.

Oksenberg, L. (1970). Machiavellianism and emotionality. In R. Christie & F. L. Geis (Eds.). *Studies in Machiavellianism.* New York: Academic Press.

Pacht, A., Kuehn, J., Bassett, H., & Nash, M. (1973). The current status of the psychologist as an expert witness. *Professional Psychology, 4,* 409–413.

Padawer-Singer, A. M., Singer, H., & Singer, R. (1974). Voir dire by two lawyers: An essential safeguard. *Judicature, 57,* 386–391.

Penrod, S. (1980). *Evaluating social scientific methods of jury selection.* Paper presented at the meeting of the Midwestern Psychological Association, St. Louis, MO.

Penrod, S., Rosenblum, S., Stefek, D., & Hastie, R. (1979). *Modeling jury selection strategies, computer simulations, and attorney behavior.* Paper presented at the meeting of the American Psychological Association, New York.

Petrella, R. C., & Poythress, N. G. (1983). The quality of forensic evaluations: An interdisciplinary study. *Journal of Consulting and Clinical Psychology, 51,* 76–85.

Petty, R. E., & Cacioppo, J. T. (1981). *Attitude and persuasion: Classic and contemporary approaches.* Dubuque, IA: William C. Brown.

Pollock, A. (1977). The use of public opinion polls to obtain changes of venue and continuances in criminal trials. *Criminal Justice Journal, 1,* 269–288.

Poythress, N. G. (1978). Psychiatric expertise in civil commitment: Training attorneys to cope with expert testimony. *Law and Human Behavior, 2,* 1–24.

Poythress, N. G. (1980). Coping on the witness stand: Learned responses to "learned treatises." *Professional Psychology, 11,* 139–149.

Poythress, N. G. (1982). Concerning reform in expert testimony: An open letter from a practicing psychologist. *Law and Human Behavior, 6,* 39–43.

Poythress, N. G. (1983). Psychological issues in criminal proceedings: Judicial preference regarding expert testimony. *Criminal Justice and Behavior, 10,* 175–194.

Prettyman, E. B. (1960). Jury instructions—First or last? *American Bar Association Journal, 46,* 1066.

Reed, J. P. (1965). Jury deliberations, voting and verdict trends. *Southwestern Social Science Quarterly, 45,* 361–370.

Rice, G. P. (1961). The psychologist as an expert witness. *American Psychologist, 16,* 691–692.

Robinson, D. N. (1980). *Psychology and law: Can justice survive the social sciences.* New York: Oxford University Press.

Robinson, E. (1935). *Law and the lawyers.* New York: Macmillan.

Roesch, R., & Golding, S. L. (1980). *Competency to stand trial.* Champaign: University of Illinois Press.

Rogers, R., Wasyliw, O. E., & Cavanaugh, J. L. (1984). Evaluating insanity: A study of construct validity. *Law and Human Behavior, 8,* 293–304.

Rosenthal, R. (1983). Assessing the statistical and social importance of the effects of psychotherapy. *Journal of Consulting and Clinical Psychology, 51*, 4–13.

Rothgeb, C. L. (Ed.) (1973). *Abstracts of the standard edition of the complete psychological works of Sigmund Freud.* New York: International Universities Press.

Sage W. (1973). Psychology and the Angela Davis jury. *Human Behavior*, January, 2, 56–61.

Saks, M. J. (1976a). The limits of scientific jury selection: Ethical and empirical. *Jurimetrics Journal, 17*(1), 3–22.

Saks, M. J. (1976b). Social scientists can't rig juries. *Psychology Today, 9*, 48–50, 55–57.

Saks, M. J., & Hastie, R. (1978). *Social psychology in court.* New York: Van Nostrand Reinhold.

Sales, B. D., Powell, D. M., Van Duizend, R., & Associates. (1982). *Disabled persons and the law.* New York: Plenum.

Sales, B. D. (Ed.) (1981). *Perspectives in law and psychology: Vol. 2. The trial process.* New York: Plenum Press.

Sampson, E. E. (1983). *Justice and the critique of pure psychology.* New York: Plenum.

Sannito, T. (1981). Psychological courtroom strategies. *Trial Diplomacy Journal*, Summer, 4, 30–35.

Schulman, J., Shaver, P., Colman, R., Emrich, B., & Christie, R. (1973). Recipe for a jury. *Psychology Today, 6*, 37–44, 77–84.

Schulman, R. (1966). The psychologist as an expert witness. *Kansas Law Review, 15*, 88–97.

Selkin, J., & Loya, F. (1979). Issues in the psychological autopsy of a controversial public figure. *Professional Psychology, 10*, 87–92.

Shapiro, D. L. (1984). *Psychological evaluation and expert testimony: A practical guide to forensic work.* New York: Van Nostrand Reinhold.

Sharp, A. (September–October 1983). Postverdict interviews with jurors. *Case and Comment, 88*, 3, 4, 6, 8, 10, 12–14.

Silas, F. A. (1983). Graphoanalysis: Choosing jurors by penmanship. *American Bar Association Journal, 69*, 1609.

Silver, D. (1978). A case against the use of public opinion polls as an aid in jury selection. *Rutgers Journal of Computers, Technology and the Law, 6*, 177–196.

Simon, R. (Ed.) (1967). *The jury and the defense of insanity.* Boston: Little, Brown.

Skolnick, J. H. (1966). *Justice without trial: Law enforcement in democratic society.* New York: Wiley.

Slobogin, C., Melton, G. B., & Showalter, C. R. (1984). The feasibility of a brief evaluation of mental state at the time of the offense. *Law and Human Behavior, 8*, 305–320.

Smith, B. S., Bruner, J. S., and White, R. W. (1956). *Opinions and Personality.* New York: Wiley.

Smith, S. (1967). The ideal use of expert testimony in psychology. *Washburn Law Review, 6*, 300–306.

Sperlich, P. W., & Jaspovice, M. L. (1979). Methods for the analysis of jury panel selections: Testing for discrimination in a series of panels. *Hastings Constitutional Law Quarterly, 6*, 787–852.

Stephan, C. (1975). Selective characteristics of jurors and litigants: Their influence on jury verdicts. In R. Simon (Ed.). *The jury system in America* (pp. 95–122). Beverly Hills, CA: Sage.

Stern, W. (1939). The psychology of testimony. *Journal of Abnormal and Social Psychology, 34*, 3–20.

Streeter, L. A., Krauss, R. M., Geller, V., Olson, C., & Apple, W. (1977). Pitch changes during attempted deception. *Journal of Personality and Social Psychology, 35*, 345–350.

Strodtbeck, F. L. (1962). Social process, the law, and jury functioning. In W. M. Evan (Ed.) *Law and sociology.* New York: Free Press.

Suggs, D., & Sales, B. D. (1978). The art and science of conducting the voir dire. *Professional Psychology, 9*, 367–387.

Suggs, D., & Sales, B. D. (1981). Juror self-disclosure in the voir dire: A social science analysis. *Indiana Law Journal, 56*, 245–271.

Swenson, R. A., Nash, D. L., & Roos, D. C. (1984). Source credibility and perceived expertness of testimony in a simulated child-custody case. *Professional Psychology: Research and Practice, 15,* 891–898.

Tapp, J. L., & Levine, F. J. (1978). Legal socialization: Strategies for an ethical legality. *Stanford Law Review, 27,* 1–72.

Thibaut, J., & Walker, L. (1975). *Procedural justice: A psychological analysis.* Hillsdale, NJ: Lawrence Erlbaum.

Thompson, W. C., Cowan, C. L., Ellsworth, P. C., & Harrington, J. C. (1984). Death penalty attitudes and conviction proneness: The translation of attitudes into verdicts. *Law and Human Behavior, 8,* 95–114.

Van Dyke, J. M. (1977). *Jury selection procedures: Our uncertain commitment to representative panels.* Cambridge, MA: Ballinger.

Vidmar, N., & Judson, J. (1981). The use of social science in a change of venue application. *Canadian Bar Review, 59,* 76–102.

Vinson, D. E. (1982). The shadow jury: An experiment in litigation science. *American Bar Association Journal, 68,* 1243–1246.

Vinson, D. E., & Anthony, P. K. (1983). Psychological tips for persuading the jury. *Case and Comment, 88,* 24–26.

Vinson, D. E., & Anthony, P. K. (1985). *Social science research methods for litigation.* Charlottesville, VA: Michie.

Wagner, W. (1981). *Art of advocacy: Jury selection.* New York: Matthew Bender.

Walker, L. E. A. (1984). Battered women, psychology, and public policy. *American Psychologist, 39,* 1178–1182.

Wells, G. L., Lindsay, R. C. L., & Ferguson, T. J. (1979). Accuracy, confidence and juror perceptions in eyewitness identification. *Journal of Applied Psychology, 64,* 440–448.

Wells, G. L., & Loftus, E. F. (Eds.) (1983). *Eyewitness testimony: Psychological perspectives.* London: Cambridge University Press.

Werner, C. M., Strube, M. J., Cole, A. M., & Kagehiro, D. K. (1985). The impact of case characteristics and prior jury experience on jury verdicts. *Journal of Applied Social Psychology, 15,* 409–427.

Whipple, G. M. (1909). The observer as reporter: A survey of the psychology of testimony. *Psychology Bulletin, 6,* 153–170.

White, R. K. (1966). Misperception and the Vietnam War. *Journal of Social Issues, 22,* 1–164.

Wicker, A. W. (1969). Attitude vs. actions: The relationship of verbal and overt behavioral responses to attitude objects. *Journal of Social Issues, 25,* 41–78.

Wicklund, R. A., & Brehm, J. W. (1976). *Perspectives on cognitive dissonance.* Hillsdale, NJ: Erlbaum.

Widman, E. H. (1980). The use of a suicidologist in accidental death litigation. *Insurance Counsel Journal, 47,* 219–223.

Wigmore, J. (1909). Professor Munsterberg and the psychology of testimony: Being a report of the case of Cokestone v. Munsterberg. *Illinois Law Review, 3,* 399–445.

Williams, G. R. (1983). *Legal negotiation and settlement.* St. Paul, MN: West.

Wolfgang, M. E. (1974). The social scientist in court. *The Journal of Criminal Law and Criminology, 65,* 239–247.

Woodward, J. (1952). A scientific attempt to provide evidence for a decision on change of venue. *American Sociological Review, 17,* 447–453.

Wrightsman, L. S. (1978). The American trial jury on trial: Empirical evidence and procedural modifications. *Journal of Social Issues, 34,* 137–164.

Yarmey, A. D. (1979). *The psychology of eyewitness testimony.* New York: Free Press.

Zajonc, R. B. (1968). Attitudinal effects of mere exposure. *Journal of Personality and Social Psychology Monograph Supplement, 9,* 1–27.

Zajonc, R. B. (1984). On the primacy of affect. *American psychologist, 39,* 117–123.

Zeisel, H. (1960). The uniqueness of survey evidence. *Cornell Law Quarterly, 45*, 322–346.

Zeisel, H. (1968). *Some data on juror attitudes toward capital punishment*. Center for studies in Criminal Justice, University of Chicago Law School, Chicago, Illinois.

Zeisel, H. (1983). The surveys that broke Monopoly. *University of Chicago Law Review, 50*, 896–909.

Zeisel, H., & Diamond, S. S. (1976). The jury selection in the Mitchell-Stans conspiracy trial. *American Bar Foundation Journal, 1*, 151–174.

Zimbardo, P. G., Ebbesen, E. B., & Maslach, C. (1977). *Influencing attitudes and changing behavior* (2nd ed.). Reading, MA: Addison-Wesley.

Ziskin, J. (1981). *Coping with psychiatric and psychological testimony* (3rd Ed). Venice, CA: Law and Psychology Press.

Author and Case Index

Addington v. Texas, 100
Adorno, T.W., 48
Ajzen, I., 43, 92, 136
Alfini, J.J., 153
Albermale Paper Co. v. Moody, 106
Allen v. United States, 10
American Bar Association, 67, 68, 69, 163
Andrews, L.B., 149
Anthony, P.K., 62, 137
Anti-Monopoly, Inc. v. General Mills Food Group, Inc., 101
Apple, W., 42
Arnold, S., 90
Austin, A.D., 143, 144, 145

Bailey, F.L., 54
Bartol, C.R., 4, 6
Bassett, H., 99
Bazelon, D., 97, 98, 102
Becker, K.L., 62
Begam, R.G., 137, 148
Belli, M., 54
Bennett, C.E., 21
Berger v. United States, 5
Bergman, P., 118, 126, 129
Berk, R.A., 20, 21, 22, 63
Berman, J., 21
Berscheid, E., 144
Bersoff, D.N., 101
Biro v. Prudential Insurance Co., 101
Blau, T.H., 99, 109
Blauner, R., 21
Blondis, R.H., 97

Boehm, V., 44, 48
Bohannon, W.E., 44
Boice, R., 42
Bonnie, R.J., 97
Bonora, B., 26, 28, 31, 62, 77
Borreliz, M., 101, 108
Bray, R. M., 4, 44, 150, 154
Brehm, J.W., 136, 139, 143
Brodsky, S.L., 52, 109, 113
Broeder, D.W., 3, 29, 41, 54, 164
Bronson, E.J., 32
Brown, M., 2
Brown v. Board of Education, 106
Bruner, J.S., 151
Bryan, W.J., 39
Buckhout, R., 4, 21, 37, 104
Bukaty, R.M., 32
Burger, W.E., 97
Burgess, J.A., 68
Burgoon, J.K., 129
Burtt, H., 2
Bush, N., 28
Byrne, D., 144

Cacioppo, J.T., 131, 146, 147, 148
Cahn, E., 64, 65
Campbell, D.T., 22, 146, 147, 157
Cannito, J.A., 62
Castaneda v. Partida, 36
Cavanaugh, J.L., 100
Christie, R., 20, 21, 22, 29, 42, 49
Clarke, B.M., 28
Cole, A.M., 54, 154
Colley, M.F., 137, 141, 145

Colman, R., 20
Constantini, E., 73, 91
Cook, T.D., 22, 157
Cowan, C.L., 33

Dancoff, J., 64
Dane, F.C., 155
Darrow, C., 39
In re David, 101
Davis, J., 44, 150, 154
Deleon, P.H., 101, 108
De Paulo, B.M., 41, 42, 43, 129
Diamond, S.S., 21, 158
Dillehay, R.C., 3, 23, 28, 29, 30, 41,
   43, 48, 54, 55, 56, 57, 60, 63, 65,
   81, 154, 158
Dittman, A.T., 51
Dixon, T.E., 97
Duren v. Missouri, 37
Durham v. United States, 100, 102
Dusky v. United States, 100, 103

Ebbesen, E.B., 131, 135, 158
Edinger, J.A., 42
Egeth, H.E., 98, 100
Ekman, P., 41, 42, 50
Ellison, K.W., 4, 37, 104
Ellsworth, P.C., 32, 33, 145
Elwork, A., 153
Emerson, C.D., 44
Emrich, B., 20
Ennis, B.J., 97
Estelle v. Smith, 100, 103
Estes v. Texas, 69
Etzioni, B.J., 17, 21

Farmer, M.W., 35, 36
Fenster, C.A., 101
Ferguson, T.J., 129
Fersch, E.A., 166, 168
Feyerabend, P.K., 6
Finkelstein, M., 36
Finlay, B., 66
Fiora-Gormally, N., 101
Fishbein, M., 43, 92, 136
Fitzgerald, R., 32, 145

Ford, T.R., 157
Fortune, W.H., 28
Frederick, J., 20, 90
French, J.R.P., 137
Frenkel-Brunswick, E., 48
Freud, S., 1, 49
Friesen, M.V., 1, 42, 50
Fritz, J.G., 42
Fromm, E., 48
Fugita, S.S., 42

Gaines, I.D., 99, 100
Garfield, S.L., 105
Gass, R., 97, 101
Geis, F.L., 42
Geller, V., 42
Gerbasi, K.C., 44
Gerber, G.L., 101
Ginger, A.F., 28, 29, 62
Gold, A., 90
Goldberg, F., 33
Golding, S.L., 100, 103
Grange, J.J., 128
Graves, J.K., 54
Green, R.G., 128
Greenberg, M.S., 4
Griggs v. Duke Power Co., 101, 106
Grisso, T., 100, 104
Groppi v. Wisconsin, 69

Hafemeister, T., 101, 107
Haller, T., 62
Hammer v. Rosen, 101
Haney, C., 4, 28, 33, 34, 100, 104
Hans, V.P., 92, 93
Harmon, D.L., 54
Harper, R.G., 50
Harrington, J.C., 33
Harrison, A.A., 42
Harvey, J.H., 137
Harvard Law Review, 162
Hastie, R., 4, 14, 21, 22, 28, 44, 135,
   141, 146, 154, 155
Havalek, M., 42
Hawthorne v. Florida, 101
Heider, F., 137, 162

Hennessy, M., 21, 63
Hepburn, J.R., 22
Hernandez v. Texas, 36
Hidden v. Mutual Life Insurance Co.,
	98, 100
Himelein, M.J., 30, 57
Hocking, J.E., 42
Hogrebe, M.C., 42
Holt, R., 44, 150, 154
Horowitz, I.A., 4, 21, 90, 104
*Hovey v. Superior Court of Alameda
	County*, 34, 100
Hovland, C.I., 135, 146
Hunt, R.G., 42
Hutchins, R.M., 3

Irvin v. Dowd, 64, 66

Jaspovice, M.L., 37
Jenkins v. United States, 98, 99
Joint Committee on Standards for
	Educational Evaluation, 165
Jones, R.A., 139, 143
Judson, J., 91, 92, 96
Jurow, G.L., 33

Kagehiro, D.K., 54, 154
Kairys, D., 36, 62
Kalven, H., 57, 65, 153, 164
Kaplan, M.F., 4, 150
Kassin, S.M., 4, 153
Katz, D., 151
Kelley, H.H., 6, 144, 162
Kelman, H.C., 142, 151
Kerr, N.L., 4, 54, 154
King, J., 73, 91
Kohlberg, L., 52
Konecni, V.J., 158
Krauss, E., 26, 28, 62, 77
Krauss, R.M., 42
Kuehn, J., 99
Kuhn, T.S., 6

Larry P. v. Riles, 101, 106
Lassen, G., 99
Lawson, R.G., 137, 147

Leathers, D.G., 42
Lee, H., 123
Lelos, D., 100
Lerner, M.J., 144
Lessard v. Smith, 100
Levine, A.G., 21
Levine, F.J., 52
Levine, M., 6
Levinson, D.J., 48
Levitt, E.E., 99, 101
Lidz, C.W., 105
Lind, E.A., 146, 147
Lindsay, R.C.L., 129
Lipsitt, P.D., 4, 100
Littlepage, G.E., 42
Litwack, T.R., 92, 101
Loftus, E.F., 98, 100, 104, 148
Loh, W.D., 2, 3, 4, 11, 101, 163
Louisell, D.W., 99
Lower, J.S., 99
Lowery, C.R., 107
Loya, F., 101
Luchins, A.S., 146, 147

Marshall, J., 4
Marshall v. United States, 69
Maslach, C., 131, 135
Matarazzo, J.D., 50
Mauet, T.A., 118
McCarty, D.G., 2
McClintock, C.G., 42
McCloskey, M., 98, 100
McConahay, J.B., 20, 90, 93
McElroy, T., 62
McGarry, A.L., 100
McGuire, W.J., 135, 141, 147, 148
McNaghten, 100, 102
McReynolds, P., 49
Mehrabian, A., 51
Melton, G.B., 100
Michela, J.L., 144, 162
Miller, G.R., 146
Miller, N., 129, 147
Mills v. Board of Education, 106
Mills, C.J., 44
Miranda v. Arizona, 104

Monahan, J., 4, 100, 105, 166, 167
Moon, T.H., 42
Moore, M., 44
Morse, S.J., 4, 97, 98
Mullin, C.J., 20, 90
Mulvey, E.P., 105
Munsterberg, H., 1, 2, 3
Murphy v. Florida, 66

Nash, D.L., 101
Nash, M.N., 99
Neises, M.L., 41
Nemeth, C., 154
Nietzel, M.T., 3, 23, 28, 29, 30, 43,
    54, 55, 56, 57, 60, 63, 65, 81,
    154, 158
Nisbett, R.E., 43, 73, 162

O'Barr, W.M., 141, 148
Okpaku, S., 101
Oksenberg, L., 42
Olson, C., 42

Pacht, A., 99
Padawer-Singer, A.M., 29
Painter v. Bannister, 101
Patterson, M.L., 42
Patton v. Yount, 67, 69
Pennington, N., 4, 154, 155
Penrod, S.D., 4, 21, 22, 154, 155
People v. Hawthorne, 98
People v. Powell, 37
People v. Shelton, 115
Petrella, R., 114
Petty, R.E., 131, 146, 147, 148
Pineault, M.A., 42
Pollock, A., 91, 92
Powell, D.M., 101, 107
Poythress, N.G., 97, 98, 110, 111, 114
Prettyman, E.B., 153

Raney, D.F., 42
Raven, B., 137
Reed, J.P., 54
Reese v. Naylor, 100
Reis, H.T., 44

Rice, G.P., 99
Rideau v. Louisiana, 66–67, 68
Robey, A., 109
Robinson, D.N., 4, 100
Robinson, E., 3
Roesch, R., 100, 103
Rogers, G., 65
Rogers, R., 100, 102
Roos, D.C., 101
Rosenblum, S., 21
Rosenthal, R., 23, 41, 42, 43, 129
Rothblatt, H.B., 54
Rothgeb, C.L., 1
Ruback, R.B., 4

Sage, W., 21
Saks, M.J., 4, 14, 21, 22, 28, 44, 135,
    141, 146
Sales, B.D., 4, 21, 28, 40, 50, 52, 60,
    101, 107, 138, 153
Sampson, E.E., 157
Sanford, R.N., 48
Sannito, T., 137
Schenitski, D.D., 6
Scherer, K.R., 42
Schreiber, J., 103
Schulman, J., 20
Schulman, R., 99
Schweber-Koren, C., 21
Seabord Coastline R. R. v. Hill, 101
Selkin, J., 101
Shapiro, D.L., 99, 101, 105, 108, 110
Sharp, A., 162, 163, 164
Shaver, P., 20
Sheppard v. Maxwell, 69
Showalter, C.R., 100
Silas, F.A., 44
Silver, D., 21
Simon, R., 44
Sindlinger, A., 76
Singer, H., 29
Singer, R., 29
Skolnick, J.H., 58
Slesinger, D., 3
Slobogin, C., 97, 100, 102
Smith, B.S., 151
Smith, S., 99

Sperlich, P.W., 37
Stefek, D., 21
Stephan, C., 44
Stern, W., 1
Stotland, E., 151
Streeter, L.A., 42
Strodtbeck, F.L., 164
Strube, M.J., 54, 154
Suggs, D., 21, 28, 40, 50, 52, 60, 138
Swain v. Alabama, 37
Swan, J., 21, 63
Swenson, R.A., 101
Szasz, T., 97

Tapp, J.L., 52
Taylor v. Louisiana, 36
Thibaut, J., 3, 6, 147, 152
Thiel v. Southern Pacific Co., 35
Thompson, W.C., 33

United States v. Amaral, 100, 104
United States v. Barnes, 19
United States v. Brawner, 100, 102
United States v. Cauble, 163
United States v. Driscoll, 162
United States v. Guzman, 36
United States v. Haldeman, 76

Van Duizend, R., 101, 107
Van Dyke, J.M., 36
Vidmar, N., 91, 92, 93, 96
Vinson, D.E., 62, 64, 65, 137

Wagner, W., 39

Wainwright v. Witt, 61
Walker, L., 3, 4, 6, 147, 152
Walker, L.E.A., 101, 109
Walster, E.H., 144
Wasyliw, O.E., 100
Weary, G., 137
Wells, G.L., 100, 129
Werner, C.M., 54, 154
Wexley, M.C., 42
Whipple, G.M., 1
White, R.K., 151
White, R.W., 122
Wicker, A.W., 43
Wicklund, R.A., 136
Widman, E.H., 101
Wiens, A.N., 50
Wigmore, J., 2, 5
Willging, T.E., 4, 90, 101
Wilson, T.D., 43, 73, 162
Witherspoon v. Illinois, 29–34, 61
Wolfgang, M.E., 100, 103
Wood, J., 44
Woodward, J., 90
Wrightsman, L.S., 4, 47, 153, 155
Wyatt v. Stickney, 101, 106

Yarmy, A.D., 100

Zajonc, R.B., 58, 144
Zeisel, H., 21, 32, 33, 57, 62, 65, 92, 101, 153, 164
Zimbardo, P., 131, 135, 147
Ziskin, J., 97, 98, 99, 111
Zuckerman, M., 42, 44, 129

Subject Index

Adoption, 101, 108
Adversary system, 5–7, 59, 121, 134, 139, 166, 171
Allen charge, 10
"Alternative juries," 13, 65–66
Association of Trial Behavioral Consultants, 118
Authoritarianism, 44, 48–52, 54
Attitudes
    see also Jury selection, juror sentiments
    assessment of, 26
    change of, 131, 135, 150–151
Aussage experiments, 1

Bias
    actual, 18, 93
    implied, 18, 93

Challenges
    for cause, 18, 29–32, 61, 91, 150
    peremptory, 18–19, 29, 34–35, 40, 67–68, 150
Change of venue, 25, 159
    case examples of, 77–90
    criteria for, 64–66, 68–69, 93
    and media analysis, 70
    questionnaires used in surveys for, 70–74
    surveys for, 63–96
    training interviewers to conduct surveys for, 74–75
Chicago Jury Project, 3, 164
Child custody, 101, 107
Civil commitment, 100, 104–105

Civil trial procedure, 11, 137–149, 152–154
Class action suits, 101, 106–107
Competence to stand trial, 100, 103
Composition challenges, 35–37
Continuance, 67
Courtroom consultation
    ethics of, 16, 59, 166–171
    fees for, 169–170
    goals of, 13–14, 24, 54
    how consultants should be identified, 59–61, 120
    research on, 30–34, 156–165
    training for, 12–14, 130, 156, 159
Cognizable groups, 36–37
Criminal trial procedure, 7–11, 137–149, 152–154

Death penalty
    attitudes toward, 29–34, 45–47, 61
    bifurcated trials, 32–33, 103, 140, 145, 154
    and voir dire, 29–34
Death qualification, 29–34, 46–47, 61
Deception, 41–43, 51, 129

Ethics
    in adversary system, 5–7
    of courtroom consultation, 16, 59, 166–172
    of expert testimony, 166–170
Evaluation research, 159–165
    and jury selection, 20–23, 30–34, 60, 169
    and witness preparation, 131–133

Expert testimony, 4, 16, 32, 58, 117, 146
and cross-examination, 97–98, 109–114
criticisms of, 97–98
ethics of, 166–170
and "learned treatises," 110
and partianship, 114
preparation for, 109–114
status of psychologists, 98–99
topics for, 99–109
Eyewitness identification, 6, 100, 104

F-Scale, 48–49

Guardianship and conservatorship, 101, 107

Imported venires, 68
Inquisitorial system, 5–7
Insanity, 99, 100, 102

Juror questionnaires, 18, 25, 151, 173–174
Jury deliberations, 40, 53, 57, 65–66, 150–151, 153–154, 161–163
Jury instructions, 9–10, 153
Jury selection
and demographic variables, 44–48, 53, 59, 144–145, 154
effects of, 23
evaluations of, 20–23, 30–34, 60, 169
influence of foreperson, 55–58, 154
intelligence of jurors, 58–59
interactions among jurors, 53–54, 151
models of, 39–59, 66, 150
prior jury experience, 54–58
profiles of jurors, 25–27, 40–41, 150–151
sentiments of jurors, 40–52, 150–151
social influence of jurors, 40, 53–54, 152–153
use of informants in, 27
use of nonverbal cues in, 49–52

Legal Attitudes Questionnaire, 44, 48
"Legal realism," 2

Machiavellian personality, 42
McNaghten rule, 102
Malpractice, 101, 108

National Jury Project, 31, 77
Negligence and product liability, 101, 105–106
Nonverbal cues, 41–43, 49–52, 127, 129, 153

Persuasion and communication, 134–155
and attribution theory, 137, 144–145
and characteristics of communicaors, 135–136, 141–143
and characteristics of persuasive messages, 135–136, 148–149
in closing arguments, 152–153
credibility, 141–142, 148
and defendant's testimony, 145
and evidence, 145–148
and juror characteristics, 144–145
jurors as audience, 150–152, 154
and jury instructions, 153
and language style, 148–149
one- vs. two-sided arguments, 139–140
order of presentation of evidence, 146–148, 152
in voir dire, 138–139
Psychological autopsies, 101, 105
Psychological damages, 100, 105
Psychologist–attorney interactions, 2–4, 12–14, 28, 40, 119, 134–135, 160–161, 169, 171
Public opinion surveys, 25–26
analyses of, 76–77, 79–90, 91–94
for change of venue, 25–26, 63–96
and the death penalty, 45–47
for jury selection, 25–26, 44
methodological problems of, 22, 90–94
sampling for, 75–76, 92–93
testifying about, 77, 92–96
uses of, 62–63, 69

Research and courtroom consulta-
    tion, 5, 156-165
  archival research, 3, 28, 54-58, 159
  disciplinary (basic) research, 3, 28,
    157-158
  evaluation research, 20-23, 60,
    159-165
  external validity, 157-158
  internal validity, 60, 157
  mock jury research, 22, 28, 44, 54,
    147, 150, 158
  policy-action research, 28, 60, 159
  post-trial juror interviews, 3, 41,
    54, 60, 153-154, 159, 161-165

Sentencing, 100, 103
Seventh Amendment, 4
Sixth Amendment, 4
Social issues at litigation, 101,
    108-109
"Struck system," 34-35

Task Force on Role of Psychology in
    the Criminal Justice System, 166
Trademark litigation, 60, 101, 106
Trial simulations, 26-27, 63, 64-66

Voir dire
  in capital cases, 29-34
  in criminal trials, 8, 20-21

definition of, 17, 60
improving conditions of, 27-39
interviewing skills in, 38-39
preparation for, 24-27
purposes of, 17-20, 129, 138-139,
    150-151
sequestered vs. open-court, 28-35,
    38, 67
type of questions asked in, 19,
    38-39

Witness preparation, 116-133
  consultant preparation for , 118-119
  credibility of witnesses, 128-129
  for cross-examination, 125-127, 132
  for direct examination, 124-125
  emotional issues in, 122-123, 131
  ethics of, 116, 170
  evaluation of, 131-133
  familiarity with court procedures,
    123-124
  on factual matters, 121-122
  and nonverbal communication, 127,
    129
  physical appearance of witnesses,
    127-128
  preparation of attorneys, 117-118
  timing of, 132
  videotaping in, 125, 132-133

About the Authors

Michael T. Nietzel received his PhD from the University of Illinois (Champaign-Urbana) in 1973. Currently, he is Professor of Psychology at the University of Kentucky. He is author of *Crime and Its Modification* and *Introduction to Clinical Psychology* (with Douglas A. Bernstein).

Ronald C. Dillehay earned his PhD degree in 1962 in the Department of Psychology at the University of California, Berkeley. He is presently Professor of Psychology at the University of Kentucky. He coauthored *Dimensions of Authoritarianism* with John P. Kirscht.

Psychology Practitioner Guidebooks

Editors
Arnold P. Goldstein, Syracuse University
Leonard Krasner, SUNY at Stony Brook
Sol L. Garfield, Washington University

Elsie M. Pinkston & Nathan L. Linsk—CARE OF THE ELDERLY: A Family Approach

Donald Meichenbaum—STRESS INOCULATION TRAINING

Sebastiano Santostefano—COGNITIVE CONTROL THERAPY WITH CHILDREN AND ADOLESCENTS

Lillie Weiss, Melanie Katzman & Sharlene Wolchik—TREATING BULIMIA: A Psychoeducational Approach

Edward B. Blanchard & Frank Andrasik—MANAGEMENT OF CHRONIC HEADACHES: A Psychological Approach

Raymond G. Romanczyk—CLINICAL UTILIZATION OF MICROCOMPUTER TECHNOLOGY

Philip H. Bornstein & Marcy T. Bornstein—MARITAL THERAPY: A Behavioral-Communications Approach

Michael T. Nietzel & Ronald C. Dillehay—PSYCHOLOGICAL CONSULTATION IN THE COURTROOM

Elizabeth B. Yost, Larry E. Beutler, M. Anne Corbishley & James R. Allender—GROUP COGNITIVE THERAPY: A Treatment Approach for Depressed Older Adults

Lillie Weiss—DREAM ANALYSIS IN PSYCHOTHERAPY

Edward A. Kirby & Liam K. Grimley—UNDERSTANDING AND TREATING ATTENTION DEFICIT DISORDER